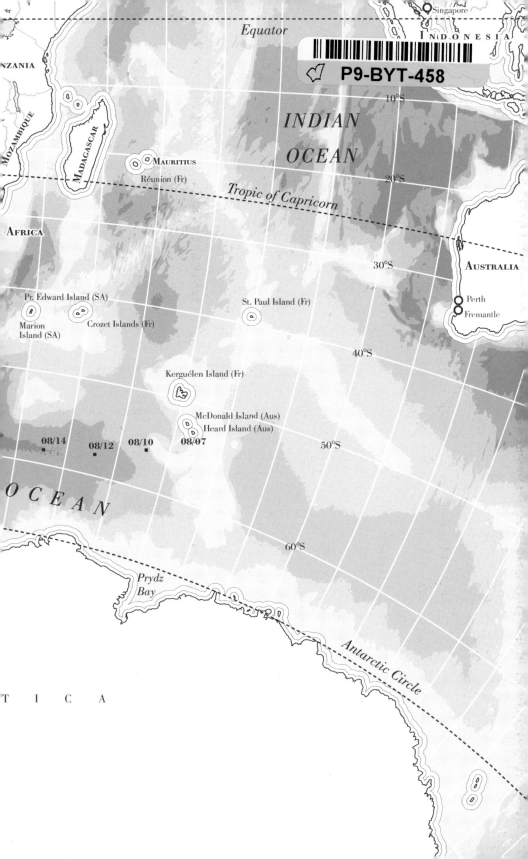

HOOKED

HOOKED

PIRATES, POACHING,
AND THE PERFECT FISH

G. BRUCE KNECHT

RODALE

Photographs appear courtesy of the Australian Fisheries Management Authority

Book design by Joanna Williams

Library of Congress Cataloging-in-Publication Data

Knecht, G. Bruce.
    Hooked : pirates, poaching, and the perfect fish / by G. Bruce Knecht.
       p.   cm.
    ISBN-13 978–1–59486–110–9 hardcover
    ISBN-10 1–59486–110–2 hardcover
    1. Law enforcement—Antarctic Ocean—Case studies. 2. Patagonian toothfish industry—Corrupt practices—Case studies. 3. Poaching—Antarctic Ocean—Case studies. 4. Patagonian toothfish—Conservation—International cooperation—Case studies. I. Title: True story of pirates, poaching, and the perfect fish. II. Title.
    HV7914.K54 2006
    363.259′33—dc22   2005036632

Distributed to the trade by Holtzbrinck Publishers

2   4   6   8   10   9   7   5   3   1   hardcover

RODALE
LIVE YOUR WHOLE LIFE™

We inspire and enable people to improve their lives and the world around them

For more of our products visit **rodalestore.com** or call 800-848-4735

FOR SARAH

CONTENTS

PROLOGUE

*S*outhern Supporter* was in silent mode as it closed in on its target. The external lights were off, the portholes had been blackened, and no one touched the radio. The radar was activated only twice an hour, each time for less than a minute, to check for icebergs. One day earlier, a sensor on the Australian patrol boat had picked up outbound radar emissions from three nearby vessels. All of them appeared to be just west of Heard Island, an uninhabited scrap of land halfway between South Africa and Australia, nine hundred miles north of Antarctica. It was the dead of winter, and the island, virtually barren and almost completely covered by glaciers, was buffeted by air so cold that wind-borne saltwater had formed horizontal icicles against the rails of the ship.

Stephen Duffy, the Australian Customs officer who was leading the patrol, knew exactly what the three vessels were doing. The waters near Heard Island contain one of the world's largest populations of Patagonian toothfish. For most of their existence, the prehistoric-looking gray-black creatures, which can live for fifty years and grow to six feet in length, had thrived in near-frozen obscurity. That was before a little-known businessman in Los Angeles coined an inaccurate though vastly more appealing name and chefs fell in love with a white flesh that seemed to accept every

1

spice and hold up to every method of cooking. It was also before fleets of fishing vessels—many of them pirates—sought to capitalize on the burgeoning demand.

"I don't want to have an intercept before dawn," Duffy told Andrew Codrington, *Southern Supporter*'s captain. "For now I'd like to head slowly toward them, six knots or less. If they happen to see us, they'll assume we're a pirate, too."

Nautical confrontations were nothing new to Duffy. He had conducted forced boardings of more than one hundred ships during a distinguished naval career, after which he joined Customs to help create a marine patrol unit. Duffy did not really look like the kind of person who would be battling modern-day pirates. At forty-two, after many years at sea, his face was surprisingly unlined. He looked more like an overgrown Boy Scout.

When he was growing up in Tasmania, he liked nothing more than the ferry voyages his family took across Bass Strait, the treacherous body of water that separates Tasmania from the Australian mainland. Duffy spent those passages exploring the ship—everything from the engine room to the bridge, where an officer once let him turn the wheel. The workings of the ship, the vast expanse of the sea, and the possibility of traveling to faraway places had an almost intoxicating effect. Duffy decided that he too would command a ship someday. He made his first visit to the naval recruiting office when he was fifteen, and he joined four years later.

Duffy was also driven by a deeply felt sense of duty. It probably came from his father, a city planner, who told his son about the importance of "Environmental Impact Statements" and always spoke about the world in terms of "the public good." But Duffy could also be difficult to read. His speech is rapid, sometimes clipped, and his expression almost never changes.

After the three ships were detected, Duffy and Codrington spent the entire night on *Southern Supporter*'s bridge, where the illuminated instrument panels and tensor lights produced a high-tech orange glow. If it were not for the heaving motion, the compartment, which stretched from one side of the ship to the other, would have looked like the control room of a power plant. The two forward-facing chairs near the front, each covered with well-worn terry cloth, were the control positions. Codrington was seated in the one on the port side, and from there he could oversee a profusion of multicolored levers, buttons, and knobs, as well as a twenty-four-inch radar screen. The delicate controls seemed incongruous in relation to the ship's powerful mechanical systems: the captain could steer the 250-foot-long vessel with a single finger, either by turning the small dial on an "automatic pilot" or nudging a joystick that looked like it was part of a video game.

Early the next morning, *Southern Supporter* was still thirty miles away from the closest vessel, the one Duffy had decided to arrest. It had been almost stationary throughout the night, so he assumed it had been retrieving a longline, an array of equipment that can stretch for more than a dozen miles and hold fifteen thousand baited hooks. A single longline can take a full day to retrieve and extract more than twenty tons of fish—making it the marine equivalent of strip mining.

At 5:00 a.m., Duffy told Codrington to head toward the target at the ship's best speed, about twelve knots.

At 6:57 a.m., Codrington, who was monitoring the radar screen, had bad news: "The contact is altering course to the south and picking up speed rapidly. They're currently moving at seven knots." A couple of minutes later, the captain added, "They're up to at least ten knots—they're going flat out."

Now that the target had fled, Duffy's job had become infinitely more challenging. He had hoped to catch the pirate in the act. Once the fish was processed in the onboard factory and frozen, it would be virtually impossible to prove its origin. The pirates would undoubtedly say the fish came from somewhere else.

Duffy *knew* the ship had been fishing in Australian waters—why else would it have traveled so far to be there?—but he needed evidence. And he needed it quickly. *Southern Supporter* is powered by three enormous Caterpillar diesel engines that drive a ten-foot-wide propeller with 3,600 horsepower, but it is only marginally faster than most fishing vessels. And unlike others that had fled from Heard Island, the target was running to the south. It would not take long before it crossed the "iceberg line," a dotted line on one of the charts that indicated where glacial ice is most prevalent. Perhaps the pirate thought the brutality of the deep Southern Ocean would be too much for a government patrol boat. But from Duffy's perspective, that strategy only increased the stakes: if this pirate found an effective escape route, others would surely follow.

CHAPTER 1

Valparaiso, Chile
1977

L ee Lantz, a young fish merchant from Los Angeles, was climbing between the colorfully painted fishing boats that had recently returned to Chile's largest port. There were more than fifty boats, all of them made of wood and less than forty feet long. They had been tied to docks and then to one another, side by side, so Lantz could go directly from one boat to another to examine the piles of fish that were lying on the decks. Lantz was disappointed with the tour. The key to his business was, as it always had been, finding new things to sell, but he saw nothing but congrio, which he had begun importing to the United States a couple of years earlier, and a few other familiar species.

Then, just as he was about to leave, Lantz did spot something new: an exceptionally large, fearsome-looking gray-black fish that had been separated from the others. Close to five feet long, it looked as if it weighed well over one hundred pounds. With its dark skin and bulging eyes, a protruding lower jaw that was studded with teeth so pointy they looked as if they had been honed by a pencil sharpener, even this lifeless specimen looked menacing.

"That is one amazing-looking fish," Lantz declared. "What the hell is it?"

"They call it bacalao de profundidad—which means cod of the deep," replied Eduardo Neef, a tough-minded businessman who owned the plant that processed congrio for Lantz. Neef said fishermen had never seen the fish until they started using deep-water longlines a few years earlier. "It's an accidental catch. Nobody knows what to do with it."

"Can you eat it?"

"No—it's too oily."

Lantz was intrigued. He guessed it was a previously unknown type of sea bass. If he was right about that, its flesh would be flaky and white, the characteristics many Americans look for in a fish. He was not concerned about its gruesome outward appearance. Congrio, after all, looked even worse—its tail narrows into a slender tubelike shape that looks like it should belong to an eel—but he was selling 40,000 pounds of it every month. Nor was Lantz put off by the Chileans' lack of interest in bacalao de profundidad or Neef's comment about its oiliness: American seafood eaters prefer fish with a lot of fat, and a species' lack of popularity in one market means little in others. Swordfish, which was abundant near Chile's coast, was a perfect example: although it was extremely popular in the United States, no one seemed to like it in Chile.

Two days after he first saw the mysterious big fish, Lantz came across another one during a predawn visit he and Neef made to Santiago's bustling central market. Because Lantz had been talking about it ever since he saw the first one in Valparaiso, Neef asked the man behind the counter to cut into this fish to expose its flesh. Now Lantz was really excited: just as he had hoped, it was white, its oiliness very much apparent. It looked almost as if it had been marinated.

The color also told Lantz a lot about the fish's basic nature. This was not a fish that chased its prey—that would require the kind of stamina that could come only from a circulatory system that would distribute blood much more liberally through its body, which would cause its flesh to be at least tinted with red. The metabolism of white-fleshed fish is geared for short bursts of energy, fueled by stores of oxygen. Clearly, this was a fish that ambushed, waiting until its prey was near before it sprinted forward with its razor teeth ready and its outsize mouth agape. Given its size—it was as big as some adult human beings—it had obviously been very successful until it fell for a baited hook.

Neef bought a few pounds of the fish so he could take it to his apartment for a taste test with Lantz later that day. The sample cost just a couple of dollars, but Neef was already thinking about much larger sums. The congrio business had become a real success, but because that fish was also extremely popular in Chile, there were sometimes shortages and price spikes. A second product would reduce Neef's business risks and enable him to use his processing plant more efficiently. And a fish no one else wanted, assuming it could be caught in commercial quantities, should be easy to buy and inexpensive.

Neef's apartment, located in a beachside community north of Valparaiso, had an expansive view of the Pacific, but the kitchen was basic, equipped with a small two-burner gas stove. Removing the fish from the newspaper in which it was wrapped, Neef carved it into several small pieces and gave them to his housekeeper, who placed them in a frying pan with a small amount of cooking oil. Looking over her shoulder, Lantz was amazed by the amount of water the fish released as it sizzled in the pan. He worried about what that would mean to its texture and what people in his industry called mouthfeel. By then, Neef had opened a bottle of red wine and Lantz was holding a plate, impatient for his first taste.

It was anticlimactic. Whereas most big fish have a lot of flavor, this one had almost none. With as much surprise as disappointment, Lantz said, "It's bland."

Without sharing his own impression, Neef said, "It doesn't matter—when they cook it in the north, they'll find a way to make it interesting."

"You're right about that—the blandness could even be a plus."

In fact, Lantz's enthusiasm was much greater than his words might suggest. Although he was unimpressed by the fish's flavor, he thought its attributes were a perfect match for the American market. It had a texture similar to Atlantic cod's, the richness of tuna, the innocuous mild flavor of a flounder, and a fat content that made it feel almost buttery in the mouth. Lantz believed a white-fleshed fish that almost melted in your mouth—and a fish that did not taste "fishy"—could go a very long way with his customers at home. But he was careful in what he said to Neef: he wanted to express enough optimism to cause the Chilean to secure a supply of the fish, but not so much that Neef's expectations rose to unrealistic heights.

Lantz worked with his father, Alvin, a Kentucky native who had moved west after World War II and become a fish salesman before starting his own business, A. R. Lantz Company, in 1949. Its strategy was to import seafood—a new concept for a country that had mostly relied on domestic sources. It began by importing shrimp from Mexico, and its biggest success came in the early 1960s when it linked up with shrimp fishermen in El Salvador who harvested the very large shrimp that many restaurants in the United States liked to serve. The younger Lantz, a large man who likes to ride motorcycles along the California coastline in his free time, joined the firm in 1971, shortly after graduating from Utah State University, and he made his first trip to Chile four years later.

Lantz knew he could not sell Americans something called bacalao de profundidad. He had never heard of the species' other common names— mero, merluza negra, or Patagonian toothfish—and he did not know its scientific name, *Dissostichus eleginoides*. But he would not have wanted to use those either. Lantz needed to create his own name, one that would spark some sort of favorable recognition in the American market.

"Sea bass" was an obvious choice. Although it is not a particularly meaningful term—it is included in the names of more than one hundred species—it has broad resonance among American seafood eaters. And in some sense it would not be entirely inaccurate: While toothfish are not bass, they do have the white, flaky flesh that is characteristic of bass. Toothfish also have triangular tails, which enable them to accelerate rapidly, another feature common to bass. Lantz's initial ideas for Americanized names were "Pacific Sea Bass" and "South American Sea Bass," but he later thought they were so geographically imprecise that they sounded almost generic.

A reference to Chile was the perfect solution. In spite of the turmoil that had rocked the country after President Salvador Allende was killed in a 1973 coup, most Americans knew very little about the country. They knew it was far away, though, and Lantz thought "Chilean" would convey a touch of exoticism that might be helpful in the marketplace. And so he settled on Chilean Sea Bass.[1]

---

[1] *Many years later, in 1994, the U.S. Food and Drug Administration refused to change the fish's official common name from Patagonian toothfish to Chilean Sea Bass. However, by then the Chilean Sea Bass name had become so widely used that the agency said it could be used as an "alternative market name."*

But Lantz's main customers, seafood wholesalers in Los Angeles, were initially unimpressed. A couple of months after he returned from Chile, he took samples to each of the wholesalers—more than thirty small, mostly family-run businesses—and offered to sell it for just $1.25 a pound, but no one placed an order. "Why would anyone want to eat this thing?" asked Bill Merry, a wholesaler who supplied seafood to Chasen's, the then famous celebrity hangout, and several large country clubs. "It tastes like nothing—and I don't think it's a bass."

While Lantz was struggling to sell Chilean Sea Bass in the States, Neef was pushing fishermen to catch more of it, and promising to buy it for forty-five cents a pound. Tension between the two men was inevitable. Neef bought whatever the fishermen caught, and he had no use for it other than to butcher it into filets that he froze and sent to California. Lantz thought Neef occasionally shipped more fish than they had agreed, and Lantz also resented the fact that he was bearing all the costs. For every pound of fish, he paid about ninety cents to Neef, seventeen cents to have it shipped to Long Beach, six cents to have a truck carry it to a warehouse, four cents for the first month of storage, and another penny per pound for each month after that.

By 1980, Lantz was desperate. "Selling seafood is like shooting ducks with a shotgun," his father frequently said. "Just keep firing and something will eventually fall from the sky." But even though he had given free samples to everyone who would take them, Lantz had made just a handful of small sales. Running out of ideas, he went to see Roger Mooreheart, one of the executives of Young's Market Company, which sold a broad array of food, including shrimp it bought from Lantz. He had already pitched Chilean Sea Bass to Young's—unsuccessfully—but Mooreheart had a reputation for being a creative marketer, so Lantz planned to play up his youth and ask the older man for advice.

As soon as Lantz stepped into the office, Mooreheart pointed to the plastic-wrapped piece of fish he was carrying and asked, "What's that?"

"You've seen it before—it's the Chilean Sea Bass."

"Can I take some? I might be able to use it."

"I thought you weren't interested—what happened?"

"We have a problem," Mooreheart said. Halibut, the main ingredient for one of Young's products, "Fish Fingers," was becoming ever more expensive. Although the two fish did not taste the same, they were both white, and Mooreheart thought the difference in flavor might not be noticed in breaded fish sticks. For the first time in months, Lantz was hopeful. He tried to temper his optimism as he drove back to his office, but he could not stop himself from feeling that something good was about to happen.

Just a few hours later, Mooreheart was on the phone. "How much of your Chilean Sea Bass do you have?" he asked.

"About 40,000 pounds."

"I'll take it—all of it!"

Young's subsequently became a regular buyer, ordering about 25,000 pounds of the new fish every couple of weeks. For Lantz, it was a crucial break. Frozen fish sticks would do nothing to enhance the stature of Chilean Sea Bass in the marketplace—the boxes they came in did not even mention the name—but he had finally found a way to move some product and justify his efforts.

During the next couple of years, the wholesalers slowly began to warm up to Chilean Sea Bass, particularly during the winter, when West Coast fishermen caught fewer fish. As with Young's, all of the initial orders resulted from shortages of some better-known fish, but Lantz used every sale to prod other wholesalers, telling them how one of their competitors had found a niche for the inexpensive product. Eventually, some restaurants actually began requesting the fish.

Many of them were Cantonese-style restaurants that used toothfish as a substitute for black cod, which cost twice as much. In San Francisco, the Hong Kong Flower Lounge used toothfish to create a dish it called "Smoked Filet of Black Cod." The restaurant's chefs marinated black cod—and later toothfish—in a mixture of onion, lemon, soy sauce, scallions, and celery as well as a small amount of egg that caused the fish to turn a reddish brown when baked, making it look as if it had been smoked. Toothfish took on the spices at least as well as black cod, and it was also more forgiving: its oiliness made it virtually impossible to overcook. The chefs also liked the thick portions they could cut from toothfish, so much so that they would continue to use it even after toothfish became far more expensive than black cod.

The Cantonese restaurants, which served mostly Asian clienteles, generally did not mention Chilean Sea Bass on their menus. The Hong Kong Flower Lounge has always described it as black cod. Other Chinese restaurants steamed toothfish with spices and soy sauce, but they called it "Steamed Black Cod with Black Bean and Ginger." In fact, even if they had called it Chilean Sea Bass, it probably would not have been noticed by the larger culinary world. This was in the days before "fusion," a time when Asian and other cuisines rarely overlapped. But while toothfish's expanding popularity was not being detected by the usual culinary radar, it registered in increasing orders for Lantz, who, in 1982, started selling frozen filets to wholesalers on the East Coast.

Neef did not have any difficulty keeping pace with the demand. He built a larger processing plant and began chartering its own fishing vessels. And, in 1982, he got a lucky break. One of the boats his company operated, the forty-foot *Catalina*, was fishing for congrio, but the captain made a fortuitous mistake: he had intended to set a longline in a place where the water was about 1,200 feet deep, but a portion of the line, which had about two thousand hooks, ended up in water twice as deep. What resulted was a mediocre congrio catch but more than a dozen toothfish. After Neef asked the captain to return to the deep water, the ship hit the jackpot—a single longline captured seven tons of toothfish. In previous trips, the same boat had never caught more than two tons of any fish on a longline.

It was eventually determined that toothfish could be found in substantial numbers just thirty miles away from an eight-hundred-mile stretch of Chile's lengthy coastline. For fishermen, the narrowness of the country's continental shelf, which provided them ready access to deep-water fish, was almost too good to be true.

CHAPTER 2

South Indian Ocean
August 7, 2003

"I have a visual!"

It was 7:45 a.m., a few minutes after sunrise, and Scott Webb, one of two fisheries enforcement officers aboard *Southern Supporter*, spotted a small speck of red through the haze and low-lying clouds. *Southern Supporter* was steaming at twelve knots on a course that would cause it to converge on its target in about two hours. As the gap continued to narrow, Webb, who was twenty-eight, trained a powerful pair of binoculars on the other vessel. What he saw looked like a Japanese-built longliner. He guessed it originally had been built for hunting tuna and was later retrofitted for toothfish.

Michael O'Dea, the senior fisheries officer, was in the "communications center," an area near the back of the bridge that was equipped with a trio of radio transmitters, several hand-held radios, and a pair of satellite phones. Picking up a telephone-like handset for the main radio, he read a script over Channel 16, the VHF frequency used for emergencies and to initiate maritime communications: "This is the Australian Customs and Fisheries Patrol Vessel *Southern Supporter*. We are patrolling the Australian Fishing Zone of Heard Island on behalf of the Australian government. I need you to reply on VHF Channel 16. I am an authorized officer." Hearing no response, he broadcast the message again. And again.

At about the same time, a radio direction finder aboard *Southern Supporter* began picking up signals from what seemed to be one or more fishing beacons, suggesting that the target had fled before it had time to recover a longline. O'Dea knew that fishing beacons, which ensure that the equipment can be found again a day or two after it is left in place, were the very best kind of evidence: each one employs a frequency that can be matched to the ship from which it came.

It is impossible to recover a toothfish-targeted longline quickly. Its central component is the "mainline," which must be positioned above a seabed that is 2,000 to 5,000 feet below the surface of the water. Each end of this line is connected to a "riser," a thick rope that is held in place by an anchor at the bottom and a buoy at the top. As many as two hundred "branch lines" dangle from the mainline, each one carrying dozens of baited hooks.

As a longline is hauled over the side of the ship, each of the branch lines is detached and pulled between a U-shaped stainless steel frame that is wide enough for the line and hooks to pass but too narrow for toothfish. As the line goes through the frame, the fish's head, with the hook still in place, smashes into the metal, forcing the prominent teeth that give the species its name forward until the hook rips through the mouth. The fish then falls into a metal chute that leads to a large, unheated compartment near the front of the ship that is called the factory, even though the work there is devoted to disassembly.

When a fish flops onto a long table, a crewman uses a circular saw to sever the head and tail. The risks of the job are all too obvious: There is a guard over the top of the eighteen-inch-diameter blade, but the front is unshielded. Although this enables the operator to slide the fish rapidly through the spinning blade, there is nothing to protect him if a wave unexpectedly jolts the ship or if he becomes so cold or exhausted that one of his hands ends up in the wrong place.

When the cutting is done, the head and tail are pushed into a long bin that empties directly into the sea. The next worker on the line uses a curved knife to carve into the fish's underside. Reaching inside, he finds the fish's stomach, grips it between his thumb and index finger, and tears it out, along with the liver, heart, and intestines. Once the gory mess is dropped into another disposal bin, what remains is placed onto a black conveyer belt that passes through what looks and sounds like an industrial dishwasher, where the fish is cleansed with a blast of saltwater. The carcasses are then sorted by size and packed into plastic-lined cardboard boxes, three to six per box. The cartons are stacked in a super-cold "snap freezer," where the fish are frozen so rapidly that the moisture in their bodies does not crystallize, which would cause the flesh to become mushy when it is thawed. Once the fish are rock solid, the boxes are moved again, this time to the fish hold, a frozen compartment near the bottom of the hull that stretches almost the entire length and breadth of the ship.

Mike O'Dea had a plan. "We need to head toward their initial position," he told Stephen Duffy, "so we can retrieve their equipment and then follow in their wake to look for fish guts and whatever else they've left behind."

But Duffy was intent on catching up with the target in the least amount of time. "There's no use chasing after evidence if we end up failing to get the ship it came from."

"If we don't get into their wake, we're not going to find any evidence," O'Dea replied.

Duffy refused to budge. "If we go to their current position and muck around in their wake, we'll lose a couple of hours. We'll never see them again."

The relationship between Duffy and O'Dea was complicated. While O'Dea had led three previous Heard Island patrols, now, as a result of a series of policy changes, he had to defer to Duffy, who was on his first. And they had different priorities: while both men wanted to arrest the ship, O'Dea was more focused on obtaining evidence that would stand up in court.

The two men's styles and personalities also differ. Duffy is sure-footed and precise, and he dresses carefully. O'Dea, who has a long face, marked by a furrowed brow and deep wrinkles, is often disheveled. He speaks slowly, and often looks drawn and melancholy. But there is also a bit of the renegade about him. His wife says he, now fifty years old, is the quintessential Australian, a "bloke" who rolls his own cigarettes and likes nothing more than camping in the outback with his teenage son and dog. Although O'Dea makes friends easily and likes almost everyone, there are exceptions—and he rarely hesitates to say what he thinks.

Fisheries enforcement is not exactly what O'Dea's father, a judge, had in mind for his son, Michael. He grew up in Perth and went to a series of academically rigorous Catholic schools, but he decided early on that he would never be a lawyer. He wanted to do something that allowed him to spend much of his time outdoors.

O'Dea was not sure what to do. "It's reasonable for us to assume it's a fishing vessel," he said to Duffy, "but there is no real evidence as such that he has been fishing."

Duffy did not respond, in part because he knew that everything was being recorded for possible use in a trial and that any words of doubt or dissent would be damaging if they ended up being replayed in a courtroom. Duffy had no doubt that the other ship had been fishing—why else would it have been stationary for so long and why had it fled and refused to respond to repeated radio calls?—but his options were limited. Because he had reason to believe the other ship had been fishing illegally, he had the right to board it and force it to an Australian port for investigation. But because of budgetary constraints, *Southern Supporter*'s twenty-two-man crew did not include an armed boarding party.

When the ships were about a mile apart, Scott Webb noticed that birds were swooping back and forth behind the fishing vessel. It is not unusual for birds to follow a ship, but Webb believed these birds were there because pieces of fish had recently been dumped over the side. Not long after that, once *Southern Supporter* had assumed a parallel course about two hundred yards away from the other boat, Webb noticed something else.

"Check it out," he declared. "They've blacked out their name."

In his fifteen years at sea, Duffy had never seen a large commercial vessel that had hidden its identifying markings. When he picked up a pair of binoculars, he saw that the area near the bow where he would expect to see a name was covered by what looked like black paint. He also saw a large black rectangle on the white superstructure just behind the vessel's bridge, the place where the ship's call letters would typically be displayed. The ship's officers were also hidden from view. The windows on the side of the bridge were covered by metal shutters, perhaps because of the foul weather—or perhaps to conceal their faces. A few minutes later, a very large man briefly stepped out onto the stern deck. He was wearing a white chef's apron.

Continuing his broadcasts, O'Dea said, "Vessel on my port bow. You are now in Australian waters. I have reasonable grounds to believe you have been using your boat to conduct fishing operations. Therefore, in accordance with my powers under the Australian Fisheries Act of 1991, I order you to stop your vessel and follow instructions to allow Australian officers to exercise their powers under the Act. Do you understand?" *Southern Supporter*'s crew also used signal flags and the ship's Morse Code–blinking Alden Lamp to ask the other ship to tune into Channel 16, but nothing produced a response.

The only remaining strategy Duffy could think to try was based on a bluff, which carried its own risk: if it failed, it would be even more difficult to establish any authority over the pirates. "How would you feel about launching one of our chase boats?" he asked Andrew Codrington. "If we could get close enough, we might be able to see the ship's name through the over-painting."

With the understatement that is typical of professional mariners, Codrington said, "It would be a bit bouncy, but I'd be happy with that."

Since Duffy wanted the fishing vessel to believe the chase boat would carry an armed boarding party, he added, "When we get ready to launch the boat, I want to have a lot of our guys on the deck wearing their foul-weather gear and helmets so they look as formidable as possible." He then went to his cabin to put on his own gear—first thermal long underwear, waterproof socks, boots, and overalls; then a fleece jacket; and, finally, a dry suit and a black helmet that was equipped with built-in goggles. While Duffy was away from the bridge, Webb saw another suggestion of misbehavior: crewmen on the fishing vessel threw two green bags over the side. Webb had a few guesses as to what might be inside—log books, fishing records, computer disks.

As a crane lifted one of the chase boats from the deck and swung it into position over the water, Mike O'Dea transmitted a new message over the radio. "Fishing vessel, this is the Australian vessel *Southern Supporter.* We order you to stop. We are currently preparing to launch our chase boat, and it will approach your vessel. You should not interfere with this craft."

Almost immediately after that, at 10:21 a.m., a gruffly accented voice came to life over Channel 16: "You have no permission to come aboard! No permission to come aboard."

"You must stop your vessel!" O'Dea replied.

"We will not stop—we are underway," the voice said. Then, almost shouting, he added: "You have no permission to come aboard!"

"You are required to provide certain information to us. If you do not, we will be required to send our boat to you."

After a pause, the voice said, "We will answer your questions."

During the next few minutes, O'Dea learned that the fishing vessel was *Viarsa-1,* a 175-foot-long ship that was registered in Uruguay. O'Dea knew that probably did not mean much: a ship registered there could be owned by people who live elsewhere.

"Can you tell me the name of the master of the ship?" O'Dea asked.

"The master is Ricardo Ribot Cabrera."

"Thank you very much. Are *you* the master?"

"Yes, I am the master."

"How many people are onboard your vessel?"

"Forty-one."

"Where are they from?"

"Uruguay, Chile, Portugal, and Spain."

Although Cabrera was answering all of O'Dea's questions, his responses to the most pointed queries were halting and sometimes repetitive. His tone suggested that he was under stress. It was easy to imagine why. A ship like *Viarsa* could carry three hundred tons of toothfish, which would be worth $3 million, about twice the value of the ship. If Cabrera was apprehended and successfully prosecuted, the fish as well as the vessel would be confiscated, the captain would be fined, and his career would probably be over.

But if the risks of illegal fishing were great, so too were the potential rewards. At a time when most fisheries are so depleted that profits are sometimes impossible, toothfish offer the kind of returns that inspired whalers to undertake their perilous expeditions centuries before. But, unlike a whaling ship, the chances that a toothfish vessel will be lost to the elements are relatively small; for toothfish pirates, the greater risk is getting caught. And for the owners, that risk is quite manageable. The loss of the occasional ship is mostly just a distraction, another cost of doing business. Owners do not have to worry much about going to jail because most of them are invisible, hidden behind corporate shells. Even if they are identified, they are insulated from legal action because they live in countries that are unlikely to extradite them. In any event, it would be extremely difficult to prove their personal complicity. The owner could, for example, claim he had no idea that his employees were fishing in places where they did not have a permit—even though most owners give their crews every incentive to go to the richest fisheries by pegging their compensation to the value of what they catch.

The crucial player is not the ship's master or captain but the "fishing master," the person who determines where the vessel goes and where longlines are set. Whereas most crewmen are paid about $800 a month, fishing masters are generally paid an amount equal to 5 percent of the value of what they catch—$150,000 for a single expedition on a vessel like *Viarsa*.

Knowing this, O'Dea assumed Cabrera was subservient to someone else but that that person would be unlikely to speak over the radio.

Onboard the fishing vessel, Antonio Garcia Perez, one of the world's most successful toothfish hunters, was struggling to contain his fury. Standing near the middle of the fishing vessel's bridge, a narrow space that was thick with cigarette smoke, Perez was watching *Southern Supporter* and speaking over a satellite telephone to his boss, *Viarsa*'s owner, who was back in Riviera, the fishing town near the northwest corner of Spain where both men had grown up. Cabrera was a fifty-eight-year-old mariner who had logged one and a half million miles at sea, but Perez was issuing the orders. He had already given the captain very specific instructions: "Speak to them—but tell them they have no permission to come onboard."

Perez was angry because he believed it was the Australians who were in the wrong. The thirty-nine-year-old Spaniard believed he was being pursued because Australia was trying to protect not fish but domestic fishermen who were not good enough to handle world-class competition. He regarded the two-hundred-mile exclusive fishing zones that many nations declared during the 1970s—claims that legally barred Spaniards from 90 percent of the world's known fisheries—as unnatural and unfair, and all the more so when the line was drawn around a remote and uninhabited territory. Except for fish living within a few miles of a country's inhabited coastline, Perez believed marine life should belong to whomever finds it first. "This is crazy," he would later say. "No one lives on Heard Island. And Australia has nothing there—no hospital, nothing."

There was never much doubt that Perez would become a fisherman.

When he was just fourteen, his father told him, "You don't want to study, so you're going to fish." It was true: Perez was only going through the motions at school. Given the near certainty that he would, like almost every male member of his family for generations, make his living from the ocean, academics seemed irrelevant. It was the kind of circular logic that the government had attempted to break by encouraging companies to build factories that would do something other than process fish or construct more fishing boats. But Riviera's most ambitious sons still do what they have always done—they go to sea, as far as it takes, farther now than ever before, to find the fish that offer the greatest rewards.

Spanish vessels began crossing the Atlantic to harvest cod near Canada in the 1400s, even before Christopher Columbus was credited with discovering America. It was the beginning of an industry that was still sustaining Spanish fishermen and their families when Perez's grandfather worked on a trawler near Canada's Grand Banks in the 1950s. But by the time Perez made his first voyage there in 1983, the world had begun to turn against its greatest nation of fishermen. Helped by ever-improving fish-catching technologies, they had been too successful. Most of the cod were gone, and Canada, eager to save what was left for its own fishermen, had asserted its two-hundred-mile fishing zone. Perez later spent more than three years, 1989 to 1993, living in New Bedford, Massachusetts, so he could work on ships that fished within the United States' two-hundred-mile zone, but the Atlantic's supply of cod and other species continued to dwindle. It became so difficult to earn a living that he was forced to spend time between fishing trips driving a New Bedford taxi before he returned to Riviera in 1993.

Just twenty-nine at the time, Perez was in trouble. He had married a few years earlier, his twin daughters had just celebrated their third birthday, and the career he believed to be a birthright was disappearing. This was reflected in Riviera's harbor: the trawler fleet that was based there, more than three-hundred strong when Perez was a child, had dropped to fewer than forty.

The only sensible solution, Perez quickly realized, was to shift his sights to the less intensively fished waters of the Southern Hemisphere. Toward the end of 1993, he flew to Punta Arenas, a Chilean port near the tip of South America, and embarked on his first toothfish expedition. During the next decade, he completed thirty voyages and captured about thirty million pounds—more than one million toothfish. His latest trip had already yielded ninety-six tons, which was worth about $1 million, and he had made it clear to Cabrera that he was not about to let the Australians take it away.

The captain was of exactly the same mind. He had spent most of his career working on bulk carriers and tanker ships, and he qualified to be a captain in 1993, but in 1998 his employer replaced its South American crewmen with Ukrainians, who were paid much less. Cabrera could not find another job until two years later when *Viarsa*'s owner hired him to work as a toothfish vessel captain. While working on fishing vessels was more demanding than freighters and Cabrera disliked the grueling conditions of the Southern Ocean, he liked the rewards that toothfish provide. He had completed seven successful voyages and was earning $5,500 a month, plus bonuses. He was about to pay off the mortgage on the house he shared with his second wife and son in a resort community outside of Montevideo, and he hoped to continue working until he was sixty-five.

"They can follow me," he told Perez. "They can follow me all the way around the world if they want to—but they're not going to board the vessel."

"Are you aware," O'Dea asked Cabrera, "that you are in the Australian Fishing Zone?"

"Yes."

"Did you undertake any fishing in the area?"

"No sir, we did not."

"Then can you explain why you stopped about twenty-five miles from Heard Island and also why you departed at speed when our vessel approached you?"

"We had a mechanical problem. We slowed down for only about fifty minutes. When the motors were ready again, we started sailing."

This, of course, was inconsistent with *Southern Supporter*'s observations. According to the radar detection equipment, *Viarsa* had been in the same area for at least ten and a half hours.

"We detected fishing beacons in the area where you had stopped," O'Dea said. "Can you report any reason why there would be fishing equipment deployed in that area?"

"Sorry sir, we didn't see any fishing equipment in the area. Nothing."

Certain that the captain was lying, O'Dea saw no reason why he should not reply by stretching the truth himself. "We can confirm we detected fishing gear in that particular area," he claimed. "It was deployed and there was no other fishing vessel in the vicinity, and I believe that fishing equipment was deployed by your vessel."

"I don't understand now what you say. What did you say? I don't understand what you say? Please repeat slowly because my English not very good."

"When did you come in the Australian Fishing Zone?"

"On Wednesday, August 6, at 4:00 a.m."

Duffy walked a few steps to the chart table to determine whether *Viarsa* could have entered the zone at that time and made it to where it had been detected the night before. It was, Duffy quickly concluded, theoretically possible but highly improbable: *Viarsa* would have had to be traveling in a straight line at an average 9.2 knots during the twenty-seven-hour period between when it claimed to have entered the zone and when it fled. Since Duffy believed it had been virtually stationary for at least ten and a half hours of that period, he suspected that Cabrera had concocted a fiction based on the ship's maximum speed.

Continuing with his questions, O'Dea asked, "Where are you licensed to fish?"

"Areas of the world—no one place in particular."

When O'Dea ran out of questions, he repeated his earlier demand: "You are violating the requirements of the Australian Fisheries Act. You must stop your vessel, turn it to the north, and follow us back to the position where we first detected you."

"I have to tell you that we are not going to stop. We are still underway."

"You are inside Australian waters, and we have reasonable grounds to believe an offense may have been committed. It is our intention that you stop your vessel and allow us to investigate."

"I tell you again—for the last time—we don't stop the vessel. We don't stop the vessel."

CHAPTER 3

Los Angeles
October 1984

Lee Lantz realized that he would ultimately lose control of the business he had pioneered. As Chilean Sea Bass became increasingly popular, other importers rushed to get in on the action—and Eduardo Neef started selling toothfish to some of them. Lantz, who knew the competition would reduce his profit margin, was outraged by what he viewed as Neef's disloyalty, but there was not much he could do about it.

A much more powerful tide had also begun to turn against Lantz. In the early 1980s, Americans were becoming more sophisticated about food, and this had led to a growing perception that frozen fish is a second-class product. All of Lantz's Chilean Sea Bass was frozen, and he did not want to deal in fresh fish, which requires advance sales and exacting transportation logistics. Instead, in October 1984, he went to see Doug Harbison, an executive at R. M. Sloan, which specialized in fresh fish. Sloan's owner and Lantz's father were longtime friends, and they had helped each other's businesses out in a variety of ways over the years. Lantz had two objectives: he wanted to introduce an ally to a promising business opportunity—and he wanted more of the Chilean Sea Bass that Neef was sending to the United States to be fresh, so it would not go to his competitors in the frozen business.

After driving to Sloan's offices, which were south of downtown Los Angeles in San Pedro, near the tuna canneries that had long given the area a distinctive aroma, Lantz met with Harbison and Wayne Deardon, a longtime Sloan executive. The meeting was a disaster. As soon as Lantz began describing what he liked about the fish, Deardon shook his head and said, "That shit will never sell!" Before Lantz could respond, Deardon added: "We already have a white fish with dark skin—it's called halibut."

Lantz was furious. Given the long and happy history between the two firms, he could not believe he was being treated so ungraciously. Harbison was also annoyed, but rather than reproach an older colleague, he broke up the meeting and offered to walk Lantz to his car. Harbison thought Deardon, perhaps because of his age, had totally missed the point. Given how stocks of most of the favorite species were becoming depleted, Harbison believed the industry needed to do exactly what Lantz was attempting—find new ones. Harbison also believed America's heightening interest in food and a new generation of restaurants would make it easier to introduce previously unknown fish to the market.

Ever since the French Pavilion at the 1939 World's Fair in New York introduced French cuisine to America, an inordinate number of America's best restaurants had been French. Although many diners found them to be intimidating and too expensive, they did not have many choices: French cuisine had become virtually synonymous with fine dining. Most of the chefs did not seek to be innovative. Instead, they sought to distinguish themselves on the basis of how they prepared a relatively limited number of dishes. In many restaurants, the seafood offerings were limited to crustaceans and a couple of fish, which were prepared in ways that were unchanging and well understood. More often than not, it was "Dover Sole Meuniere" and "Salmon Verte."

But by the early 1980s, some chefs, emboldened by the burgeoning economy and a growing interest in health and nutrition, were attempting to step out of the mold. Many of them were turning the basic culinary equation inside out by shifting the emphasis away from the preparation and back to the food itself.

This was particularly true in California, where a chef named Alice Waters, who had grown up in Chatham, New Jersey, and gone to Berkeley during the 1960s, had opened a restaurant that was almost totally focused on the excellence of its ingredients. Chez Panisse did everything they could to find the best possible raw materials, hiring a "forager," who searched for produce, and Paul Johnson, a former chef, who scouted the fish market. Waters celebrated her ingredients by describing on the menu exactly where they came from and limiting herself to simple methods of cooking. She once found peaches that were so perfect, she served them without any preparation whatsoever: They were placed at the center of a plate without even being peeled or sliced.

Waters's single-minded passion turned Chez Panisse into what *Gourmet* magazine called America's best restaurant—and she played a crucial role in creating a nationwide trend. Menus started going to sometimes exhaustive lengths to explain the origins of their ingredients, and chefs attempted to make their mark by finding new ones. Traditional French restaurants, with their rich sauces and familiar menus, were on the way out.

"Exotic" and "new" were becoming virtues—and Doug Harbison thought that would have a profound impact on the seafood business.

CHAPTER 4

South Indian Ocean
August 7, 2003

S hortly after noon, about five hours after *Viarsa* turned south to begin
its flight, the weather suddenly worsened. The first sign was a dramatic change in the wind direction, from the northwest to the southwest,
a sure sign that another low-pressure system was on the way. In this part
of the world, radical changes and generally miserable conditions—it snows
250 days a year—are the only constants. But the most recent forecast was
even worse than normal, calling for near-hurricane-strength winds and
heightening seas, so Codrington slowed his ship long enough to put about
one thousand yards between it and *Viarsa*.

Over the next several hours, the wind strengthened relentlessly, until,
late in the afternoon, it was howling at fifty knots and gusting up to sixty-
five. The wind in turn had whipped the sea into a monstrous frenzy. Like
the wind, the waves were coming from the southwest, so the ships were
heading almost directly into them. Every wave set up a violent confrontation between ship and sea. At an average height of forty-five feet, with some
of them climbing to more than sixty, the waves looked like liquid mountains. It seemed impossible that water could be made to stand so tall.

Most of the waves were invisible as they approached. The wind was so
strong that it sheared off the tops of the waves and hurled them into the

windows of the bridge to produce a visibility-eliminating torrent. The wind had also torn away the windshield wipers that were supposed to sweep the windows clean. The heavy metal grates that had formed a narrow walkway in front of the bridge had also been swept away.

The very biggest waves, which arrived every four or five minutes, set off a particularly violent pattern. Codrington, who had remained on the bridge throughout the day, always knew when the cycle was about to begin: The ship's speed slowed to almost nothing as it ascended one of the giants. Then, as it passed over the top, the ship seesawed into descent. The angle of the fall was sometimes greater than thirty degrees, so steep that the two-thousand-ton vessel sometimes felt as if it had become an enormous, out-of-control surfboard. It was difficult to comprehend that waves could be powerful enough to toss the ship around so capriciously. But the worst part came when the bow plunged into the trough. It felt as if it had literally struck a wall. Earthquake-like shudders moved from the front of the ship to the back. Cabin walls shifted and bent, creating the impression that the hull was being pressed together like an accordion. The impact also produced a thunderous noise. It sounded like nothing Duffy had ever encountered on a ship. At first, he likened it to a heavy bookshelf crashing to the floor; later, he decided it was more like the sound of crashing automobiles.

The proximity and steepness of the next waves determined how far *Southern Supporter*'s bow would plunge into each oncoming wall of water, but in every case the wave rolled over the ship before the bow had fully reemerged. Some of those waves, unimpeded when the bow was buried, were so large that they crashed directly into the windows of the bridge, thirty-two feet above the ship's waterline. The glass briefly looked like it had become part of a murky aquarium. It was only then, after the water receded and before the wind-borne foam returned, that the windows offered a nightmarish glimpse of what was coming next.

It was just as bad for those who could not see anything. Allan McCarthy, the ship's second officer, had gone off duty, but he was so worried that he would be catapulted from his bed that he had moved his mattress to the floor. Other members of the crew had gathered in the mess, where they were sitting at four long dining tables on chairs that had been chained to the floor. Still others were on couches that faced a television set near the side of the room. The mess is situated near the middle of the ship, where the turbulence is theoretically minimized, but under these conditions it did not make any difference. The heated serving table was loaded with lunch, soup and spaghetti Bolognese, but it was almost impossible to eat or drink.

Even though *Southern Supporter*'s engines were working at top speed, the ship's forward progress had been reduced to an average of less than six knots. In normal circumstances, Codrington would have further reduced his speed, to four knots or less, giving him enough momentum to climb over the waves but not so much that he launched off their peaks. "This is ridiculous," he said. "This guy is just trying to see if we can hang on."

Duffy assumed *Viarsa* was steaming at its top speed, but others were not sure. A few months earlier, the Spanish captain of an illegal toothfish vessel had told a television interviewer that he had been instructed to flee from an Australian patrol boat at something less than full speed to give his pursuers a false sense of superiority while allowing several other illegal fishing ships enough time to retrieve all of their equipment and get out of the area. "Maybe they have been told to take us a few hundred miles away to give the other pirates a chance to get away," said Arthur Staron, *Southern Supporter*'s first mate. "And then they'll accelerate to a speed we can't match." Duffy did not buy that, in part because the billowing smoke he had seen pouring from *Viarsa*'s stack suggested that its engines were working at full strength.

But by late afternoon, it appeared that *Viarsa* actually did have a speed advantage. The waves had steepened further, and the increasingly inhospitable conditions seemed to favor the relatively narrow fishing vessel. Obviously weighed down with fish, the low-riding ship sometimes looked as if it were more underwater than above, as if it were boring a hole through the waves rather than riding on top of them.

"It looks like a submarine!" O'Dea said.

"More like a roller coaster," Duffy said. "They must be having a horrendous time."

Since *Viarsa* was smaller than *Southern Supporter*, Duffy had initially hoped the violence of the fishing vessel's ascents and descents would be so great that Cabrera would find it necessary to turn back. But *Viarsa*'s ability to pierce through the mountains had changed things. By late afternoon it had pulled three miles ahead of *Southern Supporter*, creating a much larger gap than the thousand-yard separation Codrington had hoped to maintain. By sunset, the gap had expanded to six miles.

"We're losing them," Codrington declared. "We're at our maximum speed, but we're still not keeping up."

"There's nothing else we can do," Duffy said. "Just keep up as best you can."

No one had logged more miles on *Southern Supporter* than Codrington. He was its first captain when it was launched by the Australian government in 1993 and had spent about half of every year onboard the ship ever since. Although it was later sold by the government to P&O Nedlloyd, one of the world's largest ship owners, not much changed: the company frequently chartered it to the Australian government, and Codrington stayed with the ship. In spite of the pounding, he had tremendous confidence in his vessel. With a hull of one-inch-thick steel, it was certified to operate in "nearly formed ice."

The captain's biggest worry was the force of the water against the windows that were just a couple of feet in front of his chair. "If we lose one piece of glass," he told Duffy, "we'll have to slow right down or change course so we aren't heading into the waves anymore—and that will be the end of the chase."

Codrington's other fear was that the pirate might take foolhardy risks, creating the potential for a search and rescue operation in seas so treacherous that it would be virtually impossible to succeed. Visibility was still almost nonexistent. The ship's spotlight was on, but most of the windows were now covered with ice. The only two windows that afforded occasional views of *Viarsa* were the "clear view windows," eighteen-inch-wide circular panels of glass that did not freeze because they had heating elements between the inner and outer panes and a small motor that caused the glass to spin.

Duffy was staring into the blank windows and glancing at the instruments. Like Codrington, his mind was running through what could go wrong. The only time he had seen anything close to these conditions was in the North Sea, but he had been on a naval destroyer then, a far larger ship. Adding to his concern, he noticed that little streams of water had begun to flow through the window frames and trickle down onto consoles that were packed full of electronic equipment.

By now, Duffy and Codrington had developed a close relationship.

Duffy had been immediately impressed by the fifty-five-year-old captain's quiet confidence. Codrington, who has the manner of someone who spends his time in the library of an exclusive men's club, comes from a long line of distinguished mariners, including Sir Edward Codrington, the legendary British admiral who commanded the *Orion* during the Battle of Trafalgar. Codrington has been working at sea since he joined the British navy at age eighteen, after which he joined the merchant marine and emigrated to the Seychelles and later to Australia. During one conversation, Duffy and Codrington discovered that they had a distant familial connection: Codrington's wife was Duffy's brother-in-law's second cousin.

After several particularly violent waves rocked the ship, Duffy leaned toward Codrington and spoke quietly to prevent anyone else from hearing. "Listen," he began. "I feel that we have a duty to keep up our pursuit. But you're the master of the ship and you're responsible for everyone, so it's really up to you: if you feel our safety is being compromised, we'll just have to bite the bullet and let him go."

"It's ridiculous what he's doing, and we're taking some real knocks, but I don't feel like I'm compromising anyone's safety," Codrington said. A bit later, he added, "But I should tell you that there is going to be some damage. It won't be structural, but it will cost money to fix."

"Yeah, I accept that. If there's damage, the government will have to pay for it."

In fact, under its contract with P&O, the government was already obligated to cover the cost of that kind of damage, so Codrington did not need to raise the issue. He was just trying to give Duffy a greater appreciation of the danger. Duffy, too, understood that the government was contractually responsible for the damages, and he, too, had responded in a way that was intended to signal something more, namely his commitment to pressing on with the chase. The message got through. *I guess the government* really *wants to get this guy*, Codrington said to himself. For the next few minutes, the two men sat in silence, staring into the darkened panels of glass, wondering, among other things, what it would be like if one of the windows broke.

A bit later, Codrington asked, "Do you think it's worth asking him to slow down?"

Picking up the radio handset, Duffy said: "*Viarsa*, this is *Southern Supporter*. The conditions are getting worse and worse—and you are proceeding at an imprudent speed. We are concerned about the safety of your vessel and your crew. We request that you slow down to a prudent speed."

Cabrera replied almost instantaneously. "Thank you very much, but we are riding very comfortably."

Without reactivating the microphone, Duffy said, "Yeah, right!"

A few minutes later, Duffy finally retired to his cabin. It was 10:00 p.m. and he had not been in bed for more than a day, but the sea was so rough that he could not sleep. At one point he tried tucking his right arm underneath his mattress, hoping that with the rest of his weight still on top, the arm would act as an anchor and prevent him from being hurled to the floor. Later, he tried using several life preservers to wedge himself into the bunk. Whatever he did, he still found himself unable to sleep and grabbing, almost incessantly, at a handhold above the bunk.

Mike O'Dea was in the "operations room," a compartment one level below the bridge where three electronic warfare specialists from the Australian military maintained the radar detection equipment. Sitting at a small desk, he was preparing to speak to John Davis, the head of law enforcement for the Australian Fisheries Management Authority, about whether *Southern Supporter* should continue its pursuit after *Viarsa* left Australian waters. O'Dea was sure his superiors would tell him to give up. *Southern Supporter*, after all, did not have the firepower to make an arrest, and even if it did, it was not at all clear that there would be enough evidence to guarantee a successful prosecution. The pirates would do everything they could to destroy evidence at sea, and their lawyers would attempt to achieve the same result in court by discrediting the circumstantial evidence and arguing that any physical evidence had not been gathered in accordance with the rules.

The laws seemed lopsided to O'Dea. Whereas he had to follow them with unerring exactitude, the pirates were free to exploit regulations that were designed to foster unfettered international maritime trade. They could fly "flags of convenience," issued by countries that do virtually nothing to regulate their ships. They could change the name and nationality of their ships while at sea. They could even transfer their catches to "legitimate" vessels on the high seas, a form of laundering that law enforcement officials, even if they were lucky enough to witness it, could do very little to stop because proving the precise origins of any given fish is virtually impossible.

"What do you think?" Davis asked when O'Dea reached him by satellite phone. "Should we continue hot pursuit?"

"I'm not sure," O'Dea replied.

"It's up to you. If you recommend that we don't, we won't. But if you can tell us you have reasonable grounds to apprehend this boat, we'll put everything in place to continue the chase."

In fact, Davis, an energetic forty-two-year-old who thinks and operates more like a risk-taking entrepreneur than a mistake-fearing bureaucrat, was appalled by the idea of letting *Viarsa* escape. His colleagues had estimated that pirates had stolen at least fifteen thousand tons of toothfish—worth more than $70 million—from the waters surrounding Heard Island since 1997. As he sometimes told friends, "It's as if someone showed up in your country and started clear-cutting one of your rain forests, packed up all the logs on a ship, and carried them away—and you did nothing to stop them." He had reason to believe that *Viarsa* was one of the leading culprits, a pirate vessel that had systematically stolen toothfish from several of its most important habitats.

Uruguay's involvement was also part of Davis's motivation. It had licensed a dozen ships to hunt for toothfish on the high seas, areas where fishing is entirely unregulated. Since fisheries scientists do not believe toothfish exist in substantial numbers on the high seas, Davis suspected that all twelve of the ships were actually poaching in waters that belong to one of the countries that still have substantial toothfish populations. Indeed, he believed that every one of the Uruguayan-registered toothfish vessels had stolen fish from the Australian Fishing Zone. They rarely brought their fish to Uruguay. Instead, the vessel owners paid Uruguayan officials to fly to ports where the fish was unloaded and to "certify" that it had been caught on the high seas. By doing so, Uruguay gave the pirates an almost surefire means to transform illegally captured fish into a product that could legally be exported to the United States, Japan, and other major toothfish markets.

Davis was also offended by the behavior of Uruguay's ambassador to Australia, Pedro Mo Amaro, who had been told earlier that day about the pursuit of *Viarsa* and summoned to an urgent meeting with Bernard Wonder, the deputy secretary of Australia's Department of Agriculture, Fisheries, and Forestry. "Something must be wrong," Mo Amaro had said.

"I do not believe the vessel you are pursuing flies a Uruguayan flag because *Viarsa* is nowhere near your zone. According to our data, the ship is currently in the Atlantic Ocean, several thousand miles away from Heard Island."

Speaking to O'Dea, Davis said, "If we have a reasonable prospect of getting a successful prosecution, we should go ahead."

"The evidence we have is purely circumstantial," O'Dea replied. "They were obviously in our zone, but they will claim that they were just passing through."

"He was less than thirty miles off Heard Island when you found them," Davis said. "And when you ordered them to stop, he ran. What does that tell you?"

"But what's the evidence? It all depends on what we find on the boat, and they'll have a lot of time to manipulate things. We may spend an awful lot of money and end up with an unsuccessful prosecution from a lack of evidence."

"It's up to you. *You* have to say if you have reasonable grounds."

O'Dea had known it would come down to that—he would have to decide. And as the senior fisheries officer onboard *Southern Supporter*, he, more than anyone else, would have to live with the consequences of the decision. Although Davis, one of the most senior officials in his department, clearly wanted O'Dea to say yes, it was not an easy decision. Everything that had happened suggested that the vessel had been fishing in Australian waters. On the other hand, it would be difficult to win a conviction without actual evidence—and O'Dea had none.

"Based on what we have at the moment, we may or may not have enough evidence for a conviction," he said. "At this point we just don't have any real evidence."

"They were 180 miles inside our zone, you detected fishing equipment nearby, and they refused to stop. What's your view? Has an offense taken place?"

"Yes."

"Well, would you recommend apprehension?"

"Okay . . . I'm prepared to say that we should go ahead—but I have a bad taste in my mouth about making it because it's a borderline decision."

"Don't worry about that. No one is going to blame you."

O'Dea found little reassurance in that. Although he had a lot of respect for Davis, O'Dea felt almost as if he had been bullied into saying yes. And regardless of Davis's reassurances, he knew that if anything went wrong, he would bear the responsibility for the final result.

CHAPTER 5

Los Angeles
October 1984

As Doug Harbison stood in the parking lot listening to Lee Lantz describe the attributes of Chilean Sea Bass, he was as excited as Lantz had been when he came across his first toothfish. In fact, Harbison's ambitions went beyond Lantz's: while Lantz had thought of his discovery as a "utility fish," a low-cost substitute for other, better-known species, Harbison believed Chilean Sea Bass could itself become one of the all-stars.

Harbison asked Lantz every question he could think of, but he had already decided that he needed to go to Chile himself. He wanted to see how the fish were processed and how unfrozen Chilean Sea Bass behaves. Different species have very different shelf lives, and their tolerance for travel and changing temperatures varies. Some virtually rattle apart on airplanes; some are quick to smell.

So, in January 1985, Lantz and Harbison traveled to Chile. Harbison spent much of his time with Neef, explaining how fish should be inspected to ensure they had been recently caught. When you press into the fish with your thumb, Harbison said, its surface should quickly pop back to its original shape. The eyes should be shiny and clear, the flesh should be translucent, and there should be no odor. "If you smell anything at all, it should be the aroma of the sea," Harbison said. He also demonstrated how he wanted the fish to be filleted—emphasizing how important it was to use the sharpest possible knives and to make a single clean cut to avoid tearing the flesh—and how filets should be wrapped and packed in containers that would be air-freighted to Los Angeles.

Fish reached California five to ten days after they were caught. The fresh product cost more than the frozen version—Harbison initially charged $2.75 a pound—but it went to "white tablecloth" restaurants that could afford to pay more. They were also the places that were written about and emulated. About a year after his initial trip to Chile, Harbison was selling twenty thousand pounds of fresh Chilean Sea Bass every month. Lantz was selling more than twice that, about five hundred thousand pounds a year. And over the next few years, the total toothfish business grew at an accelerating rate, particularly toward the end of the decade, when the fish was successfully introduced in Japan and it became more popular on the East Coast of the United States.

Like in California, many of the first East Coast restaurants that served toothfish were Chinese restaurants that used the frozen variety as a substitute for black cod. The first white tablecloth establishment to serve toothfish may have been Manhattan's Four Seasons Restaurant, where titans from the financial and entertainment industries entertain one another when they are not quietly competing for the best table. In 1990, one of its chefs, Fred Mero, started marinating toothfish in a variety of Asian spices before searing it and placing it on a plate with a black bean sauce. Like the Chinese restaurants, the Four Seasons did not use the name Lantz had given the fish. After consulting with others in the kitchen, Mero created his own: "corvina bass." Given that corvina and bass are two different kinds of fish and that toothfish is not taxonomically related to either of them, it was an odd choice. But it did not matter: it sounded good and the dish quickly became one of the restaurant's favorites.

A year later, Chilean Sea Bass had its downtown debut under its own name at Tribeca Grill, a trendy restaurant that actor Robert De Niro and restaurateur Drew Nieporent had recently opened with a group of celebrity investors that included Bill Murray, Mikhail Baryshnikov, and Sean Penn. The chef there, Don Pintabona, served the fish with a crust of crab and a port wine glaze. In 1992, another popular Manhattan restaurant, Solera, began offering Chilean Sea Bass that was covered with a red wine reduction and came with mashed potatoes and crispy shallots. "At first, there were no fireworks—it was just another fish," says Dominick Cerrone, Solera's chef at the time. "But everyone loved it and it was beginning to really take off."

Chile gave foreign fishermen the right to harvest toothfish from its waters on an "exploratory" basis from August 1991 until July 1992. The military government that had come to power after Salvador Allende's death had three goals: to estimate the size of the toothfish stocks, to expand economic activity in the mostly uninhabited southern half of the country, and to use that activity to bolster Chile's sovereignty claims over territory that had sometimes been disputed by Argentina. It seemed like a great idea: Chile's domestic fishing vessels were too small to work in the inhospitable waters off the southern coast, so no one knew how many toothfish were there. And the government could generate business activity in remote areas without going to the trouble of building cities and roads. All it had to do was issue permits.

But the bureaucrats made a terrible mistake: they gave the licenses to eleven different companies, theoretically limiting each of them to one boat. This provided some of the biggest players in the fishing industry with a tantalizing look at what turned out to be a very substantial resource at a time when Chile did not have the means to monitor, let alone control, the fishery. For organizations that did not feel compelled to abide by the rules, it was effectively open season.

The fishing vessels that began heading to Chile were nothing like the ones Lantz had seen in Valparaiso fourteen years earlier. They were large industrial ships like *Viarsa*, fitted out with onboard factories and vast freezer holds, and they could pull fish from the sea in quantities that the domestic fishermen could not have imagined. Chile's officially reported toothfish catch catapulted from about 12,000 tons in 1992 to almost 34,000 tons one year later. Since it is unlikely that illegally caught fish were reported, the actual increase was probably much greater. And it soon became apparent that the government had given rise to an unsustainable feeding frenzy: the toothfish catch plummeted in 1994. Tighter restrictions were imposed, but it was too late. Most of the fish were already gone, and the illegal operators had moved to Argentinean waters, where toothfish had yet to be exploited and there were no quotas.

This would become the template: like a pack of ravenous wolves, fleets of sophisticated fishing boats, many of them operated by pirates, would descend upon one toothfish habitat after another, poaching entire populations before government officials even knew it was happening. Chilean Sea Bass had still not become a ubiquitous bestseller, but the basic patterns had already been established: consumer demand was gaining unstoppable momentum, and the fishing industry was only too happy to respond. Lee Lantz had unknowingly created a gold rush. Indeed, at a time when much of the fishing industry had become a marginal proposition, tooth-fish was being called white gold.

Many of the first toothfish fishermen who went to South America were Spanish. One of them was Antonio Garcia Perez.

CHAPTER 6

Southern Ocean
August 8, 2003

"The chase is on!"

Keith Johnson, Steve Duffy's boss, had called Duffy early Friday morning after several senior government ministers—including those responsible for the Foreign and Defense Departments—agreed that *Southern Supporter*'s hot pursuit should be maintained even after *Viarsa* left the Australian Fishing Zone. "We're going to get this guy," Johnson said. "Make sure you tick all the boxes. And you should also look at how you would conduct a boarding if you had assets at your disposal."

"Where are the assets going to come from?"

"No idea—I just want you to think about what you would need to do to get onboard."

Like Duffy, Johnson had had a long naval career before he joined the Customs Service to take charge of its new marine unit. Now fifty years old, he frequently talked about golf and his desire to retire early, but he still looked and behaved very much like a military man. His hair was short, and he parceled out information on a need-to-know basis. It was for that reason that he said virtually nothing to Duffy at this point about the discussions he and others were having with several foreign governments.

Duffy had already begun studying *Viarsa*'s hull and superstructure to determine how he would conduct a boarding, noting, among other things, where men could be lowered onto the ship from a helicopter. "The foredeck has a mast about eight feet high, which virtually fouls the foredeck for a helicopter winch wire," he wrote in his notebook. "The aft deck has a folding crane on the port side, and there are two wires that run from the mast to the wheelhouse and then to a mast on the aft deck. I believe they will foul that area for helo winching. The wheelhouse roof is cluttered with a lot of gear and an assortment of wires. No good for winching at all." These were just the *visible* obstacles. Duffy knew almost nothing about the ship's internal architecture, and there was no way to determine how *Viarsa*'s crew or captain would react to a forced boarding.

"We know the master is stubborn," Duffy told Johnson, "but it's impossible to know how really belligerent he'll be or how much support he'd have from his crew. We haven't seen any hostile reactions—they haven't been shaking their fists at us—but we don't know very much about them."

Shortly after his conversation with Johnson, Duffy returned to the bridge, where he saw that *Southern Supporter* had managed to catch up with *Viarsa*. Although the waves were still large by just about any standard, most of them were less than twenty feet tall and not as steep as they had been the day before. It was, therefore, impossible to know if Cabrera had pulled back the throttle a bit or if his ship had lost its advantage in the less challenging conditions. In any case, the relative calm was unlikely to last. Over the previous couple of hours, the wind direction had shifted again. It was now coming out of the west, and another storm was expected to arrive within a few hours. In the early morning light, Duffy could also see that the surface of the water had taken on an oily cast, the first sign that the sea itself was beginning to freeze.

"We're going to continue with the chase," Duffy told O'Dea and Codrington before he summarized his conversation with Johnson. "Now we have to start thinking about how we would conduct a boarding. I'll take charge of the physical part of getting people over, but Mike, you have to think about how you'd go about searching for evidence and interviewing the crew."

"But we still don't know what kind of help we're going to have," O'Dea said.

"With the *South Tomi*, we had plenty of help," Codrington said, referring to an incident in 2001 in which *Southern Supporter* chased a toothfish vessel that was registered in Togo for fourteen days, until it was intercepted and boarded by Australian troops who had been delivered by a South African naval vessel. "The South Africans brought down an Australian army contingent. Maybe something similar will happen this time."

Johnson had also asked Duffy to broadcast a very specific, two-part message to *Viarsa* before it left the Australian Fishing Zone, which was expected to happen at 8:30 a.m. After reading the message to himself, Duffy showed it to O'Dea and said, "We need to have some sort of posture when we talk to this guy over the radio. You've built up a bit of rapport with him, so why don't I be the ogre. You can play the good cop and see if you can get him to give up some more information."

A few minutes later, O'Dea read the first part of the message over Channel 16: "Over the last twenty-four hours, there has been a great deal of diplomatic activity concerning your actions and refusal to abide by my instructions. The international discussions have reached the highest levels of the Australian and Uruguayan governments. I can tell you that there is significant support for our actions. This is another opportunity to resolve this matter without there being severe consequences for you personally. I am instructing you to stop your vessel and to follow my lawful directions." After waiting for a response that did not come, Duffy took the radio handset and delivered the second, tougher part of the message: "You still refuse to cooperate. Therefore, I will now call to my government and tell them they should accept the help that has been offered. And you must accept the consequences of your actions. Good-bye."

Later that morning, after O'Dea had returned to the radio and again asked *Viarsa* to stop, Cabrera finally responded. "I can't stop the vessel without instructions from the owner," he said. "I have to wait a few minutes, only a few minutes. If the head office says stop, I will stop. If head office says go, I don't stop; I will go. Are you understanding?"

"Roger that. In the meantime, while you are waiting, I advise you to stop your vessel."

"If I stop now or I stop in five minutes, it is the same, so let me speak, and after that I give you an answer. That's only four, five minutes more."

"We will be staying on station astern of your vessel and standing by on Channel 16."

When O'Dea spoke to Cabrera an hour later, the captain said he still had not heard from the owner. "I understand your problem," O'Dea said, "but I need to explain to you that you, as the master of the vessel, are in charge. You are responsible for its actions." Shortly after that conversation, *Viarsa* changed course and began heading due west, a course that would lead directly to Uruguay.

"Do you," O'Dea asked, "have any intention or destination?"

"We don't have any particular destination. We don't know. We are awaiting instruction."

At midday, the sky was overcast and the temperature was just slightly below freezing, but the wind speed suddenly dropped to less than twenty knots. And Cabrera, it appeared, wanted to do some housekeeping. "*Southern Supporter*," he said over the radio, "this is *Viarsa*. Please keep clear of my vessel. I'm slowing down to let my crew go on the deck to tie down loose gear."

In response, O'Dea asked, "Did you receive the communiqué that we read to you earlier?"

"Yes, I did."

"Do you understand that you will be held personally responsible for all the actions undertaken by your ship?"

"Yes, I understood. I am on innocent passage. I am going to continue on my current course—I will not stop."

In spite of Cabrera's request, Duffy asked Codrington to edge closer to the other ship. He was eager to get a better look at a cutaway section of the hull, the place on the starboard side where longlines are brought onto the ship. Whereas the main deck was at least twelve feet above the waterline, the base of the cutaway section was just a few feet above the water. It looked like it would not be difficult to climb from a small boat to the cutaway section and from there to the main deck. Once *Southern Supporter* was alongside *Viarsa*, about one hundred yards away, Duffy could see that several crewmen were scurrying around the deck securing various pieces of gear with lines. Codrington decided to follow the other crew's example, asking some of his crewmen to go outside with shovels and crowbars to chop away at the snow and ice that had formed on *Southern Supporter*'s deck. Sections of the bow were covered with what looked like drifts of snow, some of them more than four feet high. They were difficult to remove: the snow was covered by so much ice that it was almost rock solid.

Scott Webb was peering through a pair of binoculars. Noticing that the door to *Viarsa*'s bridge was open, he looked inside and spotted a bearded man with ghostly pale skin. The gray hair that protruded from the top of his head and much of his face stood out sharply against a dark outfit that looked like a tracksuit. He appeared to be wizened and short.

"I think I see the master," Webb said.

Duffy had conjured a mental picture of their adversary, imagining him to be broad shouldered, muscled, and tall. What he saw through the binoculars was totally inconsistent with that image. Even so, given the gray-haired man's age and his presence on the bridge, Duffy was sure that this was Cabrera. "It's got to be him," he said. "He looks a bit freaky."

Cabrera was annoyed by the observers. "You're too close!" he said over the radio. "Please maintain a safe distance. I am slowing down."

"Roger," Duffy responded. "We acknowledge your intention." He was deliberately unfriendly. If this had been a typical conversation between two vessels, he would have described his plans and asked the other captain if he was "comfortable" with them. But Duffy wanted to take every opportunity to assert himself, so he deliberately tried to sound as though he were issuing an order. "We are navigating with caution in your close proximity," he added. "You are to maintain a steady course and speed, and we will guarantee your safety."

Speculation about what Cabrera would do next had become a constant in every conversation on the patrol boat. He was obviously strong-willed and a risk taker, but how far would he go? Was he the kind of person who would stop at nothing, who would flee the scene if *Southern Supporter* were to get into serious trouble and require assistance? Or was he just a zealous fisherman pursuing what he thought of as his God-given right to make a living? Of course, it was also not at all clear to the Australians whether Cabrera was really in charge or just taking orders from the vessel's owner or its fishing master.

"If we could figure out what is going on in his head," Duffy said, "we might be able to think of something else we could do."

"I know what he's going to do," O'Dea said. "He's got a boat that's worth a million dollars and a cargo that's probably worth more than that, so he's going to run. What else would he do? Burglars with a couple of thousand dollars run from the police. This is millions. If he gets away, he'll be laughing."

But O'Dea also recognized that several variables were unknowable. For one thing, neither captain knew how much fuel the other ship had. "Maybe," O'Dea said, "he thinks we'll run out of fuel faster than he will."

"He could be right," Duffy said. "After all, they started with enough fuel to fish for months and months. We could be in a war of attrition." Duffy knew that many longliners filled their fish holds with diesel before they left port, replacing the fuel with fish over the course of their expeditions. The way they rinsed away the oil with seawater before they filled the holds with fish was obviously ecologically unsound, and restaurant patrons would not be pleased to know that their fish had spent many weeks lying in what had previously served as a fuel tank—but the extra fuel storage gave longliners much greater endurance.

Walking over to the chart table, Duffy studied the chart that covered territory ranging from Africa to Australia and Antarctica to Mozambique. In most parts of the world, the ship would carry dozens of charts for such an enormous expanse, but there was no need for more than one here. Except for areas near Antarctica's continental shelf and a small number of islands—the same places that are home to toothfish—the water was several miles deep and therefore free from navigational hazards. Codrington was also standing at the chart table, punching the latest fuel consumption numbers into a calculator. The basic equations were straightforward, but the assumptions on which they were based were not. *Southern Supporter* carries 380 tons of fuel and generally burns seven tons a day. But the distance it can cover in that time varies enormously. In perfect conditions, it travels at close to twelve knots. If it is heading into wind and waves, it might go only half that fast.

"It looks like we can make it back to Australia as long as we turn back before August 24th," Codrington said. "After that, we'll have to go somewhere else. Maybe South Africa."

CHAPTER 7

Riviera, Spain

The essential facts about Riviera have been the same for centuries. The harbor is home to a fleet of dingy-looking fishing boats, and the crooked streets leading away from the waterfront are lined with dozens of small tapas restaurants where little dishes of food are served to anyone who buys a drink. The emphasis is on seafood: mussels and calamari are the favorites. Fish is also the main topic of conversation because most of the twenty-eight thousand people who live in Riviera make their living from the sea.

Antonio Perez lives near the center of town, in a third-floor apartment that has a view of the harbor and is just a couple of blocks from where he grew up, with his wife Angeles and twin daughters. When the chase began, the girls were fourteen. One of them had decided that she wanted to be a biologist; the other had not figured it out. When Perez was their age, he was already working on his father's trawler. It was illegal to have such a job before you were eighteen, but his father did not want to wait that long; he thought it was more important to give his son an early start. For the next several years, Perez spent every weekend on the boat, helping the crew to set and pull the net and to clean the fish. He hated the work, mostly because he was prone to seasickness. It was so bad that he thought about finding another career, but he never came up with a better idea, and by the time he turned eighteen and became a full-time fisherman, seasickness was no longer a problem.

"For me, nothing else is as good," he would say many years later. "I have friends who work in construction, but I make four times as much money as they do."

Perez does not look like a fisherman. His body is slender and not muscled, and his face, pale and serious, looks like it might belong to an academic. He often creates a poor first impression because he can come across as dour and arrogant, partly because of his tendency to cock his head slightly backward, which makes it seem as though he is literally looking down at people. The way he wears his glasses—they rest well above his ears, so the temples slant downward across his dark hair before they reach his eyes—accentuates the effect. In at least one respect, Perez *is* arrogant—he believes he is extraordinarily good at what he does. But when he is with colleagues or friends, he is playful and energetic. This is reflected in the way he moves: he walks faster than some people run and often tries to hurry others along by clapping his hands and exclaiming, sometimes in English, "Let's go. Let's go!"

The possibility that an ocean could run out of fish was not something Perez considered when he started out as a fisherman. When he crossed the Atlantic for the first time as a nineteen-year-old in 1983 to fish for cod off Newfoundland, some of the old-timers were already talking about how much better it used to be, but he never really believed them. Boasting about exaggerated past conquests, after all, is hardly unusual among fishermen. And it just did not seem possible that the ocean, after providing for his family for so many generations, would ever fail. But the populations of many species were already running low. Cod was particularly beleaguered. When Perez was part of the hunt, more than half of the remaining population was being harvested every year. It was a doomsday spiral that ended in 1992, when Canada shut down the cod fisheries near Newfoundland and a year later when the United States closed fisheries near George Bank.

Perez moved back to Riviera in 1993, but the fishing on the European side of the Atlantic had never been as lucrative as the far side, and it had become even less attractive because of Spain's accession to the European Union in 1986, which led to steady reductions in fishing quotas. But Perez, who had risen through the ranks, from deckhand to officer, during the time he worked in the North Atlantic, was sure there were promising fisheries to be found somewhere else—and that he would hear about them in Riviera. The tapas restaurants had always been the best place to trade information about jobs and fisheries; they were a concentration of expertise and networking essentially no different from those that foster software development in Silicon Valley and financial wizardry on Wall Street.

"In Riviera, we know the whole world," Perez says. "If someone asks me to take a boat to Alaska, I know someone who has worked there—and he can tell me where the fish are and what gear I should use to catch them. So if I go to Alaska, I'll catch fish on the first day."

For Spain's former cod fishermen, the basic solution had already become obvious: they needed to refocus their efforts on the Southern Hemisphere's waters, which were relatively unspoiled. Perez's family has done just that. His father still trawled for fish—by then he owned two boats—but he was operating them out of Namibia. Perez's brother was fishing for hake off the west coast of Africa; one of his uncles was harvesting shellfish from Senegal. Perez went even farther south, flying to Punta Arenas.

Although Perez had been hired to work on a boat that targeted prawns, once he arrived in the Chilean port, he learned that his employer also had four boats that sought a much more lucrative species—Patagonian toothfish. The deckhands on the toothfish boats made as much money as the officers on the prawn boats. Perez said he was willing to work as a deckhand, a demotion from his previous role, but he insisted on a job on a toothfish vessel that would seek toothfish off the coast of Argentina.

It was a great opportunity: While most of Chile's toothfish had been consumed during the previous couple of years, Argentina's population had barely been touched, and the government had yet to establish a quota. Argentina's continental shelf is much wider than Chile's, so the deepwater habitats of toothfish were so far from land that the traditional fishing fleet could not reach them.

Perez reached two main conclusions during the expedition. First, he believed the crew of the ship he was on, which included an Argentinean captain who did not seem to do anything, was lazy. "They go out for forty-five days and then go back to port," regardless of whether their hold is full of fish, Perez says incredulously. He was also convinced that toothfish were extremely plentiful. It was as if he had discovered a vast new oil field, a resource as rich as Atlantic cod had been many years earlier.

Perez was offered a position as an officer for his second voyage with the company and a big raise—from $1,000 a month to $2,500 a month, plus a bonus. Over the next three years, he completed seven more trips, all of which were successful. But, like in Chile, Argentina's toothfish fishery could not withstand an unregulated onslaught of industrialized fishing. Quotas were introduced in 1995, but enforcement was limited. Indeed, although the quota was set at eleven thousand tons for that year, the officially recorded catch was more than twenty thousand tons. Catches declined precipitously after that. It had taken hundreds of years to destroy the Atlantic cod fisheries, yet it had taken just a couple to decimate Argentina's toothfish.

By then, scientists had learned that the species is particularly vulnerable to large-scale fishing because toothfish take much longer to mature and because they tend to stay in one place, though there are exceptions. In 2001, a single toothfish was found near Greenland, which meant it had undertaken an inexplicable pole-to-pole odyssey. It had presumably swum deep below the surface so that it was able to stay in water that was almost freezing. Scientists have also found that some toothfish from Heard Island have moved to another island that is more than a thousand miles away. However, other than occasional migratory urges, toothfish are homebodies, which makes life much easier for their pursuers, most of which are human; although toothfish are sometimes consumed by seals and whales, the fully grown fish are generally not threatened by marine predators.

After fishermen had plundered most of Argentina's toothfish, it was the hunters who migrated, this time across the Atlantic, to work out of ports in South Africa and Namibia as they scoured South African waters and places farther east. Perez was one of them. Indeed, although his role is as obscure as Lee Lantz's, he too was one of the toothfish industry's pioneers, playing an important parallel role in exploiting several of the fish's main habitats.

It is not surprising that toothfish and Antonio Perez came to the attention of Antonio Vidal Pego, an aggressive young fishing boat owner who is also from Riviera. From a small office that overlooks the harbor and is within earshot of the siren that announces the fish auctions that take place three times a day, Vidal and his father run Vidal Amadores SA. For most of its history, their company had operated trawlers that fished locally, but the catches and profits were steadily declining. By the time Perez began his toothfish career, Vidal, who was then just twenty years old, knew the family business would not survive unless it found some more rewarding fisheries.

What Vidal heard about toothfish was astonishing: an increasingly popular fish that could be captured in enormous quantities. He was familiar with several of the companies that had sent ships to Chile a few years earlier, and he knew most of them had been deriving significant profits from toothfish ever since. Eager to participate, Vidal hired Antonio Perez when he came home for the Christmas holidays in 1996. It was an obvious move: the two men had the same hard-charging approach, and Perez had become expert in finding and extracting the fish. Although they did not know each other before, they immediately felt comfortable with each other because of their common backgrounds. They both grew up in Riviera and their fathers, both fishing boat owners, were friends.

Vidal had already acquired a boat, a Japanese-built vessel that originally had been used for tuna long-lining, and he asked Perez to oversee a refit that would prepare it for toothfish hunting. Following the work, which took seven months, the boat was named *Merced* and was registered in Panama. In June 1997, it set out on its first toothfish voyage with Perez as its fishing master. The inaugural trip was a complete success, as were two subsequent ones. In each case, Perez filled the hold with processed toothfish, which were offloaded in Walvis Bay, a port in the West African nation of Namibia.

There was just one problem: all of the best toothfish habitats were located in waters that belonged to countries other than Spain. On the other hand, Vidal knew that the countries that had the fish did not know much about large-scale long-lining. The waters surrounding the Kerguelen Archipelago, French-owned islands a couple of hundred miles northwest of Heard Island, were a prime example. Even before Lee Lantz had come across his first toothfish in Chile, France had allowed the Soviet Union (and later, Russia and the Ukraine) to use enormous factory ships to take the fish from its waters. Since the fish were consumed only in Russia and the Ukraine, it was a commercial arrangement that went unnoticed in the rest of the world and one that was not very economically important to France. But after toothfish became popular in other parts of the world, the government decided that it would not renew permits held by foreigners. It wanted to give French vessels the opportunity to harvest the suddenly more valuable fish. That gave Vidal an opening: by forming a partnership with a French company that could get a permit but did not have much experience with long-lining, Vidal obtained a legal entry into a major toothfish fishery. In exchange for a share of the profits, he agreed to provide a crew that would guide the fishing operations.

Perez, who went to Kerguelen for Vidal, knew the area is an ideal home for toothfish. The bottom-dwelling fish live in water that is 1,000 to 1,500 feet deep until they are about two years old; then they migrate down to the depths, sometimes to places more than a mile deep. The Kerguelen Plateau, an underwater formation that surrounds both Kerguelen and Heard Islands, has both depths: water near the islands is about 1,200 feet deep; at the end of the plateau, the bottom shelves away into canyons and seamounts, which appeal to adult toothfish, before falling to extreme depths.

Like Vidal, Perez was thrilled to have a legal opportunity to seek toothfish. His only complaint was that he was unable to work as hard as he would have liked because of French work rules. "The French only work twelve hours a day, and they never work on Sundays," he said. "Even if they find a great place, they just stop. They rest! You can't do that. If the fish are there, take them. They might not be there tomorrow!"

Then it got worse: after the first year of the partnership, the French company decided that it did not need any more help from Vidal or Perez. Thanks to the partnership, the French had learned enough about long-lining that they no longer saw a need to share the profits with Spaniards. Vidal was furious. He thought the French had effectively stolen his expertise. Now the only places where he could catch toothfish were either the mostly barren high seas or in places from which he was legally barred. But he was not about to give up the toothfish business. Indeed, he expanded his effort by acquiring another Japanese-built ship and having it refitted for toothfish. He renamed it *Viarsa*.

Sometimes Vidal's ships struggled to fish on the high seas—and sometimes they ventured into waters where they did not have permits. But since Vidal and his father believed the rules were illegitimate, they did not accept the idea that they were breaking the law.

"I am not a pirate!" the father, Antonio Vidal Suarez, once told a Spanish newspaper. During an interview, he admitted that his fishermen had illegally taken fish from French waters, the same ones where they had operated legitimately in the past, but claimed that the laws were an unreasonable form of protectionism and that any accusations of piracy were therefore baseless. "Those accusations are motivated by vested interests of companies" that have the legal right to fish in areas foreign operators cannot, he said. "Legal fishermen can say whatever they like and accuse whomever they want. Why? Because they don't want anyone else to catch those fish. Who is the pirate here—me or them? There is also a legal mafia: organizations that systematically hog all quotas and exclude everyone else."

None of Vidal's toothfish hunters were as successful as Antonio Perez, who used each voyage to perfect his methodology. The first step is easy: Since toothfish live only in waters surrounding Antarctica that are less than two miles deep, a quick look at nautical charts reveals all of their possible habitats. Most areas of the ocean are several miles deep, so the only places suitable to toothfish are the deepest sections of the continental shelves that stretch out from South America and Antarctica as well as areas near the relatively small number of islands scattered around the South Indian, South Atlantic, and Southern Oceans.

Once Perez reaches a potentially promising area, he narrows his search by using sonar to locate the large protrusions from the seabed that tend to attract toothfish. Given that the fish generally stay within a tightly constricted area, he then sets four or five "short longlines," each less than a mile long, at different locations and depths. "When you pick up the lines a day later," he explains, "three may have less than half a ton of fish. One might have almost nothing. If one has two tons, that's it!"

As soon as Perez picks his spot, he directs his crew to set a full-length longline, which incorporates up to two hundred branch lines, each with seventy-six hooks. The hooks are separated by four feet, and a single longline might extend for fifteen miles. It takes surprisingly little time to deploy such a line—*Viarsa*'s crew could do it in less than two hours—but each line represents a sizable investment because every hook is baited with a sardine. *Viarsa* began the voyage to Heard Island that led to its pursuit by *Southern Supporter* with ninety-six tons of frozen sardines purchased from suppliers in Spain, Venezuela, and South Africa and delivered to Mauritius on container ships.)

Longlines can be set at any time of the day or night, and Perez might have two or three deployed at any given time, although three is unusual because the process of retrieving one can consume an entire day if the catch is large. As the fish enter the factory, Perez continues to gather information, assessing the population that remains both by evaluating the number of fish in the catch and their average size. He believes larger fish are more likely to stay in the same place than smaller ones. "If you don't get that many and they all weigh more than thirty-five kilograms, don't go back," he says. "There's no more fish!"

It is not unusual for Perez's crew to extract ten, even twenty, tons of toothfish in a single day. During one extraordinary day, he says he reeled in *forty tons*. He says he has never brought one of Vidal's vessels back to port with a hold that was not fully loaded. Indeed, even then, when his crew is desperate to get home, he sometimes delays their return trip in order to gather data for future voyages by using sonar to plot the seabed.

The only thing Perez does not like about toothfish is the fish itself. Although he likes the flavor of their cheeks, he considers the rest of the fish tasteless, not nearly as good as sole, his favorite fish, or the calamari he likes to cook when he is at home. But what was important to Perez was the money he made. During the twelve months before he was spotted by Stephen Duffy, Perez had completed three successful voyages, each one producing three hundred tons of "trunks," toothfish that had been frozen after their heads, tails, and guts were removed. He was making much more money than he ever could have from fishing cod, and there was no end in sight. Life was not perfect: he would have preferred not to be away from home so much, and to work in places that were not so remote and cold. He also knew that his health would eventually suffer for the combination of nonstop working and smoking.

"There's no way I will make it past fifty," he told friends. Even so, he was generally content. He had set out to become a fisherman, and he had become one of the world's best.

Vidal was equally pleased. Toothfish changed everything for his company, enabling him to turn a relatively small domestic company with declining prospects into a much larger international organization that is far more profitable. "He has made extraordinary amounts of money," says Lawrence Lasarow, a California-based fish merchant who bought toothfish caught by Vidal's ships and imported it into the United States. Lasarow was also pleased to have a role to play in the booming toothfish trade.

"It just doesn't get any better," he declares. "You can make so much from this fish that you feel like you're gouging the customer. It's the perfect fish!"

CHAPTER 8

*Southern Ocean
August 14, 2003*

Southern Supporter and *Viarsa* were heading toward a sea of icebergs.
Just after 3:00 p.m. on Thursday, August 14, Allan McCarthy,
Southern Supporter's second officer, spotted the first of them and pointed
it out to Duffy. *Here's one more thing we're going to have to think about,*
Duffy said to himself as he imagined how Cabrera might use the ice to his
advantage and what a collision could do. It was also an exhilarating sight.
Duffy had never seen an iceberg before, and as the ship approached the
giant mound of white, he, like every first-time Antarctic explorer, realized
that photographs do not nearly capture the beauty or enormity of icebergs. McCarthy estimated that this one was seventy-five feet high and
almost a half-mile long.

"Are we going to see more of them?" Duffy asked.

McCarthy, who was forty-six and one of the handful of Australian
mariners qualified to navigate in Antarctic ice, spends much of his time on
an icebreaker that ferries people and supplies to Antarctica. "We're supposed to see some more very soon, and there'll be a lot more if we stay on
this course," he said, noting that the ship was then on a course of 255
degrees, mostly west but slightly to the south.

A change of course came later that night, but it was not the one

McCarthy wanted. At 11:05 p.m., *Southern Supporter*'s first mate, Arthur Staron, used an intercom to wake Duffy, telling him, "I thought you might like to know that *Viarsa* just turned south." The new course would only speed the ships' progress into the ice. Turning to Bruce Noble, a forty-seven-year-old seaman, Staron said, "This guy may be a pretty competent seaman, but he's on the verge of being a madman."

When Duffy, dressed in a sweatsuit and moccasins, reached the bridge, he picked up the radio receiver. "*Viarsa*, this is *Southern Supporter*. I request to speak to the master." Hearing no response, he added, "This is Customs Officer Duffy. I request information explaining why you altered south." There was still no response, but at 12:05 a.m., *Viarsa* turned sharply to the right to resume its westerly course. Duffy went back to bed but was awakened again three hours later, this time by Allan McCarthy, who said: "*Viarsa* has altered to the south again." Returning to the bridge, Duffy tried, again unsuccessfully, to speak to someone on *Viarsa*.

"Maybe he's just trying to alter his course away from South Africa," he said to McCarthy. "But why would he make these giant zigzags?" Duffy wondered whether the course changes were the result of disagreements among *Viarsa*'s officers.

Just after 4:00 a.m., *Viarsa* returned again to a westerly course, albeit on a track that was farther to the south than it had been five hours earlier.

Early Friday morning, August 15, a beautiful, snow-white bird flew over *Southern Supporter*'s foredeck, just a few yards in front of the bridge. Stephen Duffy was amazed that such a delicate creature could exist in an environment that was so harsh. The temperature outside, which had been six below zero Celsius for the previous two days, had dipped to nine below.

"It's a snow petrel," McCarthy said. "It means we can't be far from the ice now."

A couple of years earlier, McCarthy had been visiting a small graveyard on Antarctica when he was hit by a blinding snowstorm. While he sat on a rock waiting for it to pass, he noticed two tiny, coal-black eyes staring at him through the whiteness. He later learned that they belonged to a snow petrel, which appeared disembodied and ghostlike as it hovered in the swirl. It stayed nearby throughout the storm, and McCarthy had the impression that it was watching over him. Having ridden out the storm together, he decided it was his favorite bird, and he was pleased to see another one now.

"How does it survive?" Duffy asked.

"They eat the little fish and krill that live near the edge of the ice shelf, and we're getting close to it. *Viarsa* took us twenty-five miles farther south last night, so we need to keep a very good watch. We should also get someone in Canberra to send us the ice charts."

"The what?"

"The Bureau of Meteorology publishes charts based on satellite images that give you a pretty good indication of where the ice is and how thick it is."

McCarthy knew the ice was becoming denser by the hour. It was turning into a slurry so thick it had begun to damp down the waves. The color of the sea had also changed: *Viarsa*'s wake was almost black, and the rest of the surface was a dull gray. "Just in the last few minutes we've entered some pretty serious ice," McCarthy added. "The density is about 50 percent ice."

"What does that mean?"

"It literally means that the sea is half water and half ice."

In all his years at sea, Duffy had never been in water where ice was a concern. Most naval vessels avoid ice. In spite of their formidable appearance, most of them are built for speed and are therefore too delicate to risk it.

Glancing at the speed indicator, Duffy said, "We haven't lost any speed."

"No, fifty percent shouldn't really slow us down. When the percentage gets higher, though, it also means the ice is getting deeper, so there is more interaction with the hull. That's when it affects speed."

In the progression toward solid ice, the first step is the formation of tiny ice crystals, called spicules, which give the sea the oily cast Duffy had noticed. The spicules subsequently coagulate into slush. At some point the slush gathers into small lumps, two or three inches across, called shuga. Even then, the ice is still elastic and does little to hinder a passing ship. But McCarthy said that would change. "Eventually," he told Duffy, "the pieces of shuga get bigger and start to knock into each other. When they stick together, they turn into pancakes—it's called pancake ice—circles of ice that can be a few feet in diameter. Sooner or later the pancakes freeze together and become ice floes."

Just before 8:00 a.m. on Saturday, August 16, *Viarsa* turned north. "They must be getting nervous," McCarthy said.

"I hope so," Duffy replied.

Later that morning, Duffy spoke to Keith Johnson again. "We're not far from solid-set ice," he said, before he mentioned that the temperature had fallen to 20 below zero Celsius and requested that ice charts be sent to the ship.

Johnson also had a request: He said the Uruguayan ambassador had recorded a message in Spanish that would be e-mailed to Duffy so he could play it over the radio to Cabrera. The recording had been made after Uruguayan officials belatedly acknowledged that the ship that was theoretically flying its flag was not in the Atlantic Ocean. The officials said they were unable to contact the vessel directly, so they asked that *Southern Supporter* relay a message that had been recorded by Ambassador Mo Amaro. "There's been a lot of diplomatic back and forth," Johnson told Duffy. "The message tells them that *Southern Supporter* is on lawful government business and asks *Viarsa* to obey its instructions."

Early that afternoon, O'Dea went on the radio. "We have an important message for you from the Uruguayan ambassador to Australia," he said. There was no reply, so O'Dea continued, "I will play it for you now." In the message, Ambassador Mo Amaro, speaking in Spanish, said: "This is a message from the Government of Uruguay to the master of the vessel that has identified itself as the *Viarsa*. You are required to cooperate fully with the Australian officials onboard the Australian surveillance vessel *Southern Supporter*, currently maintaining hot pursuit with you, and to comply promptly with all instructions received by those officials." O'Dea played the message twice, but it did not evoke any response until a dark-haired man stepped out of *Viarsa*'s bridge and made an obscene gesture.

"I guess they got the message," Duffy said with a chuckle. "They might be getting a bit frustrated."

The ice thickened so much that afternoon that *Viarsa* reduced its speed to about seven knots. The ice gave *Southern Supporter* an advantage: rather than cutting its own path, it could follow in *Viarsa*'s wake. Given that and the slower speed, *Southern Supporter*'s engineers were able to switch off one of the ship's three generators to reduce the rate of fuel consumption. Although Duffy believed *Viarsa* had greater reserves than *Southern Supporter*, he also worried about what would happen if it did not: if *Viarsa* ran out of fuel, *Southern Supporter* would be responsible for the other ship and he would be confronted with another set of difficult choices. Transferring fuel between the ships would be impossible unless the sea were to become unusually calm and remain that way for several hours. Towing *Viarsa* was another possibility, but the towline would probably break in the first storm.

Late that night, Duffy examined the ice charts that had just rolled out of the fax machine. They told the story in a rainbow of colors. The gradations went from "sea ice–free" areas, which were uncolored, to places where nine-tenths of the water had frozen solid, which were indicated in red. *Viarsa* and *Southern Supporter* were then about four hundred miles north of Antarctica and heading due west, and the area in front of them was almost entirely red. The temperature was still –20 degrees Celsius, and the slush had begun to gather into pancakes.

Duffy decided to try communicating with Cabrera again. "I'm concerned for your ship and your crew because we will be heading into quite dangerous sea ice," he said over the radio, "ice that could exceed the capabilities of our ships. I have ice charts from the Australian Bureau of Meteorology indicating that we are heading into thick packed ice. I strongly advise that we alter course to the north. This is for no other reason than the safety of your crew and ship." *Viarsa* did not make an audible response, but six minutes later, it altered course somewhat to the north, from 270 to 295 degrees. After examining the charts again and determining that the new course would also take them into densely packed ice, Duffy returned to the radio: "I notice that you have altered course slightly to the north. That is good—but it is not sufficient to clear the dense packed ice, so I strongly advise you to alter further north. Do you copy? Over."

Once again, *Viarsa* declined to reply, but at 11:41 p.m., it turned farther northward again, adopting a course of 330 degrees. This course, more northerly than northwesterly, would avoid the worst of the ice. The course change was also important, Duffy believed, because *Viarsa*'s crew had, for the first time, followed his instructions. However, he believed its speed, still seven knots, was too fast. The pancakes of ice were getting larger by the hour, and some of them were probably more than a foot thick. As Duffy lay in bed that night, they made a horrific metallic sound as they scraped along the hull. Unable to sleep, he thought about what his family would be doing back in Canberra. Working out the time zones, he realized it was a bit after 7:00 a.m. there, so his wife, Wendy, who was also a naval officer, and his fifteen-year-old daughter, Caitlin, and thirteen-year-old son, Regan, were probably having breakfast and getting ready for the day.

About an hour later, the scraping suddenly stopped. Minutes later, *Viarsa* reverted to a westerly course and *Southern Supporter* turned as well. Not long after that, the relative quiet was shattered by two resounding thuds. Scott Webb and Brett Lenz, a paramedic, were in the television room watching a movie.

"What the fuck was that?" Webb screamed.

"God knows—I never heard anything like that before," Lenz said.

Webb was convinced that the ship had struck an iceberg. It felt like it had lost all of its forward momentum, so he also thought the engines had failed. The ship's lights were still on and the movie continued to roll, but that did nothing to ease his fears. Indeed, he was seized by a *Titanic*-like vision—torrents of water flooding through a gaping hole in the hull. Standing, he listened for indications of damage. He heard nothing at first, and then a piercing alarm sounded.

After Webb hurried to the bridge, his concerns intensified. "It's fucking freezing down here," one of the ship's engineers shouted over the intercom from the normally overheated engine room. "If we don't get this thing started in twenty minutes, we are going to be in deep fucking trouble. Everything is going to ice up."

McCarthy, who was always in charge of the ship from midnight until 4:00 a.m., called Codrington, who was already awake. "We have problems with the main engines," McCarthy said. "They're all overheating." The captain knew what would happen next. As the temperature rose, the three engines would continue to automatically reduce their output until they shut down completely, a process designed to prevent them from seizing up. In a matter of minutes, all three could be completely out of action. If that were to happen, an emergency generator was supposed to spring to life, but it would provide only enough energy for lights and navigational equipment, not nearly enough to propel the ship or keep it warm.

Codrington raced to the bridge and scanned the alarm indicators. The ship's speed had dropped to less than two knots. The gap between it and *Viarsa*, which continued to move at seven knots, was expanding rapidly. Captains are instinctively reluctant to leave their command position on the bridge during a crisis, but Codrington left his to go to the engine room.

As Webb listened to the commotion and saw that the normally unflappable captain was obviously frightened, he thought about the cold. Ever since the ship had left Fremantle (a port near Perth on Australia's west coast) twenty-six days earlier, he had worried about the possibility of engine failure. He understood it was extremely unlikely, but now it was happening: the turbines were not producing enough heat to keep even the engine room warm. While he guessed at how long it would take for the rest of the ship to freeze and how many days it would take for help to arrive, the life rafts were also on his mind. They were compressed into barrel-size canisters, which were supposed to break open when they were needed, but they were caked with so much ice he feared they would fail to activate. Even if they were successfully deployed, he doubted that anyone could survive for very long in the cold.

By the time Codrington reached the engine room, two of the generators had shut down completely. The ship had slowed to just one knot. More than a dozen of the 240 lights on a control panel were flashing red, including ones labeled "Sea Water Pressure," "Cool Water Temperature," and "Overload." The engineers thought they knew what had caused the problem: the fourteen-inch-wide pipes that import seawater to circulate through a cooling system that prevents the engines from overheating had probably clogged. There were two intakes, one on each side of the ship, and the water had to pass through two sets of strainers, similar to those that remove leaves from a swimming pool. Codrington guessed that the strainers had been overwhelmed by a combination of ice and krill, which come to the surface at night.

"What's your assessment?" the captain asked Julian Grant, the chief engineer.

"Both of the intakes must be pretty well blocked. Two generators are down completely; we could lose the third."

Four men were already struggling to remove the fourteen bolts that held a steel plate in place over one of the strainers. The space where they were working, crisscrossed by pipes, left them with only four feet of head-room and very little space to manipulate their tools. They took turns pushing at the wrench and hammering it with their palms until their hands were bruised and numb. When they finally removed the last bolt and lifted the plate, they found what looked like solid ice. Using the wrench and a mallet, they hammered it into pieces so they could scoop it out. After replacing the bolts, they repeated the same procedure on the other strainer. Once they were done, one of the engines was successfully restarted. However, a few minutes later, the third engine, the only one that had been running throughout the crisis, suddenly shut down.

Duffy, who had returned to the bridge, was horrified as he stood in front of the radar screen watching *Viarsa* extend its lead. *Here we go*, he said to himself. *The beginning of the end.*

Under the Law of the Sea, hot pursuits require the pursuer to maintain constant contact with its target. The concept has ancient antecedents: in Roman times, if a hunter wounded a deer, it belonged to the hunter, even if it fled onto someone else's property, as long as the hunter maintained his pursuit. England adopted the same principle in relation to property rights: if a farmer did not pay his rent, the landlord had the right to enter the property. And if the tenant decided to flee, taking with him, say, a cow, the landlord had the right to pursue the farmer and seize the cow, even if they had left the landlord's property. As long as the chase was not interrupted, the law enabled the property owner to continue his pursuit indefinitely. Under the Law of the Sea as well as Australian law, *Southern Supporter* was required to do exactly the same thing: maintain contact. It could be maintained by means of radar and even radar detection equipment—but once the limits of the onboard equipment were exceeded, the patrol boat's legal rights would expire. The chase, which had already cost a small fortune, would end in public embarrassment and send the worst possible kind of message to the pirates.

Viarsa was now two miles ahead and showed no signs of slowing down. If it continued to move at seven knots, *Southern Supporter* would lose radar contact in three or four hours. A few hours after that, the radar-emissions detection equipment would also be out of range.

By 2:00 a.m. on Monday, August 18, *Viarsa* was eight miles ahead, the farthest the two ships had been apart since the start of the chase, and the gap between the fishermen and their pursuers was expanding by the minute.

CHAPTER 9

New York City
Spring 1998

For restaurants in midtown Manhattan, lunchtime is scramble hour. "You basically become an air traffic controller," says Rick Moonen, a top seafood chef. "Everyone arrives at the same time, and they want to be back out the door in an hour. If you're not standing in place with everything ready to go at 12:30, you're dead—ten minutes makes all the difference." It was for that reason that Moonen was less than happy one day during the spring of 1998 when Patricio Osses, a Chilean who worked in New York as a seafood importer, appeared in the kitchen of Oceana, where Moonen was the executive chef, just before noon.

"You've come now?" the chef boomed. "I'm about to open for lunch! What were you thinking?"

Osses, a short man with wavy black hair and an unshaven face, is almost as soft-spoken as Moonen is explosive. "I'm sorry," he said. "I just came from the airport—I couldn't get here any quicker."

Osses, who was just thirty-three, started out selling fresh fish that his father shipped from Chile to wholesalers, the same kind of customers that Lee Lantz served, but Osses later decided that they were not working hard enough to sell his fish. Too much of it spoiled, rendering it useless. He decided that he would sell fish directly to restaurants, focusing on the top-notch establishments that would pay a premium price for superior products.

Two days before he arrived at Oceana, Osses had introduced himself to Moonen. The chef was immediately interested. Like most highly rated chefs, his approach to cooking had been profoundly influenced by Alice Waters and her keen attention to ingredients. He was always on the lookout for new types of seafood, which he described in great detail on his menu. At the time, Oceana's menu offered "Wild Alaskan Sockeye Salmon Gravlax," noted that its halibut came from the Atlantic, that the mushrooms had been "foraged," and that the scallops had been harvested by a scuba diver. But although Osses had promised to bring types of seafood that Moonen had never seen, the chef was not inclined, just then, to take the time.

"I can't do it!" he said. "Unless you bring it to the kitchen."

"I can't—there's too much. Come on, my van is right down the street."

The chef glanced at his watch and then around the kitchen, checking to see that it was fully staffed and that no one was unusually panicked, before he reluctantly agreed. "Okay, okay—but it has to be quick," he grumbled as he pushed Osses toward a service door that opened onto East Fifty-Fourth Street.

A minute later, Osses was pulling Styrofoam boxes from a decrepit white van that had obviously been involved in several accidents and placing them on the sidewalk. Opening the lids, he called out a string of peculiar names—elephant fish, congrios, grenadiers, sea squirts, shoe mussels, and picorocos. The creatures were even odder than their names. The elephant fish resembled a sand shark, but it had an inordinate number of fins and its elephant-like head, huge and ugly, jutted above the rest of its body. The grenadier had what appeared to be thorns on its skin, eyes so big that they covered half its head, and a tail not much thicker than a strand of spaghetti. "Some people call them rat fish," Osses said. The shoe mussels were literally as big as a shoe. The sea squirt looked like a gray egg that had sprouted thick black hair. Moonen had heard of congrio, and he recognized the picorocos as barnacles, but with bases that were six to eight inches across, they were outlandishly big; they looked like miniature volcanoes. Oblivious to the little crowd that was gathering around the sidewalk exhibition, Moonen was shouting with childlike delight. "It's like *Twenty Thousand Leagues under the Sea*," he declared. Although Osses had been annoyed by the way Moonen had initially tried to put him off, now he was thrilled by the chef's enthusiasm.

The collection's only halfway-normal-looking creature was a Patagonian toothfish, which was also the only fish Moonen had seen before. He knew that "Chilean Sea Bass" had become popular in restaurants across the country, but he had never gotten around to buying or even tasting one. This particular fish, however, was irresistible. It was obviously capable of yielding the kind of thick filets he liked to cook. And since its head had been removed, he could see that the flesh was white.

Even Moonen's customers, many of them culinary sophisticates, had never become comfortable with non–white-fleshed fish. The toothfish's flesh was not only white but it also looked moist. Running a fingertip across its surface, Moonen could tell it was rich in the kind of oils that are found in many of the most prized fish. He quickly agreed to buy the toothfish and asked for a sample of just about everything else before rushing back to the kitchen at 12:20 p.m. By then, the dining room, an elegant space where mahogany beams and brass portholes create the impression of a luxurious yacht, was almost full, and the daily battle was very much underway. Moonen hurried through the bustling kitchen, dipping a tasting spoon into the spicy tomato sauce that would be poured over the salmon and checking the potato salad that would be topped with lobster before grabbing a microphone and asking his staff, "Are we ready to go? Do we have crab cakes?" Although the hour that followed was an action-packed blur, the chef was already thinking about what he would do with his toothfish.

Moonen spent the rest of the afternoon experimenting with filets that one of his assistants had carved from the toothfish. He began by seasoning three of them with nothing but salt and pepper and cooking each differently—grilling, sautéing, and steaming. Moonen, whom colleagues sometimes called "the palate," was enthralled with what he tasted. "It's sweet and it has great texture, a bit like cod," he said to Andrew Engle, a sous chef, "but it has so much more fat content. We need to try something more complicated.[1]"

Moonen spent several weeks refining his thinking about toothfish. Since almost everything seemed to work, there were almost too many possibilities. "It's a diamond—no matter what you do, it turns out great," he said to Engle one afternoon. "It's like a perfect date!"

---

[1] *The presence of "complicated" fish preparations on American menus is due in large part to one man. Until the mid-1980s, words like "medium rare" and "seared" were unheard of when it came to fish. All of that changed after a Frenchman named Gilbert Le Coze and his sister Maguy moved to New York in 1986 and opened a restaurant called Le Bernardin. The* New York Times *gave the restaurant four stars, the paper's top rating, just three months after it opened. Other chefs talk about Gilbert Le Coze, who died in 1994, as if he were a god. "He came here and said, 'I'm going to teach you how to cook fish in ways that you've never seen,'" says Ed Brown, the chef at the Sea Grill, a highly regarded restaurant that looks out on the skating rink at New York's Rockefeller Center. "And he did. He showed us that fish do not need to be fully cooked and introduced things like carpaccios and tartares. I had seen some of those ideas in Europe, but I couldn't imagine how to bring them to the American market. Le Coze did it in a way that was unwavering and pure—and he changed American cooking forever."*

The first rendition Moonen put on the menu was similar to the tooth-fish dishes served in Cantonese restaurants: he steamed filets in a mix of soy sauce, shredded ginger, and garlic; when it was done cooking, he sprinkled cilantro and chives over the fish and poured a bit of hot oil over the top to crisp up the skin and wilt the greens. The plate was covered with a lid, which was removed at the customer's table to release an aromatic mist of steam.

Three weeks later, Moonen came up with an approach he liked even better. Inspired by a Japanese style of cooking known as miso zuke yaki and a dish he had tried at Nobu, the trendy Japanese restaurant, the preparation began when he covered a filet in salt and left it to partially cure overnight. By drawing out the moisture, the salt made the fish firmer and flakier; it also concentrated the fish's own flavors and of course infused a salty taste. The next day Moonen rinsed the salt away with water and submerged the filet in a mix of miso (a fermented paste of soybeans and rice or barley), oranges, and a rice wine–based sweetener. Two days later, he cooked the fish under an intense broiler, which caused the sugars in the miso coating to caramelize. The flavor that resulted was rich, a perfect mix of salt and sweet. The texture was also balanced: the outside was crisp, but the rest, which separated into thick flakes, was as succulent as foie gras. Moonen placed the filet on top of a selection of stir-fried vegetables and lined the edge of the plate with mango that had been cut into matchsticklike slivers. The sweetness of the mango mirrored the fish almost perfectly. Indeed, when Moonen was asked to describe the dish, he said, "Think of eating a perfectly ripened mango—that's exactly what it's like to eat this fish."

Oceana's customers loved it too. Seven weeks after "Miso-Glazed Chilean Sea Bass" debuted on the menu, it became the restaurant's top-selling item and, not long after that, its signature dish. Moonen knew toothfish was also doing well at other top-tier restaurants and that restaurant chains, corporate food services, and airlines had discovered its many virtues. Hotels and caterers were particularly keen on the fish because it could be cooked long before being served.

"It's bulletproof," Moonen said. "You can cook it hours before you need it and rewarm it without harming its flavor or texture. Everyone had to have it: it became a gold rush."

CHAPTER 10

*Southern Ocean
August 18, 2003*

"**H**ang on, hang on!"

One of the engineers was shouting over the intercom from the engine room at 2:30 a.m. Monday, August 18, to announce that he had just restarted the third generator, the one that had failed after the strainers were cleared. Shortly after that he added, "We're all set—we can begin to bring up the speed."

On the bridge, McCarthy said, "We'll put on an extra half knot and we should catch up with them by morning."

Duffy, who had not slept more than a few minutes during the previous twenty-four hours, went to bed. When he returned to the bridge at 7:30 a.m., *Viarsa* was clearly visible, just two hundred yards ahead. Then Duffy saw something else: the ships were completely surrounded by pancake ice. Most of the formations were two to three feet in diameter, and they collectively covered about half the surface of the visible ocean.

By mid-morning, the pancakes were substantially larger—five to six feet across—and they had upturned edges from bumping into one another. By midday, some had melded into one another to create patches of what appeared to be solid ice. McCarthy steered into the unfrozen areas, which looked like twisting rivers that narrowed in the distance until they disappeared entirely. Beyond that the sea was an endless white prairie. But what most concerned McCarthy were the craggy ridges he could see about two hundred yards to the left of the ship. He knew how they had formed: pancakes of ice had been pressed together with so much force that they had buckled upward. McCarthy also knew that the mounds of ice he could see—hummocks—would be mirrored by underwater formations of ice—bummocks—and that the combination was probably so thick as to be impenetrable. Looking to the right, he saw another stretch of ice that also looked solid. It appeared that *Viarsa*, and with it *Southern Supporter*, were heading down an icebound alley toward what was likely to be a dead end.

"The density level is probably 90 percent and it's getting worse by the hour," McCarthy said to Webb early that afternoon. "We aren't going to get much farther." When Duffy arrived on the bridge a few minutes later, it looked like the ships had entered an entirely different world. They were on a heading of 270 degrees and moving at close to eight knots, but the sea did not appear to be made of water. Except for *Viarsa* and its wake, everything was white. The sight of the two ships plowing through the ice was surreal and in a way quite beautiful, but McCarthy made it clear that the situation was actually quite dangerous. "Look at that ice," he said to Duffy, pointing to the south. "It's extremely thick, almost solid. And then take a look over to the other side. It's almost as bad. I think we're getting to a stage that could exceed the navigational limits of the ship."

"How is *Viarsa* doing?"

"They're still punching through, but it won't last," McCarthy said. "Look at their wake. See how it starts out being as wide as the ship and then how it becomes narrower as the ship gets farther ahead. It's almost gone by the time we get into it. That shows you how much pressure there is. The ice will just continue to close in on us until it's solid. And if *Viarsa* hits an ice shelf at this speed, there's going to be some major structural damage. Maybe you should give them a call and suggest that they alter to the north."

"*Viarsa, Viarsa*," Duffy said over the radio. "I have a very important message for the master. You are steaming into danger. I strongly advise you to turn back. Or at a minimum you need to alter to the north."

McCarthy knew his career as an ice navigator would be over if he allowed *Southern Supporter* to become stuck. Everything he knew about the ice suggested that he should turn back. "I don't like this at all," he told Codrington a few minutes later. The captain was more than happy to defer to McCarthy's judgment. "This guy," Codrington said of Cabrera, "is pushing it too far." Turning to Duffy, he added: "With the problems we had last night, I'm not prepared to just carry on into the ice."

"It's up to you," Duffy said, trying not to let his tone reflect the frustration he felt. "Our lives are in your hands."

Duffy then returned to the radio. "*Viarsa, Viarsa*," he said. "You are steaming into danger—extreme danger. It is our intention not to proceed any farther. You are strongly advised to move to the north to get out of the solid ice. Do you copy that, over?"

As they waited for a response, McCarthy said, "He's going to get to a place where he won't be able to continue—at that point they could be trapped."

"That wouldn't do us any good," Duffy said.

"That's for sure," McCarthy said. "If he gets stuck and the ice closes up around him, there's no way we could go in and get him. We would only end up getting stuck ourselves. We could call for an icebreaker, but we're still 1,900 miles from Cape Town, so we'd probably have to wait for summer melt."

McCarthy decided to turn the ship to the north, but a few minutes later he had second thoughts. He had initially thought he would be able to head in that direction and pick his way through the ice to find clear water, but now everything looked hopelessly solid. Slowing the ship from eight knots to five, he noticed that *Southern Supporter*'s wake went from liquid to solid almost immediately. A half-mile later, McCarthy decided that he had no alternative but to retrace the ship's initial course by heading east. This would be disastrous for the chase: the two ships would be heading in opposite directions, and the separation between them would expand by at least a dozen miles every hour. *Viarsa* had already disappeared from sight, but the radar indicated that its speed had slowed to about six knots. That, however, was not good news because it probably meant it was running into thicker ice, increasing the likelihood that it might become stuck.

Less than an hour after *Southern Supporter* turned to the east, it entered a very different environment. Except for pancake ice and occasional "bergie bits," chunks of ice the size of refrigerators and cars, the ship was in relatively open water. McCarthy hugged the edge of the ice and turned to the left whenever he could in order to adopt a course parallel to *Viarsa*'s as quickly as possible. By the time he was able to do so, the ships were about twenty miles apart, and it had become so difficult to see *Viarsa* on the radar screen that the radar detection equipment was activated. The men who were watching the screen in the operations room knew what was at stake: the little blip on the screen could become their only connection. If it disappeared, the hot pursuit would be broken.

Southern Supporter's permanent crew also understood what was happening. Sitting in the mess, Allan Brownlie, who had worked at sea for forty-one of his fifty-six years, said, "We're never going to see that boat again."

"If he gets away, he's going to be a hero," said Bruce Noble. "He'll go back to Heard Island and fill up his ship with fish."

Duffy was standing at the chart table, using a compass and pencil to draw a series of circles on a chart, each one indicating the maximum distance *Viarsa* could move from its current position over a period of four hours if it were to make seven knots. Duffy only had to worry about certain sections of the arc. "They're not going to go south," he said to McCarthy, "and they'll probably have to turn north or east at some stage."

"Unless they get stuck," McCarthy said.

Duffy decided to make another appeal to *Viarsa*. "You are endangering the lives of every member of your crew," he said. "Based on our ice information, there is a real danger that you will be stuck or that your hull will be damaged. We will come to your assistance as best as we can. However, we would prefer not to engage in a rescue operation. You should progress north to safer water. Do you understand the reason for this transmission?" While he waited for a reply, Duffy thought: *They have to know that we wouldn't risk giving up the chase if the danger wasn't real.*

At 2:20 p.m. *Viarsa* disappeared completely from *Southern Supporter*'s radar screen. Now all the patrol boat had to go on was the target's own radar, which *Southern Supporter* could monitor until the ships were about thirty-five miles apart. The radar detection equipment, however, could not identify the location of the emission source with much precision. Each of the four sensors mounted on *Southern Supporter*'s bridge roof picked up signals that came from within a ninety-degree arc. A signal that came from somewhere ahead of the ship was picked up by the sensor positioned near the front of the roof but none of the others. Therefore, the only way to approximate the location of an emission source was to turn the ship and note when a signal was lost by one detector and picked up by another. By repeating the maneuver several times, the officers could approximate the signal's direction to within about twenty degrees. For this reason, *Southern Supporter* began to carve lazy circles in the sea.

Crude as it was, the detection equipment had become invaluable. Of course the signal would disappear if *Viarsa* turned off its radar or managed to get more than thirty-five miles away from *Southern Supporter*. "If he's on the ball, he'll switch off his radar and go the other way," O'Dea said. "He'd be gone."

"It would be pretty depressing to lose him now," Codrington said.

Onboard *Viarsa*, Antonio Perez told Cabrera to hold his course. The captain was not worried about the ice. He considered it much less dangerous than high seas, in part because he saw another toothfish vessel, the *Amur*, sink near France's Kerguelen Island three years earlier. He rescued twenty-six crewmen from the boat, but eight died. Cabrera knew what his boat could withstand, and he had taken precautions. The bridge was equipped with an electric heater, and he had told the crew to leave every faucet slightly open to help prevent the water in the pipes from freezing.

Cabrera thought the chase could be over. "We've lost them," he declared. "The pursuit is broken."

Hoping to make the most of the opportunity, Perez was discussing strategies with Vidal over the satellite phone. Vidal came up with the best ideas: first he suggested that two of *Viarsa*'s crewmen could be deployed in a small boat with a hand-held radio and that they could use the radio to pretend they were aboard the fishing vessel as they headed to the north. *Viarsa*, meanwhile, would attempt to escape by heading east. The only problem with the plan was that no one volunteered to get into the little boat. Vidal then suggested that an emergency beacon could be placed in the little boat and that it could be sent north by automatic pilot. After Perez explained that the boat would not be able to make it through the ice without a human pilot, Vidal had one last idea: "Just throw some of the fishing beacons into the water."

A few minutes later, three fishing beacons were bobbing in the icy water. Perez hoped *Southern Supporter* would pick up their signals, and head toward them rather than to *Viarsa*.

Ken Leggett, the army corporal who was responsible for the radar detection equipment, was sitting in front of a desk in the operations room. A large metal box that was connected to several sets of wires, some of which were connected to a laptop computer, took up much of the desk. The laptop's screen showed several small graphs and boxes, which indicated which of the four aerials was receiving the signal and data about its strength. Leggett knew when the equipment was functioning because it emitted a brief buzz—it sounded almost like a bumble bee—every time *Viarsa*'s radar was picked up by one of the sensors.

At 3:15 p.m., forty-five minutes after the radar detection equipment had been activated, Leggett noticed that the buzz had stopped altogether. Glancing at the screen, he saw that the little boxes were still visible, but they no longer held any data. The system was dead.

"We've lost the signal!" he shouted.

Duffy, who happened to be in the operations room, felt his pulse race. "Are you sure?" he asked. "Can you try another aerial?"

Leggett toggled between the boxes that were supposed to provide data from each of the aerials, but nothing changed. Every box was blank. *Southern Supporter* was flying blind.

"I'll run some tests," Leggett said in the calmest voice he could manage. No one said a word as the corporal spent an interminable couple of minutes using the mouse and keyboard to check various components. Then he removed and replaced all of the wires to ensure that the connections were secure. Finally, he said, "I think it's a software problem that has nothing to do with the hardware."

Why now? Duffy said to himself.

To Leggett, he asked, "What's the solution?"

"I'll just reboot the program—I won't be able to tell you anything until I do. It will take about ten minutes."

Duffy did not want to interfere, but he could not stomach the idea of a ten-minute wait, so he went to the bridge to brief Codrington and consider what they would do if the equipment failed to come back online. As he thought through the possibilities, Duffy focused on *Viarsa*'s options: the west and south were blocked by ice. It could stay in place, waiting for *Southern Supporter* to give up and leave the area, but Duffy thought that was unlikely. For one thing, standing in one place increased the likelihood of getting stuck: by maintaining momentum, the ship not only broke a path for itself but it also created relatively clear water in its wake for a potential escape. A stationary ship would also become very cold. The outside temperature was −10 degrees Celsius and the wind-chill factor brought it down to −20. In those conditions, it is difficult to heat a ship even when its engines are running at top speed. If *Viarsa*'s main engine stopped, Duffy was sure that conditions onboard would quickly become intolerable. It seemed much more likely that *Viarsa*'s officers would, like *Southern Supporter*'s, come to the conclusion that they had to find a way to get to the north. Maybe *Viarsa* would head directly to the north and attempt to find a way through the ice. Or maybe it would, like *Southern Supporter,* turn back to the east before going north.

But what if it turned east and kept going?

That was the doomsday scenario. If it took that course, *Viarsa* would not come close enough to *Southern Supporter* to appear on its radar. Even if the Australian government could prevail on the U.S. military to track *Viarsa* by satellite, the hot pursuit would be over because of the Law of the Sea's requirement that contact be maintained with resources that are onboard the pursuing craft. Outside assistance is not good enough. Duffy therefore devised a backup plan: *Southern Supporter* would go halfway back to the longitude where it last saw *Viarsa* and set up an east–west patrol line. If it came to that, he knew the chances that he would come across *Viarsa* again were slim. And even if he got lucky, the gap in contact might mean that the legal requirements for a hot pursuit had not been satisfied. But Duffy could not see any other options.

In the operations room, Leggett stared at the screen as the computer whirred through the lengthy start-up process. If the pursuit ended because of a technical glitch, he knew it would lead to the kind of public embarrassment that destroys careers. He knew his equipment inside and out, but in the end he did what any neophyte would have done—switch the system off, then turn it on again—and now there was nothing to do but wait.

CHAPTER 11

New York City
Fall 1999

Rick Moonen was worried about his "Miso-Glazed Chilean Sea Bass." It remained Oceana's best-selling dish, but Patricio Osses sometimes did not have any toothfish to sell. When he did, they weighed only fifteen to twenty pounds, far less than the fifty- to eighty-pound fish Osses had delivered not much more than a year earlier. It was not difficult to guess the reason: given toothfish's exploding popularity, fishermen had caught so many fully grown fish that they were now working their way through juvenile populations. Moonen knew that declining stocks would also cause fishermen to undertake ever-longer expeditions and that their catches would be farther from fresh by the time they reached his kitchen. When he went to the Fulton Fish Market to search for alternative suppliers, he found that the toothfish there were not just small, they were also frozen. No one seemed to know where they had come from.

Moonen had seen the same thing happen with swordfish. The average size of swordfish captured in the North Atlantic had fallen from 260 pounds in the 1960s to about 100 pounds two decades later. By then, most of the fish that were being taken were so young that they had not had a chance to reproduce. Although fishermen were theoretically required to release baby swordfish, most of them died before they were taken off the hook. There was no secret about what had changed: swordfish traditionally had been caught by harpoon, a method that had consistently yielded big fish and spared smaller ones. In the 1960s, swordfish hunters started using longlines, which resulted in exponentially larger catches— and the indiscriminate capture of juveniles.

In 1988, Moonen had become one of the spokesmen for "Give Swordfish a Break," a nationwide effort that enlisted chefs to help persuade the public to stop eating swordfish. The campaign ultimately caused more than eight hundred chefs to stop serving the fish.

It was a biologist activist named Sam LaBudde who proved that public opinion could affect fishing practices. During 1987 and 1988, he surreptitiously videotaped the slaughter of hundreds of dolphins by a Panamanian tuna fishing boat. After the tape was shown on several national news programs, the owners of the biggest brands in the tuna business vowed that they would buy only tuna that had been harvested by methods that were deemed "dolphin-safe."

Tuna are generally difficult to find. Unlike most fish, which live in nutrient-rich coastal waters, tuna roam throughout the great expanses of the deep oceans. However, some tunas are much easier to locate: for reasons that have never been understood, yellowfin tunas and dolphins are devoted traveling companions; air-breathing dolphins swim near the surface while yellowfins travel below. The association is particularly strong in tropical waters west of Central America and the northern half of South America. Ever since fishermen discovered this in the 1950s, they have searched for dolphins to determine where they should drop their hooks. But as with swordfish, the adoption of a new, technology-enhanced methodology changed the dynamics. Starting in the late 1950s, fishermen surrounded schools of dolphins with mile-long nets that extended several hundred feet below the surface. Once the dolphins were surrounded, the bottom of the net was gathered together. Called purse-seining, the technique was so effective that fishermen expanded their fleets and outfitted ships with helicopters, speedboats, and explosives. The helicopters searched for dolphins. The speedboats raced ahead of them and executed violent maneuvers while explosive devices were dropped in the water in an effort to stop the progress of the dolphins—and, in theory, the tuna—long enough to give the mother ship a chance to encircle them with the vast net.

It was possible to "back down" a net, lowering a section below the surface to give dolphins a chance to escape over the top, but the procedure was often ineffective, particularly at night, and was sometimes not even attempted. By the end of the 1960s, tuna fishermen were killing close to five hundred thousand dolphins every year. In 1972, the United States enacted a law that was supposed to reduce the death rate, but American fishermen were still permitted to kill as many as twenty thousand dolphins every year into the 1980s—and by then most of the big fleet owners had reflagged their ships in countries that had few, if any, regulations. The foreign-registered vessels killed at least one hundred thousand dolphins every year.

Then LaBudde made his film. The seafaring activist managed to get himself hired to drive a dolphin-herding speedboat for a Mexico-based tuna boat. Once onboard, he ended up working as the chef, an ideal position because he was not expected to work on the deck when nets were retrieved. As the very first net was gathered together and winched aboard the ship, he used his eight-millimeter Sony Camcorder to record the deaths of more than two hundred dolphins. It was a "disaster set," one that captured and killed a large number of dolphins but just one yellowfin. During the rest of the four-month voyage, LaBudde shot almost five hours of videotape, telling everyone that his father had given him the camera and that he was using it just for fun. On one day he filmed the ship's captain as he used a penknife to carve up a dolphin that was later consumed by his crew.

Following the voyage, LaBudde edited his film down to eleven minutes of slaughter. Adult dolphins and their calves swam in graceful synchronization as they approached the net. Once they sensed something was closing in on them, they panicked, and the water erupted into turbulent chaos. It looked almost as if a net had been thrown over a herd of wild horses. Some of the dolphins attempted to break through the nylon mesh, causing their fins to tear and even rip away from their bodies. Desperate for air, they struggled to press their blowholes against the net. The distress was audible in the dolphins' high-pitched shrieks. It takes only a few minutes for a dolphin to drown, and some were obviously already dead when the net was winched onto the ship. Others were crushed as the net was forced through the winches.

The documentary became a call to arms. Dolphins were different from other marine creatures. Thanks to their friendly nature, the fact that they are mammals, their favored place in the literature of the sea, and the popular television show *Flipper*, they had a special, almost sacrosanct status. After LaBudde's film was presented on the evening news programs of ABC, CBS, and CNN, and a few days later, NBC's *Today Show*, even people who were not inclined to support environmental causes were sympathetic to LaBudde's suggestion that they boycott products produced by StarKist Seafood, the world's largest tuna canner, and its parent company, H. J. Heinz. The company ultimately capitulated, calling a press conference in late 1990 to announce that it would no longer buy tuna caught by fishermen who killed dolphins. In the end, it did not have a choice: according to the Pittsburgh-based company's own polling data, 60 percent of Americans were aware of the dolphin issue. And once StarKist made its move, the owners of the other big tuna brands, Bumble Bee and Chicken of the Sea, said they too would purchase only "dolphin-safe" tuna. Within just a few months, the number of dolphin deaths was sharply reduced.

The two Washington-based environmental groups that organized the swordfish campaign, SeaWeb and National Resources Defense Council, hoped to set off a similar kind of chain reaction. The environmentalists knew the public's knowledge about marine life was extremely limited. Although people had become familiar with the health benefits of eating fish, they knew almost nothing about the impact of fishing on marine life. "The only fish they knew about were the ones that ended up on their plates," says Vikki Spruill, SeaWeb's executive director. "And that gave us an opening—chefs were our messengers."

Seventy percent of seafood sales in the United States are to restaurants, and Spruill believed chefs could affect consumer awareness far beyond their own dining rooms because of the emergence of "celebrity chefs." Until the 1980s, even the most talented cooks were not well known except among their peers and their most devoted patrons. This began to change as French restaurants lost their stranglehold over American fine dining and chefs discovered that a new generation of diners was looking for something different. "The baby boomers, who grew up eating canned vegetables and casseroles, had developed much higher standards," Moonen says. "They wanted to go to hip places, and they wanted to try new things." It took the new generation of restaurants some time to find their footing, but there was an irreversible break from the past that opened the door to less formal restaurants and culinary inventiveness. Many of the chefs who led the charge became well known. They spent more of their time visiting the dining room, and their names were printed in the menu.

The media played an important role in this. Eager to capitalize on the expanding consumer interest in food and to capture new categories of advertisers, newspapers and magazines began covering cuisine like never before. It was a symbiotic love match: the new restaurants needed to be discovered, and journalists needed new things to write about. The creation of the Food Network catapulted the trend. It began in 1993 with modest aspirations, providing basic how-to programs for a relatively small audience—mostly women who were deeply interested in cooking. Over time, the network expanded its appeal by recruiting outsize personalities to create lively programs. A young New Orleans–based chef named Emeril Lagasse, who banged pots and yelled "Bam!" in front of a live audience and a band, was followed by dozens of others as the network forged a new form of entertainment, one that appealed to people of all ages, men as well as women. The chefs were the stars.

When the swordfish campaign was launched at a press conference in New York, more than forty journalists were there, including correspondents from all three of the major television networks. Regional launches followed in other cities, attracting food writers as well as reporters covering business and environmental issues. The chefs were a crucial component because they provided journalists with colorful local angles for the larger story. And the campaign, which ended in 2000, was effective: by increasing popular awareness of what was happening to swordfish, it led to the imposition of tighter quotas and a total ban on fishing in some known nursery areas. And swordfish stocks recovered.

But Moonen was not sure how to respond to his fears about toothfish. He knew Oceana's owners would not be happy if he dropped the restaurant's runaway bestseller. On the other hand, his involvement in the swordfish campaign had given him a heightened understanding of the damage that fishermen, and by extension restaurants, were doing to marine populations. Working with a food that, unlike just about everything else sold in restaurants, came from the *wild* was one of the things he liked about being a seafood chef, but that satisfaction was ruined by the thought that he was contributing to the destruction of a species. By the fall of 1999, he knew he had to do something. He put it off until after the busy holiday season, but in January he called Susan Boa, who had coordinated the swordfish campaign for SeaWeb.

"Chilean Sea Bass is my signature dish," Moonen said, "but I think it's in trouble. I can see it: the fish are getting smaller and smaller."

"You're right—it's a total disaster!" Boa said. "There's rampant overfishing and probably 90 percent of what comes to the United States is caught by pirates."

"So I need to take it off the menu, right?"

Boa hesitated. Her colleagues at SeaWeb were well aware of the problems with toothfish, but they were reluctant to stage another full-fledged campaign. There was a limit to what they could ask chefs to do. There was also the risk that the environmentalists would end up being seen as seafood police with so many agendas that people would just tune them out.

"It's up to you," Boa eventually told Moonen. "I can only tell you what we know."

Moonen was still torn. But as he weighed the pluses and minuses, he realized that his customers knew even less about Chilean Sea Bass than he did. Globalization may have made the world a smaller place, but it had also created voids and disconnects. Because of the enormous distances between the sources and users of some products, consumers knew very little about the implications of their choices. Even Oceana's customers, most of them highly educated professionals, knew very little about where their food came from. For toothfish, Moonen realized that he was the man in the middle and he had to act.

Two days after his conversation with Boa, he told Paul MacLaughlin, one of Oceana's owners, "I'm taking Chilean Sea Bass off the menu."

Astonished, MacLaughlin asked, "Why on earth would you do that? You have a huge success going here!"

"That's exactly the problem—it's totally over-fished! I have to approach the whole sustainability thing with consistency, as much as I possibly can. If I don't, I'll be targeted for talking out of both sides of my mouth."

In early 2002, the National Environmental Trust, another Washington-based environmental group, did launch a nationwide toothfish campaign. Modeled on the swordfish effort, "Take a Pass on Chilean Sea Bass" was launched with a rolling series of press conferences. The first city was San Francisco, where Patty Unterman, the chef and owner of the Hayes Street Grill, had convinced sixty-three other chefs to sign a one-page document that said they would stop serving Chilean Sea Bass for five years or until "illegal fishing is eliminated." The chefs who signed the pledge included

Alice Waters and those at many of the Bay Area's best-rated restaurants: Farallon, Bacar, The French Laundry, Butterfly, Boulevard, Jardinière, and Roys.

"People—restaurateurs and chefs—have lost track of where their food comes from," Unterman said at the press conference. "Though Patagonian toothfish is a delicious fish, I'm giving it up."

An avalanche of publicity followed. The *San Francisco Examiner*'s story stretched all the way across the front page, and its language was nothing like most news stories. "Boy, you've really blown it this time," it began. "Those Chilean Sea Bass that have fallen victim to the unholy trinity of you, your appetite, and your Visa? They're almost kaput, you know—facing extinction. So the conservationists blame you. Sort of. Your love for one of San Francisco's most popular seafood dishes has indirectly led to a dramatic increase in the illegal fishing of Chilean Sea Bass—aka Patagonian toothfish." An article in *Time* magazine that appeared after the San Francisco launch was entitled "A Trendy Fish Gets Snubbed."

When Andrea Kavanagh, who organized the campaign for the National Environmental Trust, arrived in Chicago for the campaign's second launch at a W Hotel, she was shocked to see four satellite trucks parked outside and a pair of television reporters doing live reports from the sidewalk. As in San Francisco, the chefs who signed the pledge included those at some of Chicago's best-regarded restaurants: Charlie Trotter's, Frontera Grill, Le Francais, Naha, and Tru. In ten years of working on environmental campaigns, Kavanagh had never seen that kind of media interest. She decided that she would seek one hundred chefs for each of the ten launches that would follow: Philadelphia, Washington, New York, Los Angeles, Cape Cod, Charleston, Boston, Seattle, Atlanta, and Miami.

Many chefs refused to participate, including those who worked at places that served the fish in much greater quantities than white tablecloth restaurants ever did—hotels, food services, and caterers. Some chefs pointed out that the boycott would unfairly penalize fishermen who worked as part of legitimate toothfish operations. Others admitted that they just did not want to give up such a popular item. "We sell so much of it, I honestly don't think we'd take it off the menu," Shawn Maher, the manager of the Red Rock Café, told the *Milwaukee Journal Sentinel.*

Others believed their customers would understand. "Most consumers wouldn't go out and buy California condor on a menu if they saw it," Michael Cimarusti, the executive chef at Los Angeles's Water Grill, said in reference to the endangered bird. In New York, Eric Ripert of Le Bernardin said, "So often we talk about how fish affect our health. We have heard that a diet rich in fish is good for our health. But maybe we need to start thinking about how we affect the health of fish—fish populations, that is."

The official campaign launches attracted so much attention that they inspired chefs in other places to organize their own pledge-signing efforts. In Aspen, Colorado, eighteen restaurants and the company that operates the ski resort there said they would join the boycott. "Because many people have no idea that this problem exists," said Pat O'Donnell, the president of the Aspen Skiing Company, "we have an opportunity to educate our employees, our customers, and local communities about how they can help save a species from extinction." All told, more than one thousand chefs joined the campaign. In addition, some of the largest seafood chains, including Red Lobster and Boston's Legal Seafood, also promised to stop serving Chilean Sea Bass, though they declined to sign the pledge.

But while the campaign went a long way to help consumers understand the problems of a declining "Chilean Sea Bass" population, it did not evoke the kind of broad-based behavior-changing outrage that resulted from either LaBudde's film or the swordfish campaign.

The effort to convert public concern into regulatory changes also came up short. The environmentalists asked the U.S. government to ban imports of any toothfish that was said to have been caught on the high seas, a move that would have prevented pirates from claiming that toothfish that came from places like Heard Island had been obtained from unregulated waters. "If the government banned all high-seas toothfish, it would close the biggest loophole the pirates have," Kavanagh says. The government did ban toothfish imports from two high-seas areas, but Kim Dawson, the official at the National Oceanic and Atmospheric Administration who is responsible for monitoring toothfish imports, said it could not impose a blanket ban because there are "a few, small legitimate" high seas toothfish fisheries.

Dawson says the government relies on "routine spot checks on imports" and a "catch documentation scheme." Under the program, the United States and other signatories to the Convention on the Conservation of Antarctic Marine Living Resources refuse to accept toothfish unless it was caught by a ship registered to a member nation and that nation certifies that the fish was caught legally. But the program is far from foolproof. If an official from a member country signs a piece of paper that says the fish came from the high seas, another member nation is unlikely to reject the fish. In addition, catch documents can be forged and legitimate documents can be used fraudulently. When fish from a single ship are divided and sent to several different locations, the same document is used over and over again, and it is difficult to be sure that the document relates to the fish in any one shipment.

Dawson says a new, electronic version of the system will be more effective. However, when asked to rate the government's ability to fight toothfish smuggling, she sounds far from confident: "This is going to be an ongoing battle, but we feel that the U.S. government has been able to close some of the avenues that were being used before."

Given the dismal prospects, the organizers of the Take-a-Pass-on-Chilean-Sea-Bass campaign, which was supposed to last for three years, decided to continue it indefinitely. "We've been enormously successful in one way—we've raised a lot of awareness," says Gerry Leape, the head of the National Environmental Trust's marine conservation programs. "But we won't have real success until the toothfish are actually protected. We obviously have a long way to go."

CHAPTER 12

Southern Ocean
August 18, 2003

Ken Leggett heard a buzz. To his immense relief, the rebooted radar detection equipment had come back to life. The boxes for every aerial were once again full of data, and the signal strengths were almost identical to what they had been before the malfunction. The fishing beacons that had been thrown into the water did not register on *Southern Supporter*'s equipment, but *Viarsa* itself was once again inadvertently giving away its location.

But over the next couple of hours, it was not clear where the fishing vessel was going—or if it was moving at all. At one time or another, the ship seemed to be tracking to the east, west, and north. But at 5:00 p.m. it appeared to be almost directly south of *Southern Supporter* and heading north. "Let's blacken the ship," Duffy said. "I don't want him to get so spooked when he sees us that he turns back into the ice."

By 6:00 p.m., the signal from *Viarsa*'s radar had strengthened substantially. At 7:20 p.m., McCarthy said, "I can see a bit of a light."

"Nah, you're dreaming," O'Dea said.

But *Viarsa*'s spotlight was indeed sweeping back and forth as the ship pushed its way through chunks of ice. A few minutes later, *Viarsa* reappeared on *Southern Supporter*'s radar screen for the first time in five hours. It was moving slowly, only three knots, and it was still heading directly toward *Southern Supporter*. When the two ships were two miles apart, just before *Viarsa* broke into open water, McCarthy switched *Southern Supporter*'s lights back on. *Viarsa* continued heading to the north and *Southern Supporter* resumed its pursuit position.

"Wouldn't you just love to be there right now to hear what they're saying?" O'Dea chortled. Speaking into the radio transmitter, he said, "*Viarsa*, *Viarsa*—welcome back! We will be maintaining our hot pursuit."

To no one's surprise, there was no response.

Like O'Dea, Duffy was tempted to rub it in a bit, but he knew a flippant radio message would not accomplish anything productive. He also thought the detour into the ice had been beneficial: by slowing the ship's westward progress, the chances had increased that a South African vessel could be dispatched in time to arrest *Viarsa*; in addition, Duffy thought there was a greater liklihood that Cabrera would heed future warnings. In his log, Duffy wrote, "It appears that the master of *Viarsa* gave himself something of a scare."

Viarsa continued to head north until 6:35 p.m. on August 19, when it entered water that was completely clear of ice. During the previous twenty-three hours, it had led the ships two hundred miles away from Antarctica. In spite of the higher latitude, the temperature stayed constant. It was so cold that the pipes that carried fresh water to the bathroom on *Southern Supporter*'s bridge had frozen, forcing everyone to climb down a steep set of stairs to reach another bathroom. Codrington spent more than an hour on his knees attempting to use an electric hairdryer in a futile effort to defrost the pipes. Afraid pipes elsewhere would freeze, the ship's engineer activated the pumps that sent fresh water back and forth between tanks near the bow and stern of the ship in the hope that the motion would prevent a more serious freeze-up.

One thing had changed, though: the wind and waves, which had been consistently on the nose since the start of the chase, were suddenly coming from behind, adding a knot to *Viarsa*'s speed. The favorable swell also made for much more pleasant conditions onboard—Duffy had the best night's sleep he had had since leaving the Australian mainland. But time was running out. By August 20, the ships were 1,320 miles south-southwest of Cape Town. The chances that a ship carrying an armed boarding party would be able to leave South Africa and catch up with *Viarsa* before it reached Montevideo were diminishing.

"He probably sees getting past the Cape as a kind of gateway," Codrington said.

"I'm so determined to get them," Duffy said, "I don't care if we have to follow them into Montevideo."

"And what kind of reception do you think we're going to get there?" O'Dea asked with half a smile.

"We'd probably end up in jail!"

Codrington, uncertain as to whether Duffy was serious, felt compelled to point out a couple of logistical problems: "We don't have any charts for the coast of South America. And we'd have to observe the conventions—we'd have to get a harbor pilot to go into Montevideo. If they don't give us one, we couldn't just sail into the harbor."

Undeterred, Duffy said, "We could just stick right behind *Viarsa* and follow her right up the river."

On Thursday morning, August 21, *Viarsa* suddenly changed course to head to the north again. The move did not make any sense until McCarthy looked at the radar screen and announced, "I've got a contact twelve miles to the west."

"Is it another ship?" Duffy asked.

"Unlikely—there aren't a lot of ships that come this far south. I don't know what it is."

"If it is another ship, it's got to be here to help *Viarsa*," Duffy said.

His specific fear was that a ship was on its way to refuel *Viarsa*, something he probably would be unable to prevent. Three years earlier, *Southern Supporter* had chased another toothfish pirate, *Lena*, for two weeks until it was refueled while the Australians watched helplessly. Knowing that the fishing boat would then have more range, the patrol boat abandoned the chase. While *Southern Supporter* could attempt to position itself between *Viarsa* and another ship, Duffy knew Codrington would not do anything that would put his ship in danger. The only consolation was the time it would take to conduct the refueling: it would take the better part of a day, during which time *Viarsa* would have to reduce its speed to almost nothing or stop entirely, improving the odds that a South Africa–based ship would have time to catch up.

But all of Duffy's scenarios were rendered moot when he saw that *Viarsa* was turning *away* from the blip rather than toward it. "Why did they do that?" McCarthy asked. "You'd think if this thing was coming to help him, he'd . . ."

"Maybe it's not for him. Maybe it's another fishing vessel," Duffy guessed.

"Or maybe," McCarthy said, "he thinks it's someone who is coming to help *us*."

A few minutes later, McCarthy spotted the answer, a volcano-shaped cone of white. "Ah, it's an iceberg," he said. As more of it became visible, Duffy estimated it was six hundred feet high, much taller than any of the others the ships had passed.

Within a few hours, the sea was filled with icebergs. At least a dozen were visible at any given time. They came in three basic sizes: full-blown bergs, some more than a mile long; "bergy-bits"; and "growlers," high-density formations that protrude from the water by just a foot or two. Formed by ice that has broken away from a full-scale iceberg or comprised of the remains of mostly melted bergs, growlers have survived two or three summer melts. Named for the sound water makes as it courses over them, growlers were what concerned Codrington the most. Full-blown icebergs are easily visible, but growlers can be impossible to see, particularly at night. Striking any kind of solid ice could be catastrophic. If the bow absorbed the impact, the ship might not sink; but a blow to the side, like the one that doomed the *Titanic*, would very likely be fatal.

Scott Webb was terrified. He understood that McCarthy had a lot of experience with ice navigation, but he was not reassured, because the ship was not operating in the normal way. While prudent seamen would slow down, *Viarsa*, and with it *Southern Supporter*, were traveling through an obstacle course of ice at close to top speed. To do so at night was like playing Russian roulette. Webb tried to push the subject from his mind, but he found himself assessing the odds almost constantly. He eventually decided the chance that they would hit a growler substantial enough to endanger the ship overnight was about one in three. His other concern was his cabin's position near the ship's waterline. If ice punctured the hull, he would not be able to move his inward-opening door against the weight of the water. Even if his cabin was not flooded, a collision might bend the superstructure in a way that would make it impossible to escape. So he kept his door open and made sure his survival suit was nearby.

At 1:15 p.m. that Thursday, *Viarsa* suddenly changed course again, adopting a line that would take it much farther north than what was necessary to reach its homeport. A course of 290 degrees would lead directly to Montevideo; *Viarsa's* heading was now 345 degrees. This time, there was nothing on the radar to suggest a reason for the change. The only thing Duffy could think of was that the new course was intended to take *Viarsa* to the position in the Atlantic where the Uruguayan government had initially claimed the ship had been fishing. Or perhaps it planned to enter the territorial waters of some other country, which would, according to the Law of the Sea, end the hot pursuit. Speaking over the radio, O'Dea issued another warning: "Even if you manage to elude us, you will have no safe port. Your catch will be seized. It will do you no good to re-register your vessel or change its name. Its configuration is known. You as a master will not be able to work again."

That evening, a few minutes after eight o'clock, O'Dea picked up the radio handset and, once again, ordered *Viarsa's* captain to stop. Although Cabrera had not bothered to respond to dozens of similar broadcasts, he did to this one, declaring: "I cannot. We have received a fax from the Uruguayan navy telling us our boat is under arrest by the Uruguayan government and that we must sail direct to Montevideo."

"So does this mean you intend to return to Montevideo and are not going to comply with my instructions?" O'Dea asked.

"Yes, we are under arrest by the Uruguayan government and must go direct to Montevideo."

"You are in our jurisdiction—not Uruguay's—and you must obey our lawful instructions."

"I cannot! We are in the high seas and this is a Uruguayan vessel. Uruguay has jurisdiction over us."

However, in spite of its supposed orders, *Viarsa* continued on a course that would take it far north of its homeport.

Shortly before 3:00 a.m. on Friday morning, McCarthy spotted a formation of low-lying ice on the radar. It was almost directly ahead of *Viarsa*, and he was just about to radio a warning when *Viarsa* veered to the right. McCarthy turned in the opposite direction, so the two ships passed the ice on opposite sides.

Whatever Cabrera's intent, *Viarsa* was obviously traveling much too close to the ice. Since it was impossible to know how far the underwater sections of icebergs extended, McCarthy thought the best strategy was to trace *Viarsa*'s path, staying just two-tenths of a mile behind. "I want to be as close as possible," he told Arthur Staron, who was on duty during McCarthy's watch, "so we can be sure that we're in the water he has already proved to be safe."

McCarthy had come to view Cabrera as a wily old fox who was willing to take calculated risks but who was not wantonly reckless. Whenever the other ship went over the line, as McCarthy believed it had just done in going so close to the ice, he assumed someone other than Cabrera was at the helm. Staron had a different theory. A Polish mariner who had jumped ship and emigrated to Australia before Poland's communist government fell, he had come to hate Cabrera almost as much as the Communist tyrants who had caused him to flee his country. He believed Cabrera would stop at nothing.

"I think he's trying to get us to crash into an iceberg," Staron asserted. "He'll turn away at the last minute and hope we hit the ice and sink."

"We're going between these things much too fast, but I don't think he's consciously trying to make us hit the ice," McCarthy said.

"He'll do anything," Staron said. "He's running for his life."

CHAPTER 13

Cape Town, South Africa
August 14, 2003

"That bastard!" Marcel Kroese shouted into the telephone. "I've been chasing him for two years. I'll do everything I can to help you catch them."

John Davis, the Australian fisheries enforcement chief, had called Kroese, his counterpart in South Africa, to tell him about the pursuit of *Viarsa*. Kroese was very familiar with the ship. In December 2001, a French naval vessel spotted a longline vessel it believed to be *Viarsa* near Marion Island, a South African territory one thousand miles southeast of Cape Town. The ship, which did not have a license to operate in what was known to be a toothfish habitat, had obviously been fishing: French naval personnel photographed crewmen as they attempted to retrieve a longline before they took flight. The French then picked up some fishing gear that was left behind and initiated a pursuit while Kroese struggled to come up with a South African warship that could take over. When he learned that every ship in his country's small naval fleet either was being repaired or already occupied with another mission, Kroese told the French to give up the chase.

Kroese had always been interested in fish. He grew up fishing from a beach near his home in Cape Town and went on to study marine biology in college and graduate school. He originally planned to pursue a career in research—he was particularly intrigued by sharks—but after he learned that pirates had virtually eliminated swordfish from South African waters, he became a fisheries enforcement officer. He had decided that it was more important to protect fish than to study them. Like Davis, Kroese, who was thirty-nine, was especially concerned about toothfish. Between 1996 and 1997, a fleet of about twenty pirate vessels—he believed *Viarsa* was one of them—had taken so many toothfish from near Marion Island that they were thought to be "commercially extinct." There were so few left that the companies that had permits for toothfish no longer bothered.

Davis asked Kroese if South Africa could provide a ship and possibly a boarding party that could arrest *Viarsa* on behalf of Australia.

"You have quite a robust interpretation of international law!" Kroese said.

Despite his eagerness to apprehend pirate vessels, particularly this one, Kroese was taken aback by the idea that South Africans could fill in for Australian law enforcement officers. The two nations had never developed agreements to facilitate joint operations, and it would be difficult to undertake one based on nothing more than a verbal understanding. But Kroese could not turn down the chance to help arrest a pirate vessel that had almost certainly damaged South Africa's toothfish fishery, so he agreed to do what he could to find a ship. Davis said the best choice would be a warship. The Australian navy said it might be able to provide a boarding party, but only if its personnel could be transported to *Viarsa* on a South African naval vessel.

"If our military is going to work with another country, it has to be with other defense forces," Davis explained. "They say it gets too complicated to put their people on a civilian vessel where the lines of command and control aren't as clear."

On Friday, August 15, Kroese learned that the two naval vessels capable of doing the job were both unavailable. One was in dry-dock and the other was on standby because of political upheaval in another country. But Kroese thought he could probably arrange to charter a civilian vessel, and he knew which one he wanted—*John Ross*, one of the world's fastest ocean-going tugboats. A 360-foot-long vessel that could travel at twenty-three knots in a calm sea and seventeen knots in rough waters, it was currently on call to assist ships that might get into trouble near Cape Town during a notoriously stormy time of the year. Early on Monday, August 18, Kroese spoke to an executive from the company that owns the ship, who said he would arrange for another ship to take over *John Ross*'s assignment. Barring an emergency, it could set out first thing Tuesday.

But the ship would not do any good if it did not carry an armed boarding party, and the Australian military still said it would not provide personnel unless they were carried on a military vessel. Kroese thought he could round up three of his fisheries officers for a boarding party—but Davis had said he needed at least ten armed men. Kroese then called Fidelity Springbok Security Services, one of South Africa's largest private security companies. With more than thirteen thousand guards, it provided protection for everything from airports and office buildings to shopping malls and homes.

"I have kind of a strange request," Kroese told Nurinda Shaw, an executive at the company. "I need six to eight of your guys to get on a ship early tomorrow morning. They need to be willing to go to sea for three or four weeks and arrest a ship on behalf of the Australian government."

"We don't do a lot of marine security," Shaw said. In fact, she could not think of even one example, but she ended up saying, "Let me make a couple of calls and get back to you."

Just a half-hour later, she phoned Kroese and said her company could provide a boarding party for about $35,000 and asked him to come to her office to discuss the logistics. When Kroese and Mike Flanagan, an Australian fisheries officer who went to Cape Town to help plan the operation, got to Fidelity Springbok's office, Kroese laid it out. "We're trying to stop an illegal fishing vessel called *Viarsa*," he began. "Your guys will be responsible for going on the ship first and taking control of the crew, but the Australians will be in charge. The situation could be volatile, so they need to be armed."

"What else do they need?" Shaw asked.

Kroese started reading from a list he had scribbled on the way to the meeting: "Immersion suits, sleeping bags, ration packs for twenty days, and bullet-proof vests. And they need to get passports and get their weapons approved by Customs. And they need to be onboard *John Ross* at 6:00 a.m. tomorrow."

"That's a whole lot of things to do!"

"I know, but we don't have a choice. If we wait any longer, it'll be too late."

After the meeting, Shaw called Dawie Malan, the only Springbok employee she knew of that spent any time on the water. Malan, a well-built, forty-year-old Afrikaner, owned a small boat and loved to fish. Having worked in private security for more than twenty years, he managed the Fidelity Springbok team that handled security at Cape Town's international airport. He had a reputation for being a good manager and was well liked by his colleagues. Shaw thought that was important, in

Above: The fishermen from Valparaiso, Chile who began catching bacalao de profundidad in the 1970s believed the huge deep-water fish were virtually worthless.

Below: But after Lee Lantz invented a new name for the outwardly unattractive fish and began importing them into the United States, Eduardo Neef built a processing plant.

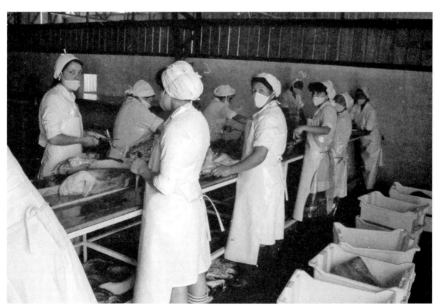

Above: It took *Southern Supporter*, an Australian patrol boat, twelve days to reach Heard Island, an uninhabited scrap of Australian territory situated halfway between Perth and Cape Town, about 900 miles north of Antarctica.

Below: Stephen Duffy, who wanted to go to sea since he was a child, went on to have a distinguished naval career and was the patrol's group commander.

Above left: Scott Webb, one of two fisheries officers aboard *Southern Supporter*, was responsible for gathering evidence of illegal fishing.

Above right: Mike O'Dea, the son of a judge and the senior fisheries officer, had arrested hundreds of pirate vessels.

Below: When *Southern Supporter* approached this nameless fishing vessel—all of its identifying markings had been blackened—it immediately fled south, toward Antarctica.

Above: During the first day of the chase, the ships encounter a violent storm and the sea steepens, but the fishing vessel—which eventually identifies itself as *Viarsa 1*—continues at top speed.

Below: The waves reach building-size heights and some of them crash over *Southern Supporter*'s bridge, which is thirty-two feet above the ship's waterline.

Above left, above right, and below: As *Viarsa* leads *Southern Supporter* closer to Antarctica, the ships enter a sea of icebergs. Some are enormous, but "bergie bits" and "growlers" are the greatest threats, particularly at night.

Above: As the temperature plunges, the sea itself begins to freeze. In the first step, the water coagulates into a slush that is readily broken up by *Viarsa*, visible in the distance.

Below and opposite page: The slush eventually solidifies into "pancakes" that will ultimately merge into solid-set ice.

Top: Ice and snow covers *Southern Supporter*'s bow and bridge.

Middle: Southern Supporter creates a wake of open water, but the gap in the ice, as seen from the stern of the patrol boat, quickly narrows.

Bottom: A life preserver is encrusted with ice and snow.

Top: The spaces between the pancakes of ice ahead of *Southern Supporter* are diminishing.

Middle: The sea looks more like a frozen prairie, and *Viarsa* almost disappears in the distance.

Bottom: When the vessels finally break out of the ice, *Southern Supporter*'s crew attempts to dig out.

Right: Members of the boarding party prepare one of the two 640s—high-speed boats that are 6.4 meters long—which will carry them to *Viarsa*.

Below: A South African vessel fires a water cannon at *Viarsa* in another unsuccessful effort to persuade the fishermen to stop.

Left: The heavily armed boarding party includes Christo Loots, who is carrying an Uzi.

Below: The sea is too rough to launch the 640s.

Left: One of the 640s is lowered into the water and makes its final approach toward *Viarsa* (*below*).

Above: A 640 heads away from *Southern Supporter* carrying four armed South Africans.

Below: Holding the 640 in a position near the fishing vessel is difficult because of the substantial swell.

Above: Stephen Duffy, standing on *Viarsa*'s bridge, shouts instructions as his team assumes control.

Below: Duffy speaks to *Viarsa*'s captain, Ricardo Cabrera, the white-haired man with the raised hand.

Left: A helicopter carries supplies to *Viarsa* for the voyage to Cape Town.

Below: Scott Webb searches *Viarsa*'s crew quarters, hop-ing to find evidence of illegal fishing.

Above: Viarsa's other officers: Jose Gonzalez Perez, whose diary appeared to say that the vessel had been poaching in Australian waters; Antonio Perez, the fishing master and one of the world's most successful toothfish hunters; and Francisco Fernandez Oliveiria, one of the first officers.

part because she assumed it would be difficult to get anyone to sign up for such a peculiar assignment. After all, they would have to leave their homes almost immediately for a long and dangerous operation for which they had no training.

Malan immediately said yes. He in turn called Karel van Niekerk, a fifty-three-year-old Afrikaner who manages security at a bank office in downtown Cape Town. A couple of years earlier, van Niekerk and Malan almost died when they were out fishing on Malan's boat and it was capsized by a wave. The boat did not sink, but it wallowed mostly underwater and the engine would not work. Neither man had a life preserver, and their radio and cell phones were lost. All they could do was hold on as the crippled boat drifted away from the coast. At times they were both certain that they would die, and by the time they were finally rescued, seven hours later, they had forged what they both believed to be a lifelong bond.

"You must come!" Malan told van Niekerk over the phone. "It will be another great adventure for us."

"For sure—I wouldn't miss it."

In fact, everyone Malan called was immediately enthusiastic. Twenty-seven-year-old Christo Loots, an athletic Afrikaner who had heard about the chase during a radio news program that morning, was particularly eager: "Of course I want to do it! I want to go—come hell or high water. I *have* to go!" It was, Shaw thought, almost as if a bunch of young boys had been given the chance to skip school to go to an amusement park. Kroese had similar success when he called fisheries officers. He asked Harry Watts, a fifty-five-year-old who normally inspects ships that harvest hake and mackerel from coastal waters, to be in charge of all of the South Africans.

The entire contingent, nine men in all, met at the Department of Home

Affairs on Monday, August 18, at 3:30 p.m. None of them had passports, so officials agreed to work past the normal closing time to issue emergency travel documents. Meanwhile, Shaw and a colleague, Lynda Lotze, drove to a large Pick 'n Pay store where they filled several carts with foul-weather gear, backpacks, sleeping bags, condensed milk, coffee, high-energy bars, and anything else that seemed useful.

"We have a boarding party," Kroese told Keith Johnson, Stephen Duffy's boss, over the phone at the end of the day. "Three fisheries officers and six 'sworn fisheries officers.'"

"What do you mean, sworn fisheries officers?"

"Private security guards who have been trained in the use of firearms."

With a military man's skepticism of "private security," Johnson envisioned a band of trigger-happy gunslingers. Since he thought of South Africa as a semi-lawless place where gunfights were commonplace, he feared their approach would be very different from Australia's, where police officers are generally told to use their weapons only in self-defense. "If one of these guys kills someone while working on Australia's behalf," Johnson told Kroese, "we're all going to be in a lot of trouble."

This is not a gentleman's game, Kroese said to himself. *These bastards are not going to say, By all means, please, come aboard.* Aloud, Kroese asked, "Do you know how big an industry personal protection is here? These men are trained. They are ex-military people whose lives have depended on knowing when to pull the trigger. It's a risk you have to take."

Without any better options, Johnson said, "Whoever they are, Steve Duffy has to be in charge. They have to operate under his instructions—and he has to decide when they can use their weapons."

"That's fine. They'll do what you want them to do as long as you give them the right to use deadly force if it's needed to protect their lives. That's all we need."

"You have it."

After the call, Johnson stared out his window at Canberra's nondescript office buildings and marveled at the magnitude of what he had just done and the disasters that could result. He had just given a band of foreign security guards who had never been to sea the right to use deadly force while undertaking a risk-filled operation on behalf of Australia. It was so easy to imagine how things could go wrong that he could not think of anything else.

Someone could fall off a boat and die in the freezing water or someone could be shot. If anyone died, a parliamentary inquiry would follow. Heads could roll and Johnson's would probably be one of the first. Eager to provide some degree of protection for himself, he drafted a classified "operations brief" describing the boarding operation and the people who would be conducting it and sent it to several senior ministers. "You should note that this is inherently dangerous," Johnson wrote. "There is a genuine risk of casualties." The memo was encrypted and sent over a secure line to Parliament House, where it was decoded and then delivered to the ministers. When Johnson had sent previous memos of this kind, the ministers had signed and returned them within a few hours. This brief, however, went unsigned. While the ministers were eager to catch the pirate, apparently none of them wanted to attach their names to a plan that carried so many risks.

On Tuesday morning, August 19, Kroese set out from his home twenty-five miles north of Cape Town well before daybreak. The weather was terrible. It was raining heavily and a radio newscaster said it was snowing in the mountains. His first thought was about *John Ross*. If the weather caused a ship to get into trouble near Cape Town, the tug's owner had reserved the right to delay its departure. Kroese's fear was realized a few minutes later. As he drove down the coast road, he saw lights in a place where there should not have been any: a massive container ship, *Sealand Explorer*, had dragged its anchor in Table Bay and was sitting on a beach just outside Cape Town's harbor with a cargo that included a large amount of unrefined uranium.

After he arrived in his office, from which he could see the grounded ship, Kroese called Flanagan at his hotel and said, "We have a big problem. *John Ross* has another job to do. We have a container ship sitting right on top of a pristine beach and there's a huge pollution hazard." Kroese and Flanagan agreed that the boarding party should still get on *John Ross* before it left the dock later that morning so the tug could head toward *Viarsa* the moment it completed its work in the harbor. And an hour later, Flanagan and the crew of South African fisheries officers and security guards were riding in a van to Simons Town, a port just north of Cape Town, where the tugboat was waiting. No one said much as the van drove through the rain. It was, Flanagan thought, a fearsome-looking group, bulky men who looked like they knew a lot about enforcing their will. But with their unmatched raincoats, jeans, and rubber boots, they did not look anything like disciplined law enforcement officers. They looked more like nightclub bouncers.

What the hell have we gotten ourselves into? Flanagan asked himself.

The ship got underway almost immediately after their arrival. The storm that drove the container ship into the beach was still in full force. The water was crawling with whitecaps, and while the giant tugboat looked strong and stable, the appearance was misleading. With a flat bottom, it was a top-heavy vessel that rolled so violently that Christo Loots became seasick shortly after it left the dock. Several others followed suit and no one could eat. Like Flanagan, most of the security guards were having second thoughts. Once the ship entered Cape Town's harbor, where the water was much calmer, steel cables were attached to the container ship, and the tug spent most of Tuesday and Wednesday attempting to pull it off the beach. But the ship refused to budge, and the cables snapped. By early Thursday, three sets of cables had broken; *John Ross* finally gave up and set out to catch up with *Viarsa*.

The trip was miserable. The boarding team had been given cabins near the front, the most unstable part of the ship. With thirty-foot waves, no one could sleep. After the ship fell from one of the bigger waves, the bunk on which Karel van Niekerk was lying collapsed onto the lower bunk where Harry Watts was trying to rest. Watts was not asleep but his eyes were closed, and the ship was so noisy that he did not even hear the disintegrating bunk until it landed on his body, briefly trapping him underneath.

Christo Loots had never felt worse. After spending most of the day in his cabin, he ventured to the video lounge in the late afternoon, but he did not stay long. The movie version of *The Perfect Storm* was on the television. Afraid that the cinematic turbulence would make him sick all over again, he retreated to his bed. Karel van Niekerk did not get sick, but the ship was moving so violently that he found it virtually impossible to walk. Like Loots, he spent almost all of his time lying on his bunk. No one was eating, leaving Flanagan with a new concern: *Are these guys going to be capable of* anything *when we get there?*

CHAPTER 14

South Atlantic Ocean
August 22, 2003

Friday morning arrived with a surprise: *Viarsa* had a name. Sometime during the previous night, its crew had apparently painted letters on the stern and side of the ship. They were precisely formed, probably with the help of a stencil. By then, the chase had consumed fifteen days and three thousand miles, but since Cabrera was still two weeks away from his homeport, it was not clear why he had decided it was time to identify his ship. Perhaps, Duffy thought, he had just taken advantage of the relatively calm conditions.

"*Viarsa*," Duffy said over the radio. "I would like to ask the master why he has identified his ship with a name that was not there before?"

"This is the *Viarsa*. We had to protect the name from the wind and waves. Now that we are going back to port, I wanted to refresh them."

After laughing at the absurdity of Cabrera's explanation, Duffy said: "I do not believe the reason you have given. Please give me the real reason."

To that, there was no response.

"I have two bits of good news for you," Keith Johnson told Duffy at four o'clock the next morning, Saturday, August 23. "We've elicited the services of an ocean-going tug named *John Ross*. It's one of the world's biggest salvage tugs, and it's on the way to meet you with Mike Flanagan and nine security people onboard—three marine conservation inspectors and six deputized fisheries officers who work for a private security firm."

"Exactly what we need!" Duffy said.

"*John Ross* has a best speed of better than twenty knots," Johnson added. "It should rendezvous with you around midnight of the twenty-fifth. And there's more: another ship—*Dorada*, a British fisheries patrol vessel from the Falklands—has also been dispatched and it should meet up with you at about the same time."

"That *is* great news!"

"I should also tell you that we don't know much about the private security people." After describing how they were hired, Johnson asked, "How do you feel about that?"

"What choice do I have? We'll just have to deal with it."

Johnson added that he had learned a bit more about *Viarsa*'s captain: he had been working for *Viarsa*'s owner for several years, had two children, and was probably a year or two away from retiring. "He wants the company to look after him when he retires," Johnson said to Duffy. "So he'll probably do anything he can to get away from us."

After Duffy told O'Dea and Webb about the other ship, O'Dea asked, "Do we have any idea who the 'security' guys are?"

"Not really. Coming from South Africa, private security could mean just about anything. But that's what we're going to have—and the timing is tight. We need to have a boarding by the twenty-eighth or we'll be too far to make it back to Cape Town. I need you to put together a detailed plan for the boarding. We're going to have ships from three governments, a variety of weapons, and a mix of government agents and private security guards, some with experience boarding ships and some with none. Also, from now until after we take control of *Viarsa*, Mike Flanagan or one of you needs to be in the operations room all the time because we could get calls from the ships, Canberra, or South Africa at any time."

"That doesn't make any sense," O'Dea declared. "We need to get all three fisheries guys onboard as soon as possible to begin searching for evidence."

"We can't," said Duffy. "I need to have an Australian officer on *Southern Supporter* in a coordinating role who can tell Canberra what's happening."

Webb was infuriated. Although he accepted that Duffy should take charge of the logistics of the boarding, he believed that when it came to the next step—collecting evidence—Duffy should defer to the fisheries officers. If an Australian officer needed to stay on *Southern Supporter* during the boarding, Webb thought it should be Duffy. "Every piece of evidence has to be tagged, numbered, catalogued, and secured," Webb said. "We have to be able to trace everything we take from the moment it's seized until we take it into the courtroom. If anything goes wrong, it could destroy the case. I can't underestimate the importance of that—and we're the ones who know how to do it."

Duffy was unmoved: he believed he would not be doing his job if he was not part of the initial boarding party. "I know evidence-gathering isn't my expertise," he said, "but we're the three who started this thing, and we're the three who should see it through."

When Webb started to object, Duffy said, "I'm sorry—no."

While Duffy and Webb clashed over the plans for the boarding, Allan McCarthy was studying the growing concentration of icebergs. Each one was different. The biggest of them had flat tops and steep, almost vertical sides; they looked like toppled office towers. That is exactly what had happened to some of them: when the underside of an iceberg melts faster than the sections above, it becomes increasingly unstable until it eventually upends. Other icebergs were much more vertical and looked like mountains; some of those had multiple peaks and looked a bit like medieval castles.

The most dangerous formations were unseen. "When the ice that's above the water melts faster than the ice below the surface," McCarthy explained, "you end up with rams," prongs of ice that can extend hundreds of feet beyond what appears to be the end of the iceberg. He also explained why some of the bergs, particularly the slab-shaped ones, carried beautiful ribbons of blue. "Any ice that's blue has survived through at least two summers and lost some of its salt content. When ice gets old, it becomes denser and it refracts light differently."

A few minutes after four o'clock, *Viarsa* turned suddenly to the left. Seconds later, McCarthy spotted a large growler directly ahead of the ships that had not shown up on the radar. Deactivating the automatic pilot, he used the joystick to turn *Southern Supporter* sharply to the right. Neither ship touched the ice, but afterward McCarthy summoned Duffy to the bridge and said, "We're getting close to nightfall and I'm concerned about the number of icebergs and growlers. I think you should ask *Viarsa* to maneuver to the north to see if we can get free of the ice."

Duffy picked up the radio immediately. "*Viarsa*, this is Customs Officer Duffy, do you read me?"

A few seconds later, Cabrera responded, "Yes, this is the master."

"Good afternoon, master. I know that you have noticed the icebergs and dangerous ice. I'm concerned about the safety of our ships and our crews—particularly the danger that we could hit ice overnight."

"Yes, I've noticed the icebergs. We are fine. We're fine with the icebergs. I will continue on my current course. It's up to you. You can go to the north, but I am maintaining my course."

"Did you notice how close you came to hitting ice?"

After Cabrera declined to reply, Duffy went back to his cabin and made a new entry in his log: "The rationality of the *Viarsa*'s master has definitely come into question. He continually accepts significant risks without showing any comprehension, and he displays scant regard for the well-being of those on his ship." Duffy spent most of the rest of the evening thinking through the boarding, trying to divide the operation into steps and imagine how things could go wrong as he drafted an operations plan on his laptop computer. There were several complications to consider. Since the pursuit boats could carry only four passengers, the initial boarding party would be limited to eight men, probably not enough if there was a violent confrontation. In addition, only Duffy and the Australian fisheries officers were authorized to drive the pursuit boats during the initial boarding, and given his decision that one of the Australian fisheries officers had to remain on *Southern Supporter*, only one Australian could be part of the first group to step onto the ship.

Would it be permissible under Australian law, Duffy wondered, *to board a foreign vessel with a boarding party of seven armed South Africans and one unarmed Australian?* Once the boarding was completed, how many Australians and South Africans would be needed to maintain twenty-four-hour-a-day control over *Viarsa* and its crew? Should they be rotated back to *Southern Supporter*? How much food should be transferred to *Viarsa*?

By Sunday, August 24, *Southern Supporter* had chased *Viarsa* for almost four thousand miles in what Duffy believed to be the longest pursuit in modern maritime history.

Remarkably, other than *Viarsa*, *Southern Supporter*'s crew had not seen another vessel since it left Fremantle thirty-four days earlier. They had been so far from civilization that they had not even seen a plane overhead.

131

But by this point, the media was providing detailed coverage of the chase. The BBC World Service was broadcasting almost daily updates. Duffy received faxes containing some of the newspaper articles, which he posted in the mess. Some of the accounts were exaggerated—one claimed that the ships had encountered ninety-foot waves—but members of the crew were pleasantly surprised by the attention. Mariners have long complained that nautical events are rarely deemed newsworthy, and their complaints have a basis: while newspapers cover almost every plane crash, even those involving small aircraft in which no one dies, the scores of ships that sink around the world every year are barely mentioned.

The ships were still in a sea of icebergs, and the wind and waves built throughout the day. The combination of turbulence and ice was treacherous, but *Viarsa* was steaming at close to ten knots. One of the bergs they steamed past looked like it was as big as several adjoined football stadiums. Duffy estimated that it was two miles long and six hundred feet high. Codrington guessed that they had passed more than five hundred full-fledged bergs in the previous twenty-four hours. The radar screen, which covered everything within twenty-four miles, had so many dots that they were impossible to count during a single sweep of the radar, leading McCarthy to suggest that four people should simultaneously make a count, one for each quadrant. The total came to seventy-two.

Despite their unease about the icy obstacles, there was a growing sense of optimism onboard *Southern Supporter*. After weeks of uncertainty and a nagging sense that the epic journey would end in failure, a positive outcome had begun to seem much more likely once *John Ross* set out from Cape Town. But it was also obvious that *Viarsa* was not going down without a fight.

Early on Monday, August 25, *Southern Supporter*'s crew noticed that the fishermen onboard *Viarsa* had attempted to create a new obstacle: a cobweb of lines now covered their ship. One arched over the full length of the vessel, starting from the bow and continuing to the forward and aft masts, before it ended at the stern. From this line dozens of others extended to the railings around the side of the ship at intervals of about ten feet. The web, which had apparently been fashioned overnight, had been made from fishing lines, but Duffy believed their purpose was less about catching than repelling—thwarting a helicopter that might attempt to land on the ship. Duffy had seen vessels in the Persian Gulf do the same thing when he was stationed there during the first war in Iraq.

Picking up the radio handset, Duffy said, "*Viarsa. Viarsa.* I've noticed that you have rigged lines over your ship. Can you tell me why?"

"The lines will help hold the mast up," Cabrera said without any hint of irony. "It was a bit loose and in danger of collapsing."

Duffy and O'Dea looked at each other in amused disbelief before Duffy responded with mock gravity over the radio: "Master, I am concerned. Are you saying that your mast could fall down?"

"Yes, it could be possible."

With obvious sarcasm, O'Dea then said, "Well then, that is a very fine example of seamanship."

When Duffy called Canberra early that afternoon, he told Johnson about *Viarsa*'s lines. Johnson explained that a South African fisheries patrol boat, the *Agulhas*, was now also heading toward the ships to assist in the boarding and that it carried a helicopter. "We've had a security breach in South Africa," Johnson added. "A government official there told the press about *Agulhas*. A Uruguayan newspaper then picked up the news, and I bet someone there figured out that *Agulhas* carries a helicopter."

133

While Duffy was pleased to learn that a third ship was coming to his assistance, the sea was too rough for any kind of mid-ocean boarding. The wind was coming from the southwest at thirty to forty knots. "I think we have a window coming up on Tuesday," Duffy told Johnson. "*John Ross* will have caught up with us by then, but *Dorada* will not yet be on the scene."

"I'm not going to stop you, but if it's at all possible, I want *Dorada* to participate in the boarding. It would provide a much better demonstration of the international community's resolve."

"I know. I would hate to do it without them, but I'm not sure how many more opportunities we're going to get."

"I understand. You're the man on the scene. If you have to go, go."

Using a satellite phone, Duffy then called *John Ross*'s captain and said, "Listen, I'm not sure how we're going to go about this because *Dorada* is still twelve to fifteen hours away. But what I'd like you to do is remain about thirty miles north of us and steam in a parallel course with us, so *Viarsa* doesn't know you're there."

"That sounds fine," the captain said. "Please keep updating us with your position, heading, and speed."

Shortly after that, Duffy sent a telex to *Dorada*: "The opportunity for a boarding may present itself on Tuesday, and your presence would be valued. If you can add speed, it would be appreciated." *Dorada* responded by giving its position, course, and speed, and estimated that its earliest rendezvous would be 4:00 p.m. on Tuesday.

Shortly after three o'clock in Canberra on Monday, August 25, Keith Johnson drove from his office to Parliament House to brief some of the most senior officials in the Australian government—Minister of Defense Robert Hill, Minister for Justice and Customs Chris Ellison, and Ian Macdonald, the minister responsible for Fisheries—along with Major General Ken Gillespie, the army's most senior officer, and several others who had gathered around an oval table in a large, wood-paneled conference room.

Johnson began by describing the ships that would be involved in the boarding, but his primary objective was to highlight the risks, the same ones he had outlined in his still-unsigned operations brief. Reflecting his long background in the military, Johnson spoke about the operation as if it were a battle, and he addressed most of his comments to Hill and Gillespie, who were sitting directly across the table from him. "We've achieved the first part of what we set out to do," Johnson said. "We've brought the overwhelming force we need. But now we're getting to the real business and it's potentially dangerous. The boarding will only occur if the man on the ground is comfortable based on what's happening on the scene—his reading of *Viarsa*'s master, the weather, what he thinks about the capabilities of the gunslingers."

It was Macdonald who asked the most interesting question: "Who are the gunslingers?"

Turning to the fisheries minister, Johnson was direct: "The boarding party is not defense personnel. They are a bunch of people I've never met and know very little about. They haven't had a chance to work together, and they're working outside their normal operating environment. They're effectively private security people who probably do a good job on land but are untried at sea."

"Do we have a contract with them?" Macdonald asked.

"No, they sailed before we could put one together."

Eager to drive the point home with maximum disclosure, Johnson shifted his focus to Gillespie and Hill and said, "You have to understand, ministers, that if we go ahead, things could go very wrong. There could be casualties."

When Duffy stepped onto the bridge early on Tuesday, August 26, the weather was, by the standards of the South Atlantic Ocean, remarkably calm. The wind had abated to twenty knots, and the swell seemed almost gentle. *John Ross* had taken up its position a few hours earlier. "The weather is continuing to improve," Duffy told its captain, "so this looks like the day. Please close in on our position at your best speed. Once you're about two hundred yards off our beam, we will bring the boarding party from your vessel over to us."

Just before 11:00 a.m., Codrington saw *John Ross*'s superstructure rise over the horizon. Cabrera, having also spotted the large tugboat, spoke over the radio: "Vessel to my north, this is *Viarsa*. Please identify yourself." But now it was Cabrera's turn to suffer the silent treatment because Duffy had asked *John Ross*'s captain to ignore any communications from *Viarsa*. When *John Ross* was about four miles away, Cabrera, apparently able to read its name through binoculars, made another appeal that also went unanswered. His tone was anxious: "*John Ross, John Ross, John Ross*, this is *Viarsa*. What are your intentions?"

At noon, a crane on *Southern Supporter*'s stern deck lifted the first of two open-hulled pursuit boats off the deck and positioned it over the water so it could pick up Flanagan and the South Africans. The powerful aluminum boat, called a 640 because it is 6.4 meters long, was equipped with two ninety-horsepower outboard engines that gave it a top speed of forty knots. But it was not well suited to rough water because its freeboard—the distance between the waterline and the top of the hull—was too small to stop waves from washing over the side. And the calm weather had vanished. The wind had picked up to forty knots, and there were much stronger gusts. The waves were not breaking, but the sea was heaving with a twenty-five-foot swell.

Eager to set off before the weather got any worse, Webb climbed into one of the 640s and headed toward the other ship. He knew it would not be an easy transfer, particularly after he approached *John Ross*, which was on a parallel course to *Southern Supporter*, and noticed the tugboat's instability. Holding the little boat next to the tug for any length of time seemed impossible. While the 640 was bobbing up and down each wave as if it were a cork, the tug had a very different rhythm, delayed because of its much greater weight. Indeed, the cycles appeared to be almost perfectly contrary: when *John Ross* surged upward, the 640 fell. During every cycle, the tug's deck went from a position twenty feet above the 640 to being virtually at the same level. Worse, when the big boat fell, it produced a wave that pushed the 640 away.

The mechanics of moving men from the ship to the 640 were also difficult to envision. Like most tugboats, the *John Ross* had a large rubber bumper that extended out over the top of its hull, creating an overhang that meant that the ladder the South Africans would descend could not rest against the hull. Instead, the ladder—and the South Africans—would have to dangle freely over the water and let go when Webb managed to position the 640 beneath them. With the movements of the boats and water, there were a lot of variables. Getting the timing wrong could easily lead to injury—or, much worse, a man overboard. The almost freezing temperature would extinguish a life in just a few minutes.

As Webb looked up at the South Africans, who were staring down from *John Ross*'s deck, and the spindly rope ladder that was hanging off the side, he had a specific vision of what might go wrong. If he let a wave carry his boat too close to the tugboat, its big rubber bumper could crash down directly onto the 640, crushing its passengers or filling it with water. The 640 could not sink—its hull contained so much solid foam that it would stay afloat no matter how much water it carried—but it could capsize. (There was a lever in the stern of the boat that would open a cylinder of gas that would right the boat, but no one had told Webb about that.) To make matters worse, a storm front was approaching. And as a dark wall of clouds—they were almost black—moved rapidly across the water, the wind was strengthening.

The second 640 was driven by Allan Brownlie. He managed to get his boat to the rope ladder before Webb, but as he got close to the ship, he spotted a problem. The bow wave, a standing wave produced by the tug's forward movement through the water, was clinging to the side of the ship just below the ladder, increasing the difficulty of holding the 640 near to the vessel.

The South Africans were more worried than the men who had come to get them. The 640 looked much too small to be in such turbulent water. It was not much bigger than the fishing boat that Dawie Malan and Karel van Niekerk capsized, and it was moving in every direction—up and down as well as side to side. It seemed like the waves had a pattern—three big ones were followed by several smaller ones—but as they studied the motions, no one could quite work out how they would get themselves onto the little craft.

Gathering his men on the deck, Harry Watts offered some advice: "The timing is the most important thing. You have to watch the waves but also where the boat is. The guy at the wheel can't control the waves—and he's going to have a hard time controlling his boat. Do you have any questions?" The men were obviously attentive, but no one spoke up, so Malan continued: "Once we get to the bottom of the ladder, we're just going to have to jump. It has to be quick. If you get to the bottom of the ladder, a swell could wash you away. So pick your moment and go. And whatever you do, hold onto the ladder. If you end up in the water, you'll only have three or four minutes before you go into hypothermia."

Christo Loots volunteered to go first. He was not trying to be brave. He just wanted to get it over with. He was wearing an oversize winter jacket and carrying his clothes in a garbage bag. An Uzi machine gun was strapped over his back. Halfway down the ladder, he stopped moving and stared down at the boat. The South African, Brownlie thought, was attempting to assess his boat handling skills. Or maybe he was looking for a bit of encouragement. One of the Australian Army troopers who operated the radar detection equipment was standing at the 640's bow with his arms spread, attempting to signal that he would break Loot's fall, but Loots did not let go.

Unable to hold his position, Brownlie waved Loots off, then turned his 640 through a tight but lumpy circle. This time, when the boat was beneath him, Loots immediately let go. His timing was perfect: the distance between him and the 640 was just a couple of feet, so he landed without injury.

Malan went next, followed by van Niekerk, Flanagan, and then Antoney Roberts, a stocky Afrikaner who normally worked as an operations manager in Fidelity's head office. Roberts did not pick the perfect moment. Falling about a dozen feet, he landed badly, bruising a leg and twisting an ankle. As soon as he found a seat, Brownlie steered the boat away from *John Ross* and pushed the accelerator as far forward as he could without drenching his crew. Because *John Ross* had slowed down during the transfer, *Southern Supporter* was now about five miles away.

Brownlie would have to head directly into the waves to catch up. Each one was a challenge. Just before he reached a crest he had to pull the accelerator back to prevent the boat from leaping off the top and crashing into the next trough with too much force. It was obvious to everyone when he did not get the timing right: the props came out of the water to produce a high-pitched whine as the boat tipped forward over the top and, seconds later, the bow plunged into the water, dousing the crew with frigid water.

Like Webb, Brownlie was watching the advancing black cloud. He wanted to beat it, but he was not nearly fast enough. The cloud was a snow-making machine, producing such a heavy onslaught that he could not see *Southern Supporter* or *John Ross*. Since he did not have a compass, he was completely disoriented. Worse still, he thought his radio had broken.

"I can't see a thing," he screamed into the receiver. Hearing no response, he shouted, "I think the skipper has pissed off and left us here!"

The South Africans were freezing. They were wearing rain jackets and had pulled hoods over their heads, but the garments were much too flimsy to defend them from the cold and wet. Loots was thinking about what it would be like to board *Viarsa* in conditions like this, specifically how easy it would be for the fishermen to push a ladder into the sea.

On the other 640, Webb was angry, both because Brownlie had set out ahead of him and also because *Southern Supporter* was invisible. After the rest of the South Africans managed to board his 640, he was unwilling to lose visual contact with both ships, so he assumed a course parallel to the tug's. He was extremely cold. He was wearing an expensive dry suit, but his boots had filled with water and he could not stop himself from shivering. Sure that his passengers were much worse off, he looked over his shoulder and asked, "Are you guys all right?" Two of them smiled and turned their thumbs up in a way that Webb judged to be artificial. The others looked terrified. They had good reason to be. They were heading into a biting wind and enormous waves, *Southern Supporter* was probably several miles away, and Webb had only a vague idea as to how to get there.

"*Southern Supporter*, this is Scott Webb," he shouted into the microphone of his radio. "I need a bearing—I can't see you!"

CHAPTER 15

Bridgehampton, New York
August 6, 2003

On the same day *Southern Supporter* first detected *Viarsa*, another toothfish-related law enforcement operation was taking shape in the Northern Hemisphere. It was a lovely summer morning near the east end of Long Island, and a five-car convoy was carrying four U.S. agents and four local police officers past the multimillion-dollar homes lining the winding roads that lead to the beach in the village of Bridgehampton. Just before 6:00 a.m., they reached Dune Road, a particularly attractive byway that bisects the narrow strip of sandy land that separates the Atlantic Ocean from Mecox Bay. Every house is on either the bay or the ocean, and most houses have views of both. Turning into one of the driveways, the officers passed through a pair of gates and past a manicured putting green, which was protected by an exceptionally deep sand trap, before they parked in front of a sprawling, cream-colored house capped with a distinctive red-tiled roof.

It would be difficult to imagine a place more different from the waters around Heard Island. As the officers stepped out of their vehicles, the early morning air was already warm. Birds were singing and gentle waves were falling against the nearby beach. Climbing the front steps, the officers reached a double set of front doors. Peering through a window, they saw a spacious living room filled with sky blue sofas, sculptures, and paintings. Most of the art was modern, although there were also several traditional seascapes. French doors on the far side of the room led to a terrace, which overlooked bulrushes and a marsh and beyond that, Mecox Bay. The bay was pristine, even more beautiful than the view of the ocean, which was visible to the officers when they looked away from the front of the house and over the golf green.

Rochelle Bengis, an attractive brunette with a deep tan and piercing blue eyes, had seen the cars, one of them a marked police car, through an upstairs window even before she heard the doorbell. Her heart was pounding. She was not entirely surprised by what was about to happen, but that did not make it any easier to accept the idea that her husband was about to be arrested and taken away. Beyond the shock, she was outraged. She knew her husband's company, once the largest privately owned fishing operation in South Africa, had broken laws there, but she believed the infractions had happened in such faraway places that they should not be a concern for the American legal system.

After she opened the door, Chris Musto, an officer of the National Oceanic and Atmospheric Administration, which is responsible for enforcing federal fisheries laws, asked, "Where is Mr. Arnold Bengis?"

"Upstairs."

While five of the officers rushed up a winding staircase, two others searched the rest of the house. The officer who stayed with Rochelle was civil, even cordial; but he refused to let her call her thirty-four-year-old stepson David, who was in business with his dad, and he was reluctant to even let her use a bathroom until she showed him that it did not have a phone.

In the hall upstairs, Musto, who had been investigating Bengis for almost two years, found his target, a bearded sixty-seven-year-old,

wearing nothing but boxer shorts. In the broad accent of his native South
Africa, Bengis declared, "You must be Musto."

Although he was taken aback by the fact that Bengis knew his name,
Musto replied, "I am—and you are under arrest."

After Musto read Bengis his Miranda rights, he was allowed to shave
and get dressed while Musto collected papers and a laptop computer from
the top of Bengis's desk and placed them into a large box. A few minutes
later, Bengis was on his way to a courthouse in lower Manhattan, where
he would be accused of masterminding one of the biggest fish-smuggling
conspiracies in American history. The indictment charged Bengis and four
other men, one of them his son, with twenty-one counts, alleging that
they "engaged in an elaborate scheme" to bring massive quantities of illegally caught Patagonian toothfish from South Africa to the United States.
The indictment also accused Bengis of submitting false documents to government agencies in the United States and South Africa, "thereby con-
cealing from United States authorities that they were importing into the
United States Patagonian toothfish that had been illegally harvested."
Bengis was also accused of smuggling vast amounts of illicit rock lobster.

But Bengis did not appear to be overly concerned as he was driven to
Manhattan, declaring at one point, "No one is going to lock up an old
man." Musto did not want to talk about the details of the case, but Bengis
pressed him for information. He wanted to know about the government's
evidence, the specific charges he would face, and the potential penalties.
When Musto told him that each of the twenty-one counts could result in
five years of imprisonment and a fine of a quarter-million dollars, Bengis's
tone was flippant, as if none of this had anything to do with him: "Wow,
that sounds like a lot of time and a lot of money!"

Musto was not surprised by the man's bravado. He knew that Bengis's organization had managed to flout South African laws for many years and that it was at one point paying bribes to fourteen of Cape Town's fifteen fisheries inspectors. When one of his business associates there asked him about the risks of getting caught, Bengis, according to court records, said, "Don't worry about that—I have fuck-you money."

What did take Musto by surprise was Bengis's knowledge about the American investigation. Of the dozens of people Musto had previously arrested, none had addressed him by name before he introduced himself. Now, in the car, Musto received another jolt when Bengis asked, "How was your trip to South Africa?" Before Musto could reply, Bengis added, "I hope you stayed in a nice hotel."

"How did you know I was there?"

"You just got back last week, right?" Since Musto did not reply, Bengis added, "Cape Town is a small place. You talked to a lot of people, and some of them still talk to me."

While Musto was amused by Bengis's brazenness, he also recognized that the businessman's skepticism about the legal system's reach was to a great extent justified. In spite of the massive amount of illegal toothfish that was flowing into the United States, none of the large-scale perpetrators had been prosecuted.

The son of a South African dentist, Bengis is intelligent, devoted to his family, and, in spite of his occasionally intemperate language, cultured. After graduating from the University of Cape Town with an honors degree in commerce, he worked as an accountant for several commercial fishing businesses until 1964, when he acquired Hout Bay Fishing Industries, then a small and struggling company. Bengis was just twenty-eight at the time, but the firm grew steadily under his management, particularly in the 1970s, when he started harvesting large amounts of rock lobster for export to the United States.

The imposition of economic sanctions against apartheid-era South Africa by the American government in the 1980s should have been a devastating blow to Bengis's business, but he devised a simple yet effective method to elude the law: the boats that harvested the lobster unloaded their catches onto United States–bound cargo ships that were registered in countries other than South Africa. The lobster never touched South African soil, and the cargos were never inspected by officials there. In fact, even if officials there knew what was going on, they would have been unlikely to do anything to enforce the American sanctions. "The South African government didn't care—they didn't believe in the sanctions—and Arnie just said the lobster came from somewhere in South America," says the owner of a large international fishing company who knew Bengis. "Everyone in the industry knew what he was doing. The real wonder is that more people didn't do the same thing." Musto and other investigators would later theorize that it was Bengis's success in sidestepping the U.S. sanctions that paved the way for his lucrative toothfish-smuggling operation.

American prosecutors found it difficult to determine exactly how much money Bengis had made from smuggling fish, but it was obviously substantial. Between 1999 and 2001, Icebrand Seafoods, Bengis's New York–based company, sent $56 million to overseas bank accounts, according to records Musto found. Bengis had accounts in South Africa, Britain, and other places with strong bank secrecy laws—Switzerland, the Jersey Islands, and Gibraltar. His Swiss account received $13 million in deposits during 2002 alone. Most of his personal assets were held in trusts, many of them registered overseas, and one of his lawyers would later say that one of the trusts was worth more than $25 million. The house in Bridgehampton was worth several million dollars, and Bengis also owned a forty-first-floor apartment on Manhattan's Upper West Side, which enjoyed a sweeping view of Central Park, as well as a home in Cape Town's exclusive Four Beaches neighborhood.

Bengis traveled widely overseas and became a generous philanthropist, contributing enough money to a Cape Town high school that a cricket field was named after his family. He also gave more than a half-million dollars to Israel's Ben Gurion University, which elected him to its board of governors and awarded him an honorary doctorate for "distinguished contributions to science and humanity."

Like Antonio Perez, Bengis got started in the toothfish business when it was still focused on coastal waters off South America. His efforts were not always successful. In 1998, one of Hout Bay's ships, *Arctic Fox*, abandoned a voyage after forty days and summarily fired its Chilean crew and left them in Punta Arenas, the same Chilean port from which Perez set out on his first toothfish expedition.

Bengis developed a convoluted method for bringing toothfish into the United States: many of the shipments were off-loaded in Walvis Bay, the Namibian port where Perez had taken three loads of toothfish. It was a perfect landing point for pirates. If the fish landed in South Africa, the inspectors who greet most commercial fishing vessels there probably would have discovered that Hout Bay did not have the necessary permits to catch, possess, process, or export toothfish. Walvis Bay had excellent infrastructure, but its regulatory capacity was extremely limited. For several years, a single inspector was responsible for monitoring every arriving fishing boat. He generally did not see the ones that visited at night.

From Walvis Bay, toothfish were taken by truck to Hout Bay's warehouse in Cape Town. The trucks had to pass through a checkpoint at the Namibia–South Africa border, but it was manned by officers who were unlikely to be familiar with the intricacies of South Africa's fishing laws or tell one type of fish from another. After the fish arrived at the warehouse, they were packed into boxes labeled "Icebrand Seafoods" and loaded into refrigerated containers. When one was full, it was trucked to Cape Town's marine terminal, just ten minutes away, and lifted onto a United States–bound ship. Hout Bay obtained export permits for each of the containers, getting around the fact that it did not have the right to handle toothfish by describing the contents as tuna or monkfish or sometimes just "frozen fish." The containers were not searched between the time they left the warehouse and when they were strapped onto the ship.

After the ship left South Africa, Hout Bay transferred ownership of the container's contents to a shell company called Black Eagle Shipping. When Bengis's New York–based employees applied for an import permit, they provided an accurate description of the fish being transported. If an American Customs agent happened to inspect the container, he would be unlikely to suspect that the fish was illegal. American Customs officers are, after all, less focused on enforcing the laws of other nations than on ensuring that importers pay the requisite American tariffs and on seizing shipments that are obviously illegal. And, unlike drugs and many other illegal items, the mere presence of a toothfish is not illegal; what matters is where the fish were caught and by whom—and even the most careful inspection would reveal nothing about that. In 1999, David Bengis said as much when he was interviewed by a reporter for the *Atlanta Journal and Constitution*: "It's impossible to track the fish that has been pirated and where it goes."

Once Hout Bay's toothfish made it into the United States, Icebrand Seafoods—which was headquartered on West Fifty-Seventh Street in midtown Manhattan, just a few blocks from Rick Moonen's restaurant—found buyers for the fish. Much of it was sold over the phone to wholesalers, some of them based at New York's Fulton Fish Market, who in turn sold it to restaurants and supermarkets.

By the late 1990s, the demand for Chilean Sea Bass had become so great that the job was less about selling than taking orders. One of Icebrand's secretaries handled some of the sales. Icebrand also employed two highly regarded seafood salesmen in the Midwest, one in Detroit and the other in Milwaukee, who had major customers throughout the region. The Detroit-based salesman sold toothfish to many of the largest hotels and casinos in Las Vegas, where the fish had become a runaway favorite. Whatever toothfish was not sold in bulk was trucked to Maine, where David Bengis ran a processing plant that carved the fish into filets that were sold to East Coast supermarket chains.

None of this attracted the attention of law enforcement officials until June 1, 2001, when Michelle Kuruc, a lawyer with the National Oceanic and Atmospheric Administration, received an e-mail from a senior South African fisheries inspector who had learned about Hout Bay's toothfish smuggling operation four days earlier. Acting on a tip, South African fisheries officers inspected a container being prepared for shipment inside Hout Bay's warehouse. In its application for an export permit, the company had said the container held 3,600 pounds of rock lobster and did not say anything about toothfish. The South African agents found that it actually held *38,000* pounds of lobster and 4,000 pounds of toothfish. The container was seized along with records indicating that another toothfish-laden container was already on its way to

New York onboard a ship called *Lobivia*, which prompted the e-mail to Kuruc.

After *Lobivia* arrived at Port Newark, Hout Bay's container was lifted off the ship by a gantry crane and placed on a truck that went to a secured warehouse where Customs Service agents search suspicious shipments. Chris Musto and several other agents from NOAA and Customs were on hand to break the numbered strip of yellow plastic that sealed the two steel doors at the end of the container. Although Hout Bay had told South African authorities that this container was filled with tuna and monkfish, Black Eagle's application for an import permit said it was filled with toothfish and lobster. An inspection confirmed that the container did in fact hold both lobster and toothfish.

Because South Africa and the United States are both signatories to the Convention on the Conservation of Antarctic Marine Living Resources, a multinational effort aimed at protecting marine life in the waters near Antarctica, a "catch document" certifying where the fish were caught should have been presented to officials in both countries. But Hout Bay never provided one to South Africa. And Musto was sure the catch document that had been given to American authorities was illegitimate because the quantity it listed did not correlate with the quantity shown on the application for an import permit, a discrepancy that had until then gone unnoticed.

Musto believed Bengis's company had violated American laws both because it had submitted a fraudulent catch document and also because of the Lacey Act, which makes it a crime to bring any wildlife into the United States that has been harvested or transported in violation of foreign conservation laws. If Hout Bay had broken South African laws by transporting toothfish without the required permits, it had, thanks to the Lacey

Act, also violated American law. Designed to counteract the powerful role that the American economy plays in driving the illegal harvesting of various types of wildlife, the act provides the perfect weapon to pursue the kind of global organizations that are behind toothfish trafficking.

Not wanting to tip their hand, Customs officers told Icebrand that the shipment could not be released because of a paperwork snafu. Meanwhile, a group of South African investigators—three attorneys, a pair of fishing inspectors, and a biologist—left for New York to gather evidence for their own legal action against Bengis and Hout Bay.

At about the same time, Bengis flew from Cape Town to New York, where an Icebrand executive had noticed that someone, whom he assumed to be a law enforcement officer, was picking up the office trash. Icebrand employees then started using a paper shredder and doing whatever else they could to hinder the investigation. Then they got a lucky break when one of Icebrand's executives phoned South Africa's Department of Marine and Coastal Management to inquire about the impounded container, and a secretary there told him that her boss was in New York and even mentioned where he was staying. Not long after that, a private detective agency followed the South Africans as they drove from the Wellington Hotel in midtown Manhattan to Port Newark. The same private detective agency, which was paid $47,000 for its work, later shadowed Musto and other American investigators.

Musto and his supervisor, Scott Doyle, were excited by the case they began developing. They knew that vast amounts of illegal toothfish were coming into the United States, but they and their colleagues around the country had found it difficult even to identify the major operators. Until the Bengis investigation, the only ones they could find were living overseas and therefore probably untouchable.

Bengis was the perfect target—a major player living in the United States. By searching through Customs Service records, they found that his organization had already brought at least eighteen other containers with 530,000 pounds of toothfish into the United States by way of Black Eagle Shipping. And all of the shipments appeared to be illegal both because Hout Bay did not have the South African permits that were required to deal in toothfish and because the company had falsely labeled the fish as something else when it left the country.

It was impossible to know exactly how much toothfish Bengis had brought into the United States because he could have easily used shell companies other than Black Eagle. It was clear, however, that it was a well-established operation and that the shipments were continuing. On August 8, 2001, another Black Eagle container arrived at Port Newark with 20,296 pounds of illegal toothfish. It was seized two days later. A subsequent America-bound shipment avoided seizure only because Icebrand's executives had enough time to divert it to Singapore and then to Hong Kong, which did not require catch documents.

Meanwhile, in South Africa, the investigation had been taken over by the Directorate of Special Operations, an elite law enforcement agency better known as the "Scorpions." In attempting to find the original sources of Hout Bay's toothfish, the Scorpions determined that some of it came from *Mare*, a 190-foot longline vessel Hout Bay owned through a company that was registered in Namibia. Investigators believed the ship had been fishing for toothfish since 1996. Records obtained from the Namibian government indicated that *Mare* had landed forty-nine tons of toothfish in Walvis Bay in 2001, a shipment that was subsequently trucked from Namibia to Cape Town. The Scorpions suspected that Hout Bay used the same method to transport toothfish purchased from other illegal operators. Indeed, some of the toothfish that passed through Hout Bay may have been caught by Antonio Perez.

By the time Bengis was arrested in Bridgehampton, Hout Bay had collapsed and Bengis had admitted that the company was guilty of twenty-eight South African fishing charges. He agreed to pay the government there a fine of about $4 million. Three of Hout Bay's ships were seized, and South Africa moved to take two others, including the *Mare*. But Bengis had not personally pleaded guilty to anything in South Africa, and prosecutors there decided not to pursue him personally because he was spending most of his time in the United States, where he had become a citizen in 1994. Afraid they would not be able to extradite him, they decided that it made more sense to assist American authorities to prosecute Bengis under U.S. law.

Following his indictment in New York, Bengis denied all of the charges and was released on $15 million bail, although he was confined to his Manhattan apartment. For someone who was accustomed to frequent travel, the restrictions on his movements and his legal prospects were depressing, so much so that he began seeing a psychiatrist and taking an antidepressant drug. As he realized that the American legal system might have the same global reach that his business operations once had—and after Marcus Asner, the Assistant U.S. Attorney who was prosecuting Bengis, threatened to add money-laundering charges to the case, which would have substantially increased the potential jail sentence—he told his lawyers that he might consider pleading guilty to some of the charges.

On March 2, 2004, Bengis entered a modern courtroom in lower Manhattan and told a federal magistrate he had agreed to plead guilty to four of the twenty-one counts for which he had been indicted, including conspiring to smuggle illegal fish into the United States in violation of the Lacey Act.

But while Bengis specifically acknowledged smuggling lobster, he did not personally admit to smuggling toothfish. During the negotiations that led to his agreement, his attorneys did not deny any of the most important toothfish allegations made against Bengis's company: that Hout Bay had possessed, processed, and exported a fish that it was not allowed to handle in South Africa and that it had concealed toothfish exports by submitting false documentation to authorities in South Africa and the United States. Nor did the attorneys refute evidence that Hout Bay had illegally caught toothfish that was later shipped to New York. But even though one of Bengis's alleged coconspirators, the Hout Bay executive who had signed the company's export applications, admitted that the company was in the business of smuggling toothfish into the United States, Bengis's attorneys claimed that Bengis himself was personally unaware of any toothfish smuggling. They later used the absence of a toothfish admission to argue that he should receive a shorter jail term than what was recommended by the federal sentencing guidelines.

Although investigators in the United States and South Africa believed there was more than enough evidence to prove that Bengis was guilty of toothfish charges, they also understood why the prosecutor accepted the plea. As strong as the evidence related to the toothfish was, the evidence for lobster-related violations was even better. Fourteen South Africa fisheries inspectors had by then admitted that they had accepted bribes to conceal the fact that Hout Bay was harvesting several times more lobster than its quota allowed. In a larger sense, the specifics of what Bengis was willing to admit did not really matter: the four counts he admitted to were enough to put him in jail for several years, and the toothfish operation had already been shut down.

Judge Lewis A. Kaplan of the U.S. District Court, who presided over the case, was obviously outraged by what he viewed to be Bengis's blatant disregard for the law. "I view his behavior as evidencing an astonishing display of the arrogance of wealth and power," the judge said. "For example, I have before me—and it has not been contradicted—that when asked by his associates about the possibility of being caught in this scheme, Mr. Bengis responded that he was unlikely to be prosecuted because he has, and I quote, 'fuck you money.'" The judge went on to cite "evidence suggesting obstruction of justice by Mr. Bengis in this investigation, including the withholding of documents responsive to a grand jury subpoena, the use of a shredder to destroy documents, and the engagement of a private investigator to shadow U.S. government law enforcement personnel who were carrying out this investigation."

When he was given a chance to speak, Arnold Bengis stood up to express a degree of remorse in front of a group of about sixty of his relatives and friends. "Your honor, I did not intend to speak today because I thought it would be too emotional," he began. "However, I feel that I have a duty to my family, who are all in court today. This is the worst day of my life."

A few minutes later, Judge Kaplan, who was not persuaded that Bengis's sentence should be reduced from the federal sentencing guidelines, sent him to prison for forty-six months, one of the longest sentences ever handed down for fishing offenses. Together with his nephew, Jeffrey Noll, who worked for Bengis and was given a thirty-month sentence, he was also ordered to forfeit $5.9 million to the government. David Bengis was given a one-year sentence and ordered to forfeit the $1.5 million he would receive from selling the toothfish-processing plant in Maine.

Prosecutors portrayed the outcome as an important victory in the battle against toothfish smuggling and as an example of what international cooperation could accomplish. But no one believed it represented an actual turning point. The fact that Bengis was still the only major toothfish operator to be prosecuted and that he had been able to avoid specifically acknowledging his role in toothfish trafficking only underlined the substantial obstacles that remained.

"Enormous amounts of illegal toothfish are still coming into the country," Chris Musto said after Bengis was imprisoned. Musto subsequently left NOAA to join the Customs Service, in part because of his frustration with the lack of resources being devoted to fish-related crimes. "The toothfish operators are big and sophisticated," he says, "and we're not doing nearly enough to stop them."

CHAPTER 16

Andrew Codrington was alone on the bridge when he heard Scott Webb shouting over the radio. Unable to see *John Ross*, let alone the 640s, the captain immediately realized that he had to temporarily break off the chase by turning around to head toward *John Ross*.

"*John Ross* is steaming in a direct line toward *Southern Supporter*," Codrington told Webb. "Keep on their bearing and you will see us."

It took Brownlie almost an hour to reach *Southern Supporter*. Webb, who spotted the ship shortly after Codrington changed course, took even longer. And when their passengers finally staggered into the mess, they did not make a great impression. Duffy was pleased to see the array of firepower—shotguns, eight nine-millimeter automatic pistols, and the Uzi—but the haphazard way they were being carried made him nervous. The condition of their weapons was also troubling: The barrels of some of the shotguns had come loose from the stocks and they were held together by knotted wires. Some of the weapons had been so heavily used that sections of their black metal stocks had worn away to silver.

The men's clothing, unmatched and inappropriate, added to the ragtag impression. So did the garbage bags that some of them were using to carry their clothes. "They look like a bunch of trigger-happy misfits," Duffy whispered to O'Dea. The combination of men who were under stress and new to the sea and who were all too comfortable firing their weapons seemed like a recipe for disaster. In spite of this, Duffy wanted to get on with the boarding as soon as possible.

"I would like to board *Viarsa* this afternoon," he told the South Africans. "We don't know how they will react. They have been consistently noncooperative throughout our pursuit, but we don't expect any violence. The important thing is that no one is to use firearms unless it is in pure self-defense."

The South Africans were skeptical. *Of course they're going to fight,* Dawie Malan said to himself. *These guys are like dogs in a fight. They know they are about to get torn apart—and it takes only one of them to set off violence.* He was also skeptical about the weather. It was snowing again, heavily. The wind had obviously picked up too because the flakes, visible through the four large portholes on the port side of the mess, were moving sideways. Harry Watts was thinking through the details of the boarding. Given that *Viarsa* appeared to be riding the waves in the same way that *John Ross* had—and that it was moving at its top speed—it seemed unlikely that the 640s could be positioned next to the fishing vessel long enough for his men to attach a ladder and get themselves onboard.

Following the briefing, Watts told Duffy, "There's no way our people can board the ship in these conditions."

"Let's see what happens," Duffy replied.

Leaving the mess, he went to the bridge, where he learned that the wind was blowing at fifty knots and gusting to sixty, just short of hurricane force. In truth, Duffy was not sure what to hope for—another sudden change in the weather that would enable him to conduct a boarding that afternoon or a delay that would give him more time to speak with the

South Africans. Returning to the mess, he sat down at one of the tables with Watts, who wanted to make it clear that his men were accustomed to violent confrontations. "Illegal fishing is a big business in my country," he said. "You have to stay on top of the poachers all the time or the place will be bare in a year or two. The pirates cleaned out our toothfish fishery— more than $100 million worth of fish—in less than two years." Watts added that most of the poachers in his country, particularly those seeking abalone, were armed and that fisheries officers, who are trained in the use of automatic weapons and shotguns, are fired on regularly. "When we approach abalone poachers," he said, "we usually arrive in armored vehicles."

"This operation has to be different," Duffy said. "We have to run it according to Australian regulations. You can defend yourselves if it comes to that. But if a South African shoots a Uruguayan on behalf of Australia, the international ramifications would be incredibly messy."

Given his fear that the South Africans would be too quick to use firearms, Duffy was eager to find another way to persuade Cabrera to give up. Going back to the bridge, he asked *John Ross*'s captain to use its water cannon, a powerful fire-fighting device, to send a blast of water over *Viarsa*. Then he got on the radio and spoke to Cabrera: "I'm maneuvering *John Ross* to be on your beam, so we can demonstrate the force of the water cannon. Now is the time—you must stop your ship and turn toward Cape Town."

"I am not going anywhere with you!" Cabrera said. "I have orders to return to Montevideo."

Dawie Malan, having just entered the bridge, asked, "What's the water cannon supposed to do?"

"It's incredibly powerful—it'll show that we mean business," Duffy said.

"That's what the Uzi is for!" Malan said. "Get a little closer and we'll shoot out their radar."

"You know we can't do that!" Duffy said. "Under our legislation, it is extremely unlikely that we would *ever* shoot at a fishing vessel. If the water cannon encourages them to be more cooperative, it will make our job easier."

"Things are different in South Africa," Malan said. "We knock them on the ground first. That way we know we're safe."

In fact, the cannon had no effect. Because of the distance and wind, the blast of water did not even reach *Viarsa*. "Let's hope we have better luck tomorrow," Duffy said to no one in particular. By 4:30 p.m., it was already dark outside and most of the South Africans had retreated to the video lounge, a windowless cabin with a dozen upholstered chairs, to watch *Thunderball*, the James Bond thriller.

Once again, Duffy tried to communicate with *Viarsa*. "We now have the capability to board you," he told Cabrera over the radio. "The weather isn't appropriate right now, but there will come a point when it will be. Therefore, it is in your own best interests to turn toward Cape Town. Now!"

"I'm sorry," Cabrera replied, "I cannot. The Uruguayan government has put me under arrest, and it is not possible for me to refuse an order from my government. You do not have authority over me."

Given the conflicting pressures Cabrera faced, Duffy felt a small degree of sympathy for him. He was not about to let it show, though, so he said: "I don't have any confidence in the orders you are receiving from your government. My orders are very clear. You must return with us. You should also know that Britain is also sending a ship to assist us—and tomorrow morning we will be boarding your vessel."

"I understand those instructions, but I tell you now that you have no permission to come aboard the vessel. I've been arrested by my government—and I must return immediately to Montevideo. That's what I am going to do."

Duffy was also thinking about Uruguay's government, most particularly its navy and the possibility that one of its ships might complicate matters by arriving on the scene. The appearance of a single naval vessel, no matter how old or decrepit, would require him to back down. Duffy's other fear was that he might never have an opportunity to board *Viarsa*. His instructions were to follow the ship all the way back to Montevideo, but under the Law of the Sea, the hot pursuit would end as soon as they entered Uruguayan waters. Aware that they would not be greeted warmly by Uruguayans, members of *Southern Supporter*'s crew had begun to joke about the possibility that they might end up in jail. Bruce Noble, who served in the Australian navy before he became a member of *Southern Supporter*'s permanent crew, cornered Duffy after dinner and asked, "In all seriousness, what's the likelihood of us getting thrown in prison?"

"If it came to that, you'd be okay. If anyone gets into trouble, it would be Andrew Codrington and me."

At 10:00 p.m., *Dorada*, the British fisheries patrol vessel, caught up with the rest of the ships and assumed a position a half mile behind *Viarsa*. With *John Ross* on its port beam and *Southern Supporter* on its starboard beam, *Viarsa* was surrounded. But the multinational constellation of ships had no apparent effect on Cabrera, who maintained his course and speed throughout the night.

When Duffy went to the bridge at 6:00 a.m. on Wednesday, August 27, it was hailing, the wind was blowing at forty knots, and the waves were consistently twenty feet high, too big to even launch the 640s. Most of the rest of the crew had gathered in the mess for breakfast. Crowded because of the extra personnel, the atmosphere was loud and boisterous. The South Africans seemed to be much more comfortable with their surroundings than they had been the day before. After breakfast, most of them returned to the video lounge to watch another movie.

By 2:00 p.m., Duffy was feeling more optimistic—at least about the weather. The wind had dropped to twenty-five knots and the sky opened to reveal a few patches of blue. "It's really beginning to come good," he said to Codrington, Watts, and several others who were on the bridge. "If it continues to abate at the same rate, by 3:30 conditions will get to the point where we can probably go."

"From what I see, I think you could go right now," Codrington said.

Shaking his head, Watts said, "My guys would never feel comfortable in this."

Undeterred, Duffy spoke to the captains of *John Ross* and *Dorada* over Channel 72, a VHF channel he did not think *Viarsa* would be monitoring. "I think we're going to have a window this afternoon," he said. "At this point, I'd like *John Ross* to maneuver ahead and take a position about five hundred yards in front of *Viarsa*. I'd like *Dorada* to put itself about two hundred yards off *Viarsa*'s port beam. While you're doing that, we're also going to move ahead, so that when the time comes, we can slow down to make it easier to launch our boats."

By 2:40 p.m., *Southern Supporter* was one and a half miles ahead of *Viarsa* and Duffy judged the conditions to be reasonable. "What do you reckon?" he asked Watts. "The weather looks pretty good now, doesn't it?"

"I don't think so," the South African replied. "It's still pretty rough out there, and it might get worse after we leave the ship."

"Okay," Duffy said. "But let's get everyone ready to go."

Duffy did not want to push too hard and certainly did not want to risk losing a man in the water, but he also did not want to lose another day. The weather might never get any better than this, and with every passing hour they were getting farther from Cape Town, closer to the point where a Uruguayan ship might reach them, and beyond the point where *Southern Supporter* could make it back to South Africa. With assistance from Codrington, Duffy did his best to convince Watts that the conditions were not as bad as they appeared. "When we slow the ship down," the captain said, "the waves won't look nearly as big. It's actually starting to get quite good."

At 2:45 p.m., Duffy called his department's duty officer in Canberra, where it was 12:45 a.m. Keith Johnson and other senior officials wanted to be in the office at the time of the boarding. "This is your forty-five-minute notice," Duffy said. "You better wake everyone up." Turning to Watts, he said, "There's still a bit of swell, but the wind is continuing to drop. It's down to just ten to fifteen knots. It's not even that cold—it's above freezing. I think we should plan on going at 3:30 p.m."

"Okay. I'm happy to go."

"Great—it's time to see what we can do!"

Picking up the radio receiver, Duffy said, "*Viarsa, Viarsa*, stop your vessel! I intend to put my boarding vessels in the water. You should not resist. The party will be armed, and I have been authorized to use all reasonable force available to me. You need to gather every member of your crew onto the aft deck in warm clothing. Do this now! You are to remain in the wheelhouse and may have one crew member to steer your ship. Do you understand me?"

Hearing no response, Duffy added, "If you fail to answer, I will have to take more severe steps. Do you understand me?"

"Please, can you repeat again," Cabrera replied. "I am taking notes and not understand all that you say to me."

"You are currently being filmed, photographed, and voice recorded. Any information that you say will be used as evidence, so it is in your best interests to comply with my instruction. I have the support of many countries and of the vessels now surrounding you. Do you understand?"

"Just a minute please."

"You do not have any time to consider. There is no time. The time has come for you to comply. This is not a request. It is an order. Do you understand?"

"Yes, yes, now I understand, but I tell you the vessel is under arrest of the Uruguayan government and Uruguayan Navy. They have ordered me to go directly to a Uruguayan port, and it is impossible for me to refuse an order directly from the government of Uruguay. So I know you come—but for me it is very, very, very difficult." After a pause, Cabrera added: "But if you come, I shall take orders. I must say, you are not authorized, but we will not offer you any resistance. And after, we will see."

When the South Africans assembled on *Southern Supporter*'s deck with thick layers of clothing and unshaved faces, Duffy told them, "The captain says he will put his crew on the aft deck and he won't resist us. But he won't assist us either, which means he probably won't slow down the ship."

Duffy did not know whether to take Cabrera at his word, but his biggest worry was the trigger-happy instincts of the South Africans—and his concern only heightened when Malan pointed to a crowbar that was lying on the deck with the equipment that would be loaded onto the 640s and asked, "What's that for?"

"If they lock the door to the bridge," Duffy replied, "we'll use it to get inside."

Waving his hand toward the Uzi that Christo Loots was carrying over his shoulder, Malan smiled and said, "We'll use this!"

Given their previous discussions about the use of firepower and Malan's expression, Duffy thought this remark was probably facetious. He could not be sure, though, so he asked, "You remember our rules of engagement, don't you?"

"Yes, yes, yes."

"We have to keep cool. No one needs to be a hero."

But Malan was clearly pumped with adrenaline. A few minutes later, he motioned toward *Viarsa* and told O'Dea and Webb, "I want those guys to know that we don't fuck around. If someone even puts their head over the rail, we're going to take it off!"

"Fucking hell!" Webb said to O'Dea. "These guys are pretty hyped up. You better go up to the bridge and ask Mike to make sure Cabrera understands that everyone needs to stay on the stern of their vessel."

O'Dea scrambled up the outside set of stairs that led to the bridge and told Flanagan what Malan had said. Rather than repeating the specifics, Flanagan radioed: "The boarding party will be heavily armed. You must make sure that no one on your crew comes anywhere near them."

Webb, who would be driving one of the 640s, had no doubt: he *knew* there would be bloodshed. He thought he was unlikely to be shot himself—he thought *Viarsa*'s crewmen were the most likely casualties—but he was unhappy about the prospect of even seeing the gore. Since Brett Lenz, the paramedic, was going to be on his boat, he knew the victims would end up on his boat.

Duffy was at the wheel of the first 640 that was lifted off the deck. As it was lowered toward the water, the four South Africans who were with him stopped talking and their eyes widened. They were awestruck by the conditions. From *Southern Supporter*'s deck, the waves had seemed distant and smaller than they really were, more like a movie than the real thing. But from their new perspective, the ten-foot mounds of water looked enormous. Once the little boat entered the water, its jerky motions were also unsettling, particularly when it fell between the waves and *Southern Supporter* was no longer visible. Duffy drove the small craft slowly, hoping to prevent his passengers from getting any wetter and more frightened than necessary. He also did his best to project an aura of confidence in order to suggest that there was nothing particularly extraordinary about what they were setting off to do.

Antonio Perez was standing on *Viarsa*'s bridge and assessing his options. He was desperate to prevent the boarding. Vidal had told him that Uruguay had agreed to send a navy ship to a point 750 miles off its coast to scare off the Australians, and Perez needed only a couple of more days to get there. The key was to keep moving. But his boat was hemmed in. If it turned to the left, it would strike the *Dorada*. If it turned to the right, it would hit *Southern Supporter*. And *John Ross*, which was directly in front of *Viarsa*, was slowing down, obviously attempting to force *Viarsa* to do the same.

Running out of alternatives, Perez ordered Cabrera to run into the tug's stern, which was then just thirty feet away. Unlike a collision with the other two ships, which would be the direct result of *Viarsa*'s action, Perez believed one with *John Ross* would be deemed to be the tug's fault.

"Whatever happens, we don't stop," Perez told Cabrera. "We just keep going."

"*John Ross*, you want a collision?" Cabrera shouted over the radio. "You are crazy!"

But then Perez saw the first of the 640s, the one Duffy was on. It appeared to be heading to a position between *John Ross* and *Viarsa*. Perez was willing to do almost anything to get away, but he would not risk running over the little boat, so he ordered Cabrera to slow the ship, temporarily, he hoped.

Seeing that *Viarsa* was no longer traveling at its top speed, Duffy said to himself, *They must understand that the game is finally up*. But he also knew that the most perilous part of any forced boarding comes during the moments after the first members of the boarding party step onto the target and before they take control. If they were attacked at that point, before they understood exactly what they were up against and how the boat was laid out, they would be extremely vulnerable. And it would be difficult for them, or the men who were still on one of the bobbing boats, to return fire effectively. Even if no one on *Viarsa* had a firearm, the fishermen could easily dislodge the ladder, causing anyone on it to fall into the water. The rest of the boarding party would then have to become a rescue squad and the operation would probably have to be aborted.

Viarsa's crew, most of them wearing dark jackets and wool hats, had assembled on the aft deck. They did not look particularly hostile. They were lined up against the rail with their hands in their pockets doing nothing but watching the approaching 640s. Duffy stared back, trying to get a read on their feelings. A couple of them waved, but their expressions seemed empty, neither angry nor welcoming. Other than the two men who he had said could remain on the *Viarsa*'s bridge, Duffy hoped he was looking at the entire crew, but it was impossible to know whether others were hiding elsewhere—or whether the South Africans would hold their fire.

Duffy's boat was carrying an aluminum ladder that had been fitted with a bracket at the top, which was supposed to hook over the rail above *Viarsa*'s deck. But after Duffy drew alongside *Viarsa*, Malan, who wanted to be the first man to board the ship, could not lift the ladder high enough to get the hooks over the rung. The ladder was not long enough. It just banged against the side of the hull without catching anything.

"Give it to me!" Christo Loots shouted.

Since the ladder could not reach the top railing, Loots secured it to a railing in the cutaway section. But he was not sure whether the connection was secure. And even if it was, bringing the 640 directly up against the ladder could easily cause the ladder to uncouple from the rail. Duffy was attempting to hold the boat in a position about a foot away from the ladder, but *Viarsa* was still moving and was riding the waves very differently than the 640, so the size of the gap varied from second to second. The South Africans would have to take that into account, summon their courage, and jump, hoping the ladder held. The timing was critical. If someone mounted the ladder at the wrong time, the next wave would be over his head.

"Wait until we're high on the swell," Duffy shouted. "Then grab the ladder at the highest point you can."

Seeing how much difficulty the men on the little boat were having, Perez shouted to Cabrera, "Let's go—let's go!"

But Cabrera saw that a man was just about to jump to the ladder. "I cannot," the captain said. "It's too late."

As he watched the man leap to the ladder and then climb onto the steel tray that normally carries toothfish into the factory, Perez knew it was over. "Fuck," he declared. "They're coming onboard exactly where the fish do!"

Loots had gotten it just right. The ladder lurched a few inches sideways when he landed on it, but the hooks remained locked onto the railing. Once he reached the cutaway section, he turned and shouted: "Follow me!" He then climbed onto *Viarsa*'s main deck, where he gripped his Uzi and swept it back and forth as he looked for anyone who might be hiding. Seeing no one, he dropped to one of his knees to make himself a smaller target. Using his other knee to brace his arm and the Uzi, he took aim at the bridge. Metal shutters covered all but two of the windows, so it was impossible to see how many people were inside, but a bearded man was clearly visible. Since Loots thought it was the ship's captain, he pointed the barrel directly at him. It was then that *Viarsa* came to a dead stop.

Malan was the second man up the ladder. Just before he left the boat, he clasped van Niekerk's shoulder and said, "Uncle, you must make sure they don't loosen the ladder. If anyone falls in the water, they're not going home." When Malan reached the deck, he drew his automatic pistol and began patrolling the perimeter of the bow, searching for hatches and other potential hiding places.

The passengers on Webb's boat, which was forty feet from *Viarsa*, were standing with their shotguns raised and their fingers on triggers. When he was not concentrating on maneuvering the boat, Webb stared at *Viarsa*'s crewmen. He had assumed that they would look evil, like hard-core criminals. But as he looked for indications of malevolence and tried to imagine

171

what it would be like to be in their shoes, he decided they looked more like average working-class men.

By the time Duffy's boat had unloaded and Webb's took its place, the ladder had been lashed to the side of the ship, making it easier for his passengers to clamber aboard *Viarsa*. Antoney Roberts had volunteered to go first. Standing at the front of the tender with his hands halfway extended, he was watching the swell, trying to time his move. But he could not do it.

"Do I go now?" he kept asking. "Now?"

Rather than trying to tell him precisely when to jump, Webb said, "Relax. Watch the swell and pick your moment."

Webb was concerned about the impression that this show of timidity would make on the *Viarsa*'s crew, but he was more worried about the possibility that Roberts might end up in the water. Even if he were quickly retrieved, he probably would have to be rushed back to *Southern Supporter*, leaving less than half the boarding party on *Viarsa*.

Just as Webb was about to suggest that someone else go first, Roberts made his move. His timing was terrible. Seconds after he stepped onto the bottom rung, his feet were swept off as half of his body plunged under water. Then, just as suddenly, the ship and Roberts, holding on with only his left hand, leapt upward out of the water. The force was so strong he felt as if someone were trying to yank the ladder out of his hand. In those seconds, Roberts thought it was all over. He knew it would be impossible for him to swim with his heavy wool jacket and the pump-action shotgun that was strapped across his back. Images of his wife with his son and daughter flashed through his mind. But then, as suddenly as it began, the upward motion stopped, and, after a pause, reversed. It was then, as he began to plunge back into the water, that his feet somehow found a rung. In the background, he heard screaming.

From the cutaway section, Gamat Solomons, one of the South Africans from Duffy's boat, was shouting, "Climb, climb!"

Someone in the 640 was also screaming: "Come back! Jump back in the boat."

Ignoring the conflicting instructions, Roberts went up the ladder until Solomons grabbed him by the arm and led him up to the deck. There Malan told him to take a position near the bow, next to a hatch that led inside the ship. As he stood there, Roberts realized that his entire body was shaking. He was not sure whether he was cold or in shock or both.

The others on Webb's boat had less trouble. O'Dea, the third man to climb up, quickly made his way up to the deck and went directly to the bridge, accompanied by Dawie Malan. Once they reached the door to the bridge, O'Dea paused, assuming that Malan would go inside first so he could secure the compartment. Instead, Malan pushed the door open and motioned for O'Dea to enter. *So much for my security*, O'Dea said to himself. Rather than objecting, he stepped into a compartment that was so thick with smoke that even O'Dea, a compulsive smoker since the age of sixteen, started coughing. A diminutive man with a flowing shock of gray hair, a full beard, and bushy eyebrows was standing impassively near the center of the bridge. Only the eyebrows were dark. His face was deeply lined, and some of his teeth were missing. Wearing a grimy tracksuit, he looked weary.

"Are you the master of the vessel?" O'Dea asked.

"Yes."

Cabrera stepped forward and extended his hand. O'Dea shook it, then opened a small black wallet to display his official identification, a badge, and a photo identification card.

"Your crew is to cooperate with our instructions," O'Dea said. "I must tell you that you don't have to say anything. Anything you do say may be recorded and used as evidence. Do you understand that?"

"Oh sure, sure . . ."

This was obviously the man O'Dea had been speaking to for the last three weeks. But given his previous recalcitrance, Cabrera's amiability—there was a hint of a smile on his haggard face—was surprising. So was the rest of his appearance. Even though the fleeting glimpses suggested that the captain was an older man, O'Dea still had it in his head that the gutsy mariner who had led *Southern Supporter* halfway around Antarctica must be young and physically robust. In reality, Cabrera was short and overweight. He had the leathery skin of someone who had spent a career at sea, but he looked more like Santa Claus than a pirate.

The bridge, which stretched across almost the entire width of the ship, was pretty much what O'Dea had expected. There were only four feet between the windows at the front and the artificial-wood paneling at the back, where a foot-tall statue of the Virgin Mary stood on a small shelf. The floor, which sloped slightly upward toward the front of the ship, was littered with cigarette butts and empty packs of Marlboro. O'Dea was standing next to the captain's chair, which looked more like a barstool, on the starboard side of the bridge. From there he had a clear view of the cutaway section as well as easy access to a sophisticated array of electronics—radar, a computer, a depth sounder, two GPS units, a pair of radio receivers, a satellite telephone, a device that could "scramble" radio conversations, and a radio direction finder that could locate fishing beacons. While the electronics were state of the art, everything else was dilapidated. A chair at the other end of the bridge was covered with cracking black vinyl and was missing part of a leg. It was next to an electric radiator that was almost completely covered with rust. Grimy metal coffee cups lined the windowsill just above a large can of Nescafé.

The chartroom, an alcove just behind the bridge, contained more than five hundred charts. There were several for the waters near Heard Island, including a bathymetric chart that indicated the depth of the seabed there. The ship's cloth-bound log was sitting on a shelf just above a large table that was designed to hold charts, not far from an additional array of communications and navigational equipment: another satellite telephone, telex and fax machines, three hand-held radios, and another GPS. O'Dea immediately seized the log along with a locked leather briefcase that sat on top of the table. Just before he left the room, O'Dea noticed something else: four screw holes in the wall just above the table and a severed wire tucked behind the shelf. He wondered if the wires had been connected to the Vessel Monitoring System, or VMS, that was supposed to automatically report the vessel's position to officials in Uruguay.

Returning to the bridge, O'Dea asked Cabrera, "Where is the fishing log?"

"We don't have one."

Turning to the younger man who was standing behind Cabrera, O'Dea asked, "Are you the fishing master?"

With a look of disgust, Antonio Garcia Perez said, "No, no. First mate. Captain is the fishing master."

O'Dea immediately formed a negative impression of Perez. Either unwilling to maintain eye contact or incapable of doing so, his face seemed to be frozen into a scowl. Everything about him suggested that he was supremely arrogant, possibly dangerous.

Scott Webb came to exactly the same conclusion. "He looks positively evil," he told O'Dea. "He is obviously the guy we have to watch."

CHAPTER 17

Vancouver, Canada

The open-air market on Vancouver's Granville Island is a lot like many retail fish markets. The concrete floor is usually wet, there is not much space in the aisles, and customers have to give way to sometimes fast-moving pushcarts. Daniel Pauly, a large, bearded black man who speaks with an indiscernible European accent, goes to the market at least twice a month, but he rarely buys anything. One of the world's foremost fisheries scientists, he goes only to see what's there. Actually, in recent years he has also spent a lot of his time pointing to what *is not* there.

Pauly believes his profession is partly to blame for what has happened to the world's fisheries, and he is determined to change things. The first step, he says, is helping people to understand the full extent of the problem. He began one of his visits to the market by pointing to a yellowish fish and said, "That's a rock fish: it's the kind of slow-growing fish that used to be found in huge numbers all along the coast of British Columbia. Now there are hardly any left. Look at what *is* here." Of a small, sardine-like fish, he said: "These are smelts: they always had been thought of as bait fish, but people started eating them about ten years ago. There's a tilapia—it came from Taiwan. The lobster over there came from Cuba. The tiger prawns came from Thailand. The scallops probably came from South America."

Pauly has never met Lee Lantz or Antonio Perez, but he would recognize both as being ahead of their time in realizing that their industry's future would depend on its ability to find new species from the Southern Hemisphere to replace the dwindling populations in the north. "That's the big story," Pauly says. "The Northern Hemisphere is running out of fish—and it's become this enormous black hole that's absorbing more and more marine life from the south."

Actually, the next stall appeared to tell a different story: it contained several types of salmon along with snapper and cod, both of which were "local" according to little signs planted in the ice. Of the salmon, Pauly said, "This is what British Columbia still has, but it may not be what you think it is because most of what you see here is farmed. Half the salmon in British Columbia is farmed now. And that isn't local cod. There is no real cod near here—and there's no snapper around here either."

Overhearing this, the man behind the counter said, "The cod is local!"

"No it isn't," Pauly said. "There's no such thing as cod here—I don't know where it came from."

Pauly's directness, his unwillingness to sugarcoat, and his penchant for cutting through discussions with definitive statements sometimes lead to confrontation. Pauly says the problems are too urgent to take the time for niceties or political sensitivities. For example, when colleagues suggest that he meet with the fishermen who are responsible for harvesting too many fish, he invariably declines: "What are we going to talk about?" he asks. "When I drive too fast in my car, the policeman doesn't initiate some kind of a *dialogue*. He just gives me a ticket."

Just around the corner from the supposedly local cod, Pauly spotted an almost luminous orange fish. "Ah, Orange Roughy," he said, sounding like he were greeting an old friend. "They used to be called slime heads. It's a fish that grows even slower than Patagonian toothfish and it can live for 150 years. In another couple of decades, they'll be gone." Saving long-lived fish such as Orange Roughy or toothfish from extinction, Pauly believes, is no different from preserving a stand of old trees, like the majestic cedars and hemlocks in Stanley Park, a preserve near the center of Vancouver. "Would Stanley Park still be a wonderful place," he asked, "if we set a quota that says you may take down 4 percent of the trees every year? Or if we let people cut down trees but only on the second Sunday of every month? Or if we told people not to buy wood that comes from trees there? Of course not! Whatever way you do it, we'd still end up with a lot fewer trees. The reason we like Stanley Park is because it is forbidden to touch the damn things. We need to do the same thing in the oceans—create some zones that are for nature and others for us. But no, we think we can fish everywhere and make adjustments as we go along. It can't be done. As a result, we lose everything."

When Pauly began his career in the 1970s, fisheries scientists spent most of their time devising ways to catch more fish rather than protecting them. Like the fishermen of Riviera, they simply could not imagine that the world would ever run out of fish. Over the next twenty years, as Pauly studied fisheries around the world, he found, over and over, that mankind had had a profound effect on fish populations. The only solution, he decided, was to reverse his profession's priorities. He had become an environmentalist. His is not the idealistic kind of environmentalism that looks at the world from the point of view of animals. His concerns are motivated by waste, the opportunities that have been lost now that the populations of many of the most desirable eating fish have been reduced by more than 90 percent from what they were fifty years ago. If fish stocks were allowed to recover and were managed more effectively, he says, fish could become a reliable—

and ultimately larger—source of food and jobs. He is also motivated by social inequities, particularly those that affect people in developing nations who can no longer afford to eat fish. "Take Angola," Pauly said as he walked away from the fish market. "It was exporting massive quantities of fish even when it was in the midst of a major famine."

Spending time with Pauly can be exhausting. He is charming and frequently funny, and his thoughts and words are invariably interesting, but he speaks in staccato bursts and fire-hose torrents. And his conclusions are depressing, so consistently dire that he is sometimes accused of crying wolf, an accusation that infuriates him. "People have to deal with the data," he demands. "Is it true that there are one-tenth as many big fish in the oceans now as there were a few decades ago? The answer is yes—and that's the only thing that matters. If people just say they don't believe the basic conclusion—if they refuse to do the science—then screw them! They don't belong. This is not a theological debate!"

Sitting down to lunch at a restaurant near the market, Pauly found a glimmer of hope halfway down the menu: halibut in a broth of coconut ginger and sweet chiles. While halibut was over-fished back when Young's Market could not secure enough for its frozen fish fingers, its population has recovered since then to provide a rare example of what proper fishery management can do. "Halibut is a beautiful fish," Pauly said, "and the halibut fishery in the Pacific Northwest is one of the best-run fisheries there is."

Pauly recognizes that most people know very little about the fish they buy and eat. He says that is part of the problem. "Everyone sees that there are plenty of fish in the market, and they don't remember what *used* to be there," he said not long after his halibut arrived, "so they say things can't be all that bad. But they're wrong: we are in a *crisis*! It's not coming—it's already here." As he said this, something lodged in his throat and Pauly's normally powerful voice slipped out of gear. He raised his arms, one of them holding an empty water glass, and waved to get the waiter's attention, but he would not stop talking. "Actually the 90-percent population decrease *understates* the problem," he said in a raspy, barely audible whisper, "because fish populations are not just declining—they're disappearing. The Hudson River used to have shad. It used to have huge sturgeon. They're not there anymore. But when the government counts the number of fisheries that are in trouble, does it include the Hudson River shad and sturgeon fisheries? No! It only counts what there is to count and forgets about what's already gone."

After he gulped down some water, Pauly's voice returned and his pace accelerated, as if he were making up for lost time: "The North Sea is a total disaster area—it contains 2 or 3 percent of the big fish it used to have. New England is just as bad. We were catching 60 percent of the Atlantic cod population every year before the fishery completely collapsed. It's as if you withdrew 60 percent of your capital from the bank every year. You can live large for a while—right up until close to the end, your consumption is going to be fine."

Pauly's global perspective—and probably his zealousness—are the products of an extraordinary personal history. He was born in Paris in 1946 to a white Frenchwoman and a black American serviceman Pauly did not meet until many years later. At the age of two, he was taken to Switzerland by a couple who befriended his mother, a factory worker who was having difficulty providing for him on her own. The Swiss couple offered to take care of Pauly for a few months, an arrangement that became a nightmare when they refused to give him back. They told Pauly's mother she had no rights because her son was born out of wedlock. They told Pauly that his mother, like his father, had abandoned him. And although they promised to treat Pauly as if he were their own son, they eventually turned him into something closer to a servant, forcing him to clean the house and to work as a delivery boy for a local bakery that turned over his wages to the couple. He was allowed to go to school, but as the only black child in the area, he never had the sense that he belonged there, either.

When he was seventeen, Pauly left his "home," taking a train to a small town in Germany where a Lutheran minister had arranged for him to work in a hospital as a nurse's aid. One year later, his life was interrupted again, this time by the French Army, which tracked him down to demand that he return to France to perform his compulsory military service. Perhaps because of his German-accented French, he ultimately was not forced to serve, and the bureaucratic tussle ended with him being turned over to his mother. Until then, Pauly had not known how to reach her. She had married a Frenchman who had, also unbeknownst to Pauly, adopted him several years earlier. Pauly also learned that he had seven half-siblings, who had all been told that they had an older brother who lived with another family. Prior to his reunion, Pauly had no specific memory of his mother—he did not even have a photograph of her—but he never believed the Swiss couple's claims that she had abandoned him. Now his conviction was confirmed as she described the threatening letters they had sent and how she set an extra place at the table on each of his birthdays.

After spending almost a year in France, Pauly went back to Germany because he was eager to see his girlfriend and return to a night school he had been attending. Once he was back at school, he thought about going on to study literature or history, but it was 1964 and he was inspired by the idealism of the day. He eventually made two tentative but potentially connected decisions: he wanted to do something that would help people in developing countries, and he wanted to go to Africa. He had, after all, never experienced anything that might be considered black culture. He had never even met a black person until he left Switzerland; his night school was all-white, and even his mother and his seven half-siblings were white.

By the time he enrolled in the University of Kiel at age twenty-three, Pauly thought he had arrived at a more specific plan: he would study agronomy. But he took several part-time jobs in order to pay his expenses, and one of them happened to be in the university's Institute for Marine Science. It was one of the scientific world's ultimate low-level positions— examining seabed samples and counting the tiny animals that lived there, which were mostly worms, mussels, and shrimp. It was a painstaking process, accomplished with spoons and tweezers. After working through several pounds of the material, Pauly came up with a better idea—a mechanical device that mixed the samples with water and pumped them through a filter. It could separate creatures from a gallon of the muck in fifteen minutes, a volume that took several hours before his innovation. Pauly was introduced to the Institute's senior professor, an unusual honor for an undergraduate in Germany's rigidly hierarchical university system. The professor urged Pauly to write an article about his invention, which he did. Pauly subsequently decided that he had, at least professionally, found a home.

The geography of his future, however, was still unclear. By the time he finished his undergraduate and masters degrees at Kiel, he had spent half a year in Ghana studying lagoons to determine whether they might be used for aquaculture, but he found that they were too polluted for raising fish. During the same trip, he also discovered that he had spent too much time in Europe to ever really feel at home in Africa. By that time he had also visited the United States, where he met his father, who was working in California as a power plant technician, and an aunt who lived in Arkansas. He could not imagine living in their country either, particularly after his aunt warned him not to run on the downtown streets of Little Rock. "She told me, 'Black kids can't run here—the police will shoot you!'" Pauly recalls. So he ended up moving to Indonesia to take a job with a German government agency that was helping develop local fisheries.

In 1979, Pauly moved to the Philippines to take a job with the International Centre for Living Aquatic Resource Management, which was founded with money from the Rockefeller Foundation. The foundation hoped the center would help Southeast Asian countries to increase seafood harvests. In fact, during the previous twenty years, catch rates had already soared throughout the region, but Pauly did not believe they were sustainable because he was sure that many fish stocks had already been demolished. It was obvious from the poverty of the fishermen: in the Philippines many worked all day to bring home just two or three pounds of fish, less than half of what they had harvested a decade earlier.

Like in other parts of the world, the introduction of trawling was the main culprit. Fishermen started dragging nets behind sail-driven boats in the Middle Ages, but the technique did not really come into its own until the Industrial Revolution. English fishing vessels were fitted with steam engines in the 1860s and steel trawl lines in the 1880s. Even then, no one understood the potential impact of mechanization. When Thomas Huxley, the famous naturalist who once served as England's fishing commissioner, addressed a gathering of fishing industry executives and scientists in 1883, he acknowledged the possibility that some fisheries might become "exhausted," and he mentioned the risk that pollution might eliminate salmon from some of England's rivers. But he saw no risk for ocean fisheries. "Probably all of the great sea fisheries," he said, "are inexhaustible; that is to say, that nothing we do seriously affects the number of fish."

Technology proved Huxley wrong. Following World War I, diesel engines and onboard ice-making machinery became widely available, enabling fishermen to get to distant fisheries more quickly and also to extend their voyages. Another wave of enhancements followed World War II—radar, acoustic fish finders, onboard fish processing "factories," nets made of synthetic fibers, and mechanically refrigerated fish holds.

The new technologies found ready acceptance in Southeast Asia, where the demand for fish had skyrocketed along with exploding populations and rising standards of living. The Philippines led the way: Using boats and engines left behind by the American military after World War II, fishermen created fleets of trawlers that accessed heretofore untapped fisheries. Thailand was not far behind: the number of trawlers there went from about one hundred in 1960 to almost three thousand in 1966. The nation's total catch soared from 146,000 tons in 1960 to 1,343,000 tons in 1970. During the same period, catches roughly doubled in Indonesia, Malaysia, the Philippines, and Vietnam (although Vietnam's total catch plummeted in the 1970s after half of its trawlers were put to use evacuating refugees).

The enhanced fish-catching technologies obscured the truth of what was happening, but a closer look at the numbers made it clear that fishermen had commenced a one-sided arms race that was nowhere near sustainable. While Thai trawlers caught about five hundred pounds of fish per hour in 1963, their hourly yield was only half as much four years later. This meant that fish populations had been halved and that they were being taken from the sea much more rapidly than they replaced themselves, but it did not lead to a reduction in fishing. On the contrary, more trawlers were launched every year. By the late 1970s, Thailand had more than six thousand of them. And they were working much harder than before: vessels that initially fished only during the day were operating around the clock.

Habitats were being destroyed along with their populations. Many fishermen in the Philippines used explosives, another legacy of World War II. An inexpensive device could kill every fish within one hundred feet, leaving fishermen with the simple task of scooping up corpses with hand-held nets. But the explosions also destroyed coral reefs and juvenile fish. Trawlers were at least as wasteful and probably even more destructive. In some places, close to half of what they captured were "trash fish" that were either discarded or fed to animals. And while some claimed that trawlers would benefit the ocean by "plowing" the seabed, nothing could be further from the truth. The coral reefs that are felled by trawler cables are crucial to many species both because they are surrounded by nutrient-rich water and because they provide protection from predators.

"Can you imagine," Pauly asks, "someone telling you that he's come up with this great way to catch fish that involves dragging a big net across the seabed that will not only catch every fish but also removes entire habitats? It would be as if someone told you they were going to hunt for deer by cutting down the forest in which they live."

CHAPTER 18

South Atlantic Ocean
August 27, 2003

Even before he pushed open the narrow door to *Viarsa*'s bridge, Stephen Duffy had decided that he would not shake hands with Ricardo Cabrera. He wanted to take every possible opportunity, particularly during their first direct encounter, to demonstrate the new order of things.

"I am Customs Officer Stephen Duffy. I have spoken to you many times before. Do you remember that?"

"I do."

Duffy then handed his identification card and a list of the boarding party members to the captain, who put his glasses on and looked closely at the names. "These personnel are acting under my direct authority," Duffy said. "You and your crew are to follow their directions. I intend that you will remain in charge of your ship and crew. But you will take instructions from me on where we go. Do you understand this?"

"So I will be in charge but I cannot go where I want?" Cabrera asked.

"Yes."

"I am in charge but not in charge?"

"You are in command, but I am in control. Are you willing to accept this?"

"Yes—I have no choice."

"Good. Now, I intend to bring supplies over to your ship for my personnel, so there will be several transfers using my boats. I don't want your crew to do anything. They should stay where they are and not come any farther forward. We will begin making our way toward Cape Town, and from there we will probably take the ship to Fremantle in Australia. Do you understand this?"

"Yes."

"Now please bring your ship to a course of 040 and a speed of four knots."

"My slowest speed is six knots."

"Okay. Come to your minimum speed and a course of 040."

After Cabrera passed along the instructions to Perez, who was steering the ship, Duffy said: "Now, you may call your owners, and I think it might be wise to do so. You can tell them everything that I have said to you."

During most of the five-minute telephone conversation that followed, the captain did most of the talking. He maintained an even tone until near the end of the conversation when he became agitated. Afterward, Cabrera told Duffy that the owner was going to contact DINARA, Uruguay's National Aquatic Resources Department. Run by an autocratic man with the unlikely name of Captain Yamando Flangini, the department was responsible for granting fishing permits and licenses and for installing government observers on fishing vessels and was also responsible for the system that is supposed to automatically report their positions.

Nodding, Duffy said, "I need to know if you have any weapons onboard."

"We have no guns. We have fishing knives throughout the ship, but no guns."

Scott Webb was listening to Duffy's conversation and watching Perez, who was smoking a Marlboro with one hand and gripping the small wooden steering wheel with the other, when he noticed a curled piece of paper that was rolling out of a telex machine. Although the words were in Spanish, Webb deduced that the Uruguayan Navy had sent the message because *Viarsa* had activated its Emergency Positioning Indicating Beacon, a distress signal that is supposed to be used only for dire emergencies. Turning to Cabrera, Webb said, "You need to reply to this and tell them you are not in distress, that you have been boarded by Australian officials and that your safety is not in danger."

"No problem," Cabrera said without saying anything about who might have set off a distress signal. Taking the wheel, the captain asked Perez to type a message on a computer near the center of the bridge.

O'Dea was eager to determine how *Viarsa*'s position had been so inaccurately reported that Uruguayan officials could initially have claimed it was in the Atlantic. Because Uruguay is a signatory of the Convention on the Conservation of Antarctic Marine Living Resources, each commercial fishing vessel registered there is supposed to be equipped with a Vessel Monitoring System that automatically transmits its position.

"Do you," O'Dea asked Cabrera, "have a Vessel Monitoring System?"

"No."

"How does your government know where you are?" O'Dea asked Cabrera.

Pointing to the computer, the one Perez was using to send a message about the false distress signal, the captain said, "We just type it in and send it to Uruguay three times a day."

"That's not the way it's supposed to work."

Cabrera shrugged. Shortly after that, O'Dea's questioning was interrupted by *Viarsa*'s satellite phone. Picking it up, Cabrera spoke in Spanish for a couple of minutes, but he mostly listened. At one point, he said, "Si, si, si" and looked at Duffy, who was standing nearby. Cupping the mouthpiece with his hand, Cabrera explained that the caller was Captain Flangini, the DINARA director, and that he wanted to speak to Duffy. "He wants to know what's going on with our ship," Cabrera added.

"You can pass along to him what I said to you—that the ship will be taken back to Australia," Duffy said. Cabrera spoke in Spanish for several more minutes before covering the mouthpiece again and saying, "The director has an interpreter and he would like you to speak with her." Taking the phone, Duffy listened as a woman who identified herself as Carmen said, "There are difficulties between the Uruguayan and Australian governments because of the time of day. We are having difficulty trying to reach people in your government."

"I understand that," Duffy said.

"Because of this difficulty, the director wants you to stop what you are doing. You can stay on the boat, but it must come to Montevideo. The director wants to make it plain that what you're doing is wrong." As she said this, Duffy heard a man in the background speaking rapidly in Spanish. Duffy assumed it was Flangini and that he was pushing the interpreter to convey his message more forcefully. "Si, si, si," the interpreter said, as if to suggest that she needed more time to translate his words, but the man did not stop talking.

"Please tell the director that I cannot heed his request," Duffy said. "I am taking the vessel to South Africa and then to Australia so that it can be investigated for illegal fishing."

When those words were translated, there was another explosion of Spanish. "My director says you must not do this!" Carmen said. "You are committing an act of piracy. The vessel is under arrest by the Uruguayan government and it must return here."

"Listen," Duffy said, "under the Law of the Sea, the vessel is under my control and it will be investigated for illegal fishing. I am not going to speak to the director any more. If he has any complaints, he should pursue diplomatic channels."

Ending the call, Duffy turned to Cabrera and asked, "Where are your other records and the fishing log?"

Cabrera repeated what he had told O'Dea: "I don't have a fishing log."

"Well, can you tell me how much fish is onboard?"

"No."

"How can you be a fishing vessel at sea and not know how much fish you have? It's just not possible."

At that point, Cabrera walked into the chart room, opened a drawer, and pulled out a manila folder that contained several green forms, each of which reported the location and amount of the ship's catches. "This is what we have," he said. According to the forms, *Viarsa* had harvested 6.8 tons of toothfish on August 2 and 8.3 tons on August 3 and nothing since. The locations where the fishing was reported to have taken place were all outside the Australian Fishing Zone—and recorded in pencil.

"Where do these positions and weights come from?" Duffy asked.

"I record the positions and the observer gives me the weights."

"Where is the observer?" Duffy asked. "We need to get him up here."

Eduardo Morello Schultz, a clean-shaven young man, was lying in his bunk in a space marked "Cabin Number Two," a cramped compartment near the bow that he shared with three of the ship's officers. Because of

CCAMLR's regulations, *Viarsa* was required to give the observer, an employee of the Uruguayan government, complete access to the ship, including its navigational instruments, and he was required to note the details about every longline—the gear that was used, where and when it was set, the species and weight of what was caught.

When Schultz arrived on the bridge, O'Dea and Webb were surprised by his youth. *He looks like a scared little mouse*, Webb said to himself. The observer spoke enough English that Webb and O'Dea tried to speak directly to him, but they occasionally had to ask Cabrera to translate. The observer said the ship was carrying about 2,600 boxes of toothfish that weighed about eighty-five tons.

"How did you get the data for your reports?" O'Dea asked.

"The captain tells me what the catches were, and he gives me a piece of paper that has our positions." This, of course, contradicted Cabrera's claim that the observer told him about the size of the catches. And the observer's comments appeared to upset Cabrera and Perez, who were both close enough to hear everything he was saying. The two began speaking to one another rapidly in Spanish. Perez, who was leaning against the wall behind the steering wheel, was playing with a piece of twine that he at one point tied into what Webb thought was intended to look like a hangman's noose. After looking in that direction, Schultz lowered his head and cradled his forehead in his hands.

"They're obviously threatening him," Webb said to O'Dea. "Let's take him outside to talk."

After Webb led the observer to the small deck just outside the bridge, he said, "Those guys are threatening you, aren't they?"

"The captain is crazy," Schultz said. "He took us into the ice; he put our lives in danger. Now he's putting a lot of pressure on me."

"What do you mean—did he threaten you?"

The observer did not answer the question directly, but he said Cabrera was particularly sensitive about the positions—the latitudes and longitudes—that had been reported to Uruguay.

"Would you like us to remove you from the vessel?"

"No, no, no. They would know I was helping you."

"Where are your records?"

"They're in my cabin," Schultz replied. "I know you're a government official and I can help you, but I can't be seen as helping. If we go to my cabin, I can show you where things are, but you have to make it seem like I'm not helping you."

Excited by the prospect of a cooperative witness who would have first-hand knowledge of illegal fishing, Webb said, "We can do that. Let's get your records."

"You must talk to Captain Flangini first. He's told me that you have no right to touch my papers, so I would like you to call him and speak directly to him. If he says I should give them to you, I will give you everything."

Although Webb agreed to make the call, he did so only as a gesture of goodwill. Regardless of what Flangini said, the fisheries officer intended to find and seize the records. Schultz used *Viarsa*'s satellite phone to call DINARA, and Captain Flangini came to the phone almost immediately. After speaking to him for a few minutes, Schultz motioned for Webb to take the phone. Carmen, Flangini's translator, was on the other end.

"We need to see your observer's records," Webb said. "We have told him that we will be seizing those records."

After speaking with her boss in Spanish, Carmen said, "The observer is not a member of the crew. He is a government official. Any information held by him is property of the Uruguayan government—and any action to take it away from him is illegal. He must be allowed to return to Uruguay with his records. He must not be taken to Australia."

"We will be securing the records and they will be taken back to Australia."

After another pause, Carmen said: "Your search is illegal!"

Cutting her off, Webb said, "I'm sorry, but the vessel was found in our zone. We will be searching for evidence and that includes the observer's records." As soon as the call was over, Webb told Schultz, "We're going to seize the records whether you give them to us voluntarily or we have to search to find them. Either way, we're going to get them." A few minutes later, Webb, O'Dea, and Schultz climbed down a steep set of stairs behind the bridge to reach the crew's quarters. They then walked down a narrow corridor that passed through the center of the ship to get to Schultz's cabin. After the three men entered the compartment and shut the door, Schultz pointed to a drawer and said, "You should look in there, but when you do your search, I don't want to be in the room."

"How did you get the ship's position?" O'Dea asked.

"The captain never lets me on the bridge. He gives me a little piece of paper with the lats and longs. I know they're wrong positions, but he tells me, 'That's what you write down.' Everything else is correct—the amount of the catch, the gear they used."

O'Dea then asked the crucial question: "What was the vessel doing the day before we found you?"

"I don't know."

"How could you not know?"

"I was sick. I didn't even leave this cabin for four or five days before then."

"Okay, but even here you would have heard the engines change speed, so you would know if you were fishing or steaming, wouldn't you?"

"No. I was very sick. I didn't leave my cabin at all."

Certain that this was a lie, O'Dea concluded that Schultz was hopelessly untrustworthy and had been in league with the pirates from the beginning or had agreed to play along at some later stage. Webb, whose assessment was less categorical, asked Schultz to leave the cabin. The fisheries officers then searched through drawers and cabinets, the areas beneath the bunks, even the bedding. They seized several items that appeared to belong to Schultz—a Toshiba laptop computer, a Kodak digital camera, and several files.

When O'Dea lifted the mattress of the bunk directly above Schultz's, he found something else—a diary bound in black and tan imitation leather. A name was written on the front page: Jose Gonzalez Perez. O'Dea and Webb knew that was the name of one of the ship's officers, a Spaniard, no relation to Antonio Perez. O'Dea immediately turned to the days just before the start of the pursuit. The text was in Spanish, but O'Dea recognized some of the words, including "pesca." He also noticed that some of the entries had been crossed out.

After they left the cabin, Schultz, who had been standing in the corridor, motioned toward a cabinet and whispered, "You might also want to look inside there. I've hidden some papers there." Anything Schultz took the trouble to hide from his cabinmates, Webb thought, sounded promising. Tucked under a vacuum cleaner, he found another set of catch documents. Each page had been overwritten with the words *posiciones falsas*, which Webb assumed to be Spanish for "false positions." Webb thought the notations, which he assumed to be Schultz's, meant he had refused to fully play along and might even be willing to testify against the crew. O'Dea remained skeptical. The documents turned out to be summary catch reports, each page containing data about catches and positions for a four-day period. When O'Dea examined the pages, he immediately recognized that the positions that had been overwritten were in the Atlantic Ocean, the same positions where the Uruguayan government had initially placed the ship.

Later, O'Dea pointed to the handwritten notes and asked Schultz, "Why did you write 'false positions' on these pages?"

"The captain told me they were false a few days ago."

"Did he explain why he had given you false positions?"

"He said he gave me false positions because he didn't want anyone to know where his best fishing spots were."

O'Dea could not believe that Schultz had so little sense of where the ship was that he could ever have thought it was in the Atlantic. In addition, while Schultz claimed he was not permitted to go on the bridge, he had also said he was allowed to use the satellite telephone, which was located in the chartroom near one of the GPS units. Since it had a digital readout that would have indicated *Viarsa*'s position, he must have known the vessel was nowhere near the Atlantic.

Back on the bridge, Webb said, "I still think if we shield him from the others and we mother him a bit, he might give us the goods and put it in a statement."

"I doubt it," O'Dea replied. "I wouldn't trust this guy as far as I can kick him."

O'Dea had concluded that the ship's cloth-bound log was equally unreliable. The first entry for the current voyage stated that *Viarsa* left Mauritius on the afternoon of June 30. That much, O'Dea believed, was probably true because he had also found a legitimate-looking document issued by the Mauritius government on that day. Mauritius is frequently used by toothfish vessels: it is relatively close to several fisheries, it has port facilities where frozen fish can be loaded into containers, and it is regularly visited by freighters. But O'Dea was skeptical about the subsequent entries in the log, which reported that *Viarsa* had spent most of its voyage on the high seas.

Unlike most ship logs, which have multiple entries for each day, often made by different people, all of the entries in this log appeared to have been written in the same hand and with the same pen. Only one position was recorded for each day, and there were seemingly no mistakes— nothing had been crossed out. O'Dea's search of the bridge turned up another red flag: while the days prior to August 4 were documented with telexes and weather reports that had been gathered into a binder, there were almost no documents of any kind for the period after that date.

Eager to gather other documents, O'Dea asked the captain for identification papers for the crew. Walking into the chartroom, Cabrera opened the locked briefcase and removed an envelope that was stuffed with passports and a crew list that noted each man's nationality, qualifications, and previous experience. The roster included sixteen Chileans, thirteen Spaniards, four Uruguayans, three Portuguese, three Peruvians, and one Romanian. One of the Chileans, a thirty-four-year-old named Roberto Enrique Reyes Guerrero, had previously served on the *South Tomi*; O'Dea wondered if he had been onboard when that ship had been arrested.

O'Dea and Webb spent the rest of the night searching other sections of the ship. They began in the "setting area," a compartment at the stern where the baitfish are hooked onto the branch lines, the branch lines are attached to the mainline, and the longline is attached to the risers and beacons, before the whole thing is lowered off the back of the ship. The quantities of every component were mind-boggling. The pale-green branch lines had been carefully coiled and placed in a red plastic tray in such a way that the twenty-five hooks, each three inches long, hung over one side of each of the containers. There were *thousands* of trays, stacked from floor to ceiling. An untold number of mainlines were stored in a seven-foot-tall wooden bin. There were several buoys on top of the lines. Most of them were orange, but several were painted dark blue—to make them more difficult for a patrol boat to see, O'Dea assumed.

The need for massive amounts of painstaking labor was obvious—every hook had to be baited by hand—and the working conditions were horrible. Like the factory, the setting area is unheated. Indeed, when longlines are ready to be deployed, two steel doors, which are four feet tall and long enough to reach across most of the ship's width, are opened, leaving workers almost completely exposed to the elements. The compartment's focal point is a large table, where hooks are driven through the mouths of the baitfish, most of which are about six inches long. When the ship is fishing, boxes of baitfish, about a ton every day, are brought from the front of the ship on a long conveyor belt that passes through an alley-like space on the port side of the ship.

Once all of the hooks on a branch line are baited, it is attached to a three- to four-pound chunk of granite to ensure that the line will dangle beneath the mainline. As soon as a section of a mainline is fitted with a branch line, the crew passes it out the window and allows it to fall into the water. Once the entire mainline is set, the ship maneuvers to either set another longline or retrieve one. For the crew, who rotate between the setting area and the factory, the work is essentially without end.

From the setting area, O'Dea and Webb walked alongside the conveyor belt and entered the factory. It had been cleaned up to some extent, but fish bones were still strewn about the floor and the stink of fish was brutal. Just aft of the factory, they found a storeroom filled with white cardboard boxes labeled: "Longline fish frozen at sea." The boxes said nothing about toothfish or Chilean Sea Bass or where the fish had been caught. Next to the storeroom O'Dea opened the heavy wood doors of the "snap freezer," a locker that contained several shelves, each one surrounded by condenser pipes to ensure that the boxes of dismembered fish were frozen as quickly as possible.

The fish hold was located down a steep ladder. With the help of flashlights, O'Dea and Webb descended to see a network of condenser pipes that snaked through the ceiling and walls of the cavernous space. Floor-to-ceiling stacks of the white cardboard boxes filled about a third of the room. Opening one of them, O'Dea saw that it contained four toothfish trunks.

Walking toward the bow, Webb reached a wall that ran from one side of the ship to the other and contained two large doors. Opening one of them, he saw that it led to another refrigerated compartment, this one filled with stacks of brown cardboard boxes labeled "sardino." It was obviously baitfish, although there was far more of it than *Viarsa* would need to catch a full load of toothfish. He guessed that the ship was carrying an additional amount that would have been transferred to a sister ship. Or perhaps *Viarsa*'s crew planned to off-load their toothfish onto another ship while at sea to disguise the cargo's origins and continue fishing without having to take time out to return to port.

CHAPTER 19

Vancouver

Daniel Pauly understands that mankind's relentless and sometimes irrational destruction of marine populations is not new. Whaling provides a poignant example. The pursuit of the earth's largest creatures began more than one thousand years ago because they provided an abundant source of fats and oils that could be used for lighting, food, soap, and eventually, various manufacturing processes.

"Right" whales—so-called because they are slow and easy to catch, have lots of blubber, and do not sink after they are killed—were particularly attractive targets. "Settlers looked at the broad backs of the right whales and saw not their grace and beauty but floating oil factories— more enticingly, floating oil factories they didn't have to maintain," Richard Ellis writes in *The Empty Ocean*. Later, as right whales became harder to find, whalers became less discriminating, chasing almost every whale they spotted. The only species that survived in significant numbers were either too fast to be captured or impossible to retrieve because their corpses sank. But in 1868, a new technology put every whale in danger: cannon-launched harpoons. Not only could they reach much farther than their hand-thrown predecessors, but they could carry tubes that pumped air into the whales to keep even the heaviest of them afloat.

One species after another, whales were hunted down until their populations were so small as to be no longer worth the trouble. It was obvious that the systematic killing would eventually eliminate whale populations as well as the human industries that depended on them—but the whalers, like the fishermen in Thailand, responded to the scarcity they created by redoubling their efforts. "It appeared that everyone knew the whales were being hunted out of existence, but nobody wanted to acknowledge it," Ellis writes. "Besides, it was clear that if one nation stopped whaling or even reduced its effort, the others would move in."

Since World War II, many of the officials who manage fisheries have been guided by the idea that the maximum sustainable catch rate for most species is achieved when the population is reduced by about half. While this is obviously not a formulation that would win the support of environmentalists, the basic principle is widely accepted by fisheries scientists, including Pauly. It works because when a population is cut, its newly hatched fish grow faster than they otherwise would have and more of them survive to maturity as the community strives to refill its niche in the ecosystem. However, once the population falls below half, there are just not enough fish to keep the ball rolling. To use Pauly's bank-account analogy, fishermen have consumed so much capital that the remaining balance cannot generate enough interest to compensate for the withdrawals.

The biggest problem with this is that it tends to set off an unstoppable chain reaction. Catch rates of course grow dramatically as the first half of the population is removed. And since fishermen's incomes and expectations escalate at least as quickly, they rush to acquire more boats and better gear. This is precisely what happened in both the Pacific and Atlantic

Oceans during the 1950s and 1960s, a process that was turbocharged by the introduction of enhanced technologies and also by governments that subsidized the construction of new vessels. "It was the age of innocence," Pauly says. "And by the time half the fish were gone, the industry had invested so much money in its fleets that it zoomed right past the point where it should have stopped. A soft landing was impossible."

In the Atlantic, the first sign of trouble came in 1971, when the enormous Peruvian anchovy fishery collapsed. However, since this was initially thought to be the result of El Niño (which was in fact partially to blame), the warning went unheeded. A surer sign came a few years later: in 1976, the total North Atlantic catch declined from the previous year.

Even then, the idea that oceans were running out of fish still seemed preposterous. Thanks to its vastness and, for some, decades of Jacques Cousteau documentaries, the sea was still thought to be a mysterious frontier with virtually unlimited resources. Even Pauly's colleagues were slow to recognize mankind's impact on ocean fisheries. This became obvious to him when he read a 1986 study that concluded that only 2.2 percent of total "marine production" was accounted for by the seafood harvested by fishermen. The strange-sounding statistic was based on the consumption of phytoplankton, the microscopic plants that are the foundation of marine food chains. People do not eat phytoplankton, but we eat fish that do. Or we eat the fish that eat the fish that eat plankton. Either way, by estimating the percentage of plankton that is consumed by seafood taken by fishermen, it is possible to estimate the portion of the oceanic resources, or "production," that is consumed by humans. Pauly was sure that 2.2 percent was wildly off the mark, in part because the study's authors did not distinguish between the relatively shallow waters above continental shelves—where about 90 percent of the world's fish are caught—and the rest of the ocean, which has always been relatively barren.

When Pauly and a colleague, Villy Christensen, conducted their own study, they found that the seafood extracted by fishermen actually consumes 8 percent of the ocean's phytoplankton. More importantly, they found that fish taken from the waters above continental shelves swallow up 25 to 35 percent of the phytoplankton there, close to what they believed to be the maximum possible amount given that a large portion of plankton settles to the bottom without ever being eaten by fish. Pauly's study, which was published in *Nature*, one of the scientific world's two preeminent journals (the other is *Science*), went a long way, at least in the scientific community, toward exploding Thomas Huxley's idea that the ocean was a giant reserve from which humans could never take too much.

The evidence has steadily mounted as catch levels in the North Atlantic have continued to decline, particularly in the early 1990s when the cod fisheries that supported Antonio Perez and his ancestors collapsed and were legally closed. Strangely, the total reported global catch continued to rise into the 1990s. Pauly was one of many scientists who did not believe the numbers. They were compiled by the United Nations' Food and Agriculture Organization, which is limited in its ability to challenge what is reported by member nations. Pauly suspected that one of the world's largest fishing nations—China—was distorting the numbers by exaggerating its catch, in all likelihood because the Chinese bureaucrats who were responsible for the catch statistics also managed the fishing industry and were rewarded on the basis of its productivity.

When Pauly and another colleague, Reg Watson, used various statistical models to analyze China's fisheries, they found that the country's reported catches were about twice as large as what was being taken from similar bodies of water elsewhere. And when they adjusted the global numbers to reflect what they believed to be China's actual yields, they concluded that the global catch peaked in 1988 and had been diminishing ever since. This was in spite of the introduction of the latest generation of technological advancements: GPS, which enabled fishermen to return to their favorite fishing positions with unerring precision; gear that made it easier to capture fish from much deeper waters; and highly detailed charts of seabeds, which helped fishermen identify the habitats of deep-water fish such as toothfish.

In 1994, Pauly, his wife, and their two children moved to Vancouver, where he became the director of the University of British Columbia's Fisheries Centre. By then, his outrage about what had happened to marine life had turned him into an insistent critic of his own profession. Because most fisheries scientists are employed either by the fishing industry or by narrowly focused government institutions, Pauly had become convinced that they were either unwilling or unable to see the larger picture. "Most of my colleagues study a single species that lives in a particular river or bay," he says. "So everyone has this idea that what they see in their specific fishery is unique. No one wants to generalize. That was fine when fish were plentiful—there was no need for anyone to put everything together then—but now it's different."

Not surprisingly, Pauly's criticism has made him unpopular with many of those colleagues. "Daniel is an incredibly creative and clever guy," says Ray Hilborn, a fisheries scientist at the University of Washington, "but very few people actively involved in fisheries management would see him as a constructive force" because he is so consistently negative. "He fails to recognize that many fisheries are working, that progress is being made, and that we do know how to manage fisheries pretty well if we can apply the right governance and incentives."

Many others admit that Pauly's criticism is fully warranted. One of them, Alan Longhurst, said so with depressing frankness in an e-mail to Pauly: "What surprises me is that you still take fish science seriously. It's a failed science and the fish industry is a failed industry. It needs someone as knowledgeable as you to stand up and say so."

Pauly has not given up hope, but the problems have become so urgent that he is now devoting much of his time to pushing for policy changes as the principal investigator of the Sea Around Us Project, a far-reaching research effort funded by the Pew Charitable Trusts. Named after Rachel Carson's best-selling book about the oceans, it came about after Pew invited Pauly and several other marine scientists to describe what they would do to produce a thorough assessment of the health of the oceans. Josh Reichert, the head of the foundation's environmental programs, opened the meeting, which took place at the foundation's headquarters in downtown Philadelphia, by explaining its goals: "No one in the environmental community is attempting to influence the government's marine policies. People speak up about pollution and urban sprawl because they see it—but since no one really sees what's happening in the oceans, no one speaks up. We want to change that."

Pauly made an immediate impression on Reichert, first because he is black, a rarity among marine scientists. But it was Pauly's approach that really set him apart from the other scientists, most of whom advocated elaborate studies that would involve years of data collection. "We don't need more data!" Pauly asserted. "Fishermen are sampling the ocean all the time. In the North Atlantic, we have been collecting information for more than one hundred years. What we need to do is analyze the data we already have."

Just a couple of months before he met Reichert, Pauly published a paper in *Science* that used Food and Agriculture Organization statistics to demonstrate that fishermen were catching much smaller kinds of fish than they had years earlier, including once unthinkable creatures such as the smelts he pointed to in the fish market. The diminishing populations of the biggest and traditionally most desirable fish—tuna, cod, and swordfish—had obviously caused fishermen to resort to other things, a fundamental change that Pauly said would irreversibly alter marine ecosystems. He called it "fishing down the food web" and predicted, with a degree of facetiousness, that it would lead to the consumption of "jellyfish sandwiches" and "plankton soup."

Pew made an initial $2 million grant to establish the Sea Around Us Project, providing Pauly with a funding source that was entirely independent of government agencies and the fishing industry. The Fisheries Centre has become a hotbed of cutting-edge research. "Daniel is a remarkable man with a remarkable history who has become hugely influential for all the right reasons," says Stuart Pimm, a prominent conservation ecologist. But Pauly is far from satisfied: "We turn out a lot of research and we are recognized by our colleagues, so by the standards scientists usually apply to themselves, we are doing incredibly well. But is that the appropriate standard to use? Obviously not, because in the real world nothing is happening. The only people who push for nature are considered marginal."

Pauly also produces a steady flow of policy recommendations, the most important of them being his suggestion that at least 20 percent of the oceans be designated as "marine protection areas" where fishing is permanently banned. He says the waters surrounding Antarctica are particularly vulnerable and says a fish that has been targeted there recently by fishermen—Antarctic toothfish—needs to be protected before its population is ravaged like Patagonian toothfish or Orange Roughy.

Pauly also wants to change the laws that have protected the owners of pirate fishing vessels from being prosecuted personally. "They're like drug dealers," he says. "We know who they are, we know what boats they own, and we know what they do with them—but we have not been able to get them if they live in a country like Spain." It does not have to be that way, he says, citing other forms of criminality. "Take child pornography— that's something nations have decided will not be tolerated. We go after the culprits of that crime wherever they live. We don't care enough about fish to do that—and that's what we really need to change."

CHAPTER 20

Antonio Perez remained a mystery to Duffy and O'Dea. Whenever they asked him a question, he either ignored them or said he did not understand what they were saying. They suspected that he understood more English than he let on, but the only thing they were sure of was that he was not who he said he was. Everything about him suggested that he was not, as he had repeatedly claimed, *Viarsa*'s first mate. They knew very little about his background or the extent of his experience with toothfish, but a crew list that Keith Johnson had sent a few days before the boarding listed Perez as the fishing master, and the leather briefcase in the chartroom contained a certificate indicating that Perez was a qualified fishing master. From other documents in the briefcase, it appeared that Ricardo Cabrera had spent his entire career working at sea, but most of it was on cargo ships and tankers. He had worked on fishing vessels only for three years.

The Australians knew that fishing master is the top position on most large-scale fishing ships. He is, after all, responsible for the most important decisions—where the vessel goes, where and when lines are set, and what gear is used. The captain is relegated to a supporting role. Consistent with this, fishing masters make much more money than captains and stay in their ship's most desirable cabin. Duffy and Webb assumed that Perez was downplaying his importance because he thought the potential penalties would be greater if it was understood that he was the decision maker.

But proving Perez's role was difficult. For example, while O'Dea and Duffy were sure that a cabin just behind the bridge belonged to Perez, he claimed that he shared a narrow, much less desirable cabin with *Viarsa*'s two other officers and the Uruguayan government observer. The cabin behind the bridge was clearly the superior accommodation, and the raised letters on a brass plaque over the top of the door said, "Patron de Pesca." It was the ship's only private cabin, and it had a generous amount of storage space—drawers beneath the bunk and nine built-in cabinets along the wall at the bunk's base. One of the drawers was filled with magazines, all of them either pornographic or related to motorcycles, publications that Perez had been seen reading more than anyone else.

The room was decorated in much the same way as the rest of the crew accommodations. A calendar hung from the back of the door; days had been slashed with a black marker as they passed. A poster of a naked woman was taped to the ceiling above the bed. A much smaller image of the Virgin Mary was hanging on the wall near the door, not far from a poster showing members of Real Madrid, a Spanish soccer team. The soccer poster was one of the reasons O'Dea was sure that Perez was the real occupant of the cabin. A framed photograph of one of the team's stars, Zenedine Zidane, which had been personally inscribed to Perez, hung on the back wall on the bridge. Duffy thought it was unlikely that a personal memento would be in the bridge unless it belonged to the man in charge. He also found a pair of jeans in one of the cabinets that contained Perez's driver's license and credit cards. And Webb found a folder of documents that belonged to Cabrera in the four-man cabin downstairs.

Shortly after he found the driver's license, Duffy confronted Perez, saying, "I understand that you are the fishing master."

"No, first mate. Ricardo is the fishing master and the captain."

"We think you're the fishing master and that this is your cabin," Duffy said, motioning to the nearby doorway.

"No, no, no."

"Why was your wallet there?"

"I don't understand your English."

"We have information to indicate that you are the fishing master—but if you want to pretend that you're the first mate, that's fine."

Duffy had another reason to be interested in room assignments. Since *Viarsa*'s crew filled every one of the ship's bunks, it was not clear where the Australians and South Africans would sleep. Duffy had initially thought he would ask the occupants of a six-man cabin to give up their bunks, but, reluctant to impose his will in a way that would be disruptive and potentially antagonizing, he had decided against it.

The South Africans had, at least temporarily, taken up residence in the factory and the conveyor belt corridor. The two spaces were connected, and they could be secured by two people, an important attribute given that the occupiers were outnumbered five to one by *Viarsa*'s crew, but it was an otherwise unattractive solution. The odor in the factory was horrible, there was no heat, and the floor was always wet. The area where the fish were gutted was covered by metal grates, and water was supposed to course underneath to remove offal, but it regularly lapped over the edges and onto the rest of the floor. The only section of the floor that was really dry was near the bow. Some of the South Africans had spread coils of rope there that were intended to create something like a mattress. They laid cardboard boxes over the coils, then covered that with sleeping bags and blankets. The result looked comfortable, almost cozy, but in reality was lumpy and shifting.One of the South Africans, Gert Du Toit, had a different idea: he cleaned out one of the tanks where toothfish were placed during the disassembly process and lined it with several cardboard boxes and a sleeping bag.

Before anyone went to sleep, Webb found a plastic bag with eighty rounds of 223-caliber bullets, the kind of high-velocity ammunition used in semi-automatic rifles, in the fishing master's cabin. Webb immediately took them to Duffy and summoned Cabrera.

"Can you explain what these are for?" Duffy asked.

"I don't know," the captain said without looking directly at Duffy. "I've never seen them before."

"If someone pulls out a rifle, they are going to get hurt."

"I have no rifle on board."

"Has there *ever* been a rifle on this ship?"

"No, I've never had a weapon on the ship."

"I'm not sure if I believe you. I need to know: is there a rifle on this ship?"

"No, there is no rifle on this ship *now*."

Duffy believed that. He suspected the ship had carried a rifle to shoot the seals that sometimes feed on toothfish that are hooked to mainlines as they are pulled to the surface. Since vessels registered in CCAMLR-member countries are prohibited from having firearms, he guessed the gun was thrown overboard sometime after the start of the chase as part of the effort to rid the ship of incriminating evidence.

Nevertheless, Duffy repeated his question: "Are there any weapons onboard the ship?"

"No. But I can't speak for the crew. Sometimes someone will buy a pistol in Mauritius."

Duffy then told Harry Watts about the ammunition and the possibility that some members of *Viarsa*'s crew had guns. "You're going to have to be very careful with the crew," Duffy said. "And you need to have your men conduct a detailed search—look in the ventilation ducts, everywhere. If there are any guns onboard, we need to find them." The guards spent several hours searching, but they knew they could never cover every possible hiding spot. They also knew the ship was carrying dozens, probably hundreds, of knives. They were everywhere. Duffy found six on the bridge, which he collected and took to the factory, although he later agreed to return one so it could be used to cut loaves of bread.

Duffy ended up sleeping only briefly, just before dawn, on the decrepit vinyl-covered chair on the bridge. Besides guns, he was worried that one of *Viarsa*'s crewmen might attempt to scuttle the ship by opening a sea valve or prevent it from making it back to Australia by damaging the engine. His first priority was to evaluate the ship's mechanics. He had walked through the engine room soon after the boarding, but he wanted to make a more thorough inspection with the help of an expert, so shortly after daybreak he asked Codrington to send *Southern Supporter*'s first engineer, Julian Grant, to *Viarsa*. A couple of hours later, Grant arrived on one of the 640s, and Duffy led him through *Viarsa*'s mess and down a steep metal ladder to the engine room.

Grant was amazed by its condition. There were no leaks in the exhaust gaskets, and even the removable steel plates that formed the floor of *Viarsa*'s engine room were free of oil and grime. Engine rooms are notoriously difficult to keep clean, particularly on older ships. Since it takes constant effort just to keep the mechanical systems running, the extra work required to make things look good is indicative of unusual diligence and an engineer who takes real pride in his work. Grant checked everything—the engine itself, the gearbox, the valves and drive shaft—without finding a problem. Looking into a small but well-equipped machine shop, he noticed that all of the tools were clean and carefully stored. But what most impressed him was the bilge: most bilges are filled with oil, rags, and indeterminate filth. *Viarsa*'s had a couple of inches of water, which is normal, but only a tiny slick of oil.

Speaking in broken English, Javier Russi, *Viarsa*'s Uruguayan engineer, told Grant that the ship did not have any major mechanical problems. He said one of the compressors that chilled the main fish hold was broken, but that he had already begun the repair. "Everything is in very good condition," Grant told Duffy. "They'll need some spare parts, some fuel filters and oil separations, but this thing could run virtually forever."

Duffy asked about the fuel. Leading his visitors back up the stairs and into the tiny, glass-walled control room, Russi pointed to a schematic drawing of the ship that indicated the location of sixteen fuel tanks. A small metal hook protruded from each of the tanks shown in the drawing, and each one held a tag—green ones for tanks that had some fuel and red for those that were empty. Russi said all but one of the tanks were less than half-full and explained that the exception was the "centerline tank," a reserve tank that also functioned as ballast. "It's full, but we can't use it because we would lose our stability." A sheet of paper sitting on the desk contained specific amounts for each of the tanks, numbers that Duffy copied onto a pad of paper.

The ships were near the center of the Atlantic, almost as close to South America as they were to South Africa. Based on what he learned from Russi, Duffy believed *Viarsa* had a bit less range than *Southern Supporter* and that it could make it to South Africa, although with almost nothing in reserve.

Before he left the control room, Duffy took the engineer's log, which he hoped would shed some light on the validity of the ship's log. Each page of the engineer's log covered a single day and was divided into several boxes. The words on the top of the page were in Spanish, but most of the information was numerical. The column on the far left side of the page indicated six time periods. Since the next column was labeled "RPM," Duffy believed the three-digit numbers beneath it indicated the revolutions per minute of the engine's drive shaft, numbers that could be used to determine the ship's speed during each of the time periods: all he had to do was find out the number of revolutions required to produce various rates of speed. Later that morning, he came up with a way to ask about the correlation that he thought was unlikely to make Cabrera suspicious.

"We need to slow down your ship, so we can transfer some supplies over from *Southern Supporter*," Duffy told the captain. "What did you say was your slowest speed?"

"Six knots."

"You can't make the engine go slower?"

"The minimum number of revolutions is 200. If you go slower, the engines stall."

"So you can't go slower?"

"No, no, that's the minimum revolutions. To go slower, you just take the ship out of gear."

"What's the maximum revolutions?"

"Three hundred forty."

"What speed can you maintain with that?"

"About ten knots."

Duffy struggled to contain a smile. He believed Cabrera had inadvertently provided evidence that contradicted his earlier assertion that he was steaming through Australian waters at top speed until shortly before he was spotted by *Southern Supporter* back on the morning of August 7. The engineering log suggested the opposite—that the ship was moving at close to its *minimum* rate of speed during the thirty-six hours before the start of the chase. Cabrera claimed that on August 6, the ship traveled at its top speed throughout the day except for the fifty minutes when he said it had mechanical problems, but the log indicated that the engine never exceeded 235 RPMs. One day later, after the chase began, the log reported RPMs consistently higher than 320. The log also included temperature readings from the exhaust fumes, and Duffy believed those readings also confirmed that the ship was moving slowly before the start of the chase.

Just before midday, Duffy visited *Viarsa*'s galley. The chef's domain was a relatively small space on the starboard side of the ship, crowded with a large oven and stove on which sat three outsize kettles and an enormous mixer. Duffy was impressed by the galley's cleanliness and by how carefully the stores were organized. Given that they had been at sea for five weeks, he was also amazed by what was in the nearby freezer. The chorizo sausages and Spanish cheeses looked particularly appealing.

The chef, a Spaniard named Jose Carlos Nogueira Boubeta, was cooking pork chops on a large griddle. Six feet tall and stout, the chef was easily the largest member of *Viarsa*'s crew. He was also one of the most important. Food always assumes an important role at sea; it is a frequent conversation topic and is crucial to maintaining morale. This was reflected in the chef's salary: he was paid $3,000 a month, more than three times as much as regular crewmen.

Thinking about how much better *Viarsa*'s crew was eating than he was, Duffy said, "That smells great."

The chef waved his hand and said, "Have some!"

Lifting his hand, Duffy said, "No thanks."

Leaving the galley, Duffy walked into the mess, a windowless space so cramped that it felt like a cave. The ceiling was so low, just five feet, seven inches above the floor, that Duffy could not even stand up. Three long tables were close together, making it difficult to maneuver through the room even when it was empty. Sandwiched between the engine room on one side and the hydraulics of the steering mechanism on the other, the room was also noisy. When the door to the engine room was open, it was impossible to hold a conversation.

Just down a corridor from the mess, Duffy opened the door of a washroom, which incorporated the ship's laundry and was, like everything else, a model of efficiency. Sinks, washing machines, and dryers lined one side of the narrow space; four shower stalls and as many toilets were on the opposite side. In spite of the heavy usage and in sharp contrast to the bathrooms on many merchant ships, the compartment was clean. There was no mold or broken pipes, and everything looked like it was regularly scrubbed.

Meeting up with Webb, Duffy then entered the narrow passageway between the mess and the setting area, which was lined with racks holding the beacons used to mark the location of longlines. Two racks contained beacons that were numbered almost sequentially, one to seventeen. Two beacons—those numbered thirteen and fifteen—were apparently missing. Webb and Duffy were thinking the same thing: the absent beacons had produced the signals that *Southern Supporter* had picked up back at

Heard Island. As Webb photographed the racks, he said, "This is some pretty great evidence!"

The two men then put on their heavy coats and went outside to inspect the forward deck. They were particularly interested in a collection of steel anchors, which were lying on their sides about thirty feet in front of the bridge. They were obviously the ones that hold longlines in place. Pointing to a pair of wooden planks under the anchors, Duffy said, "Look at the indentations and rust. It looks like three or four are missing."

Mike O'Dea was trying to find out what had happened to the VMS transponder that was supposed to send *Viarsa*'s position to Uruguay. Given Ambassador Amaro's initial claim that the vessel was in the Atlantic Ocean, the equipment obviously had not been working. Or it had been somehow overridden, either onboard *Viarsa* or in Uruguay. O'Dea suspected that the transponder had either been disabled or removed entirely. Examining the severed wire and empty screw holes in the chartroom, he had an idea where the transponder equipment had once been mounted. When he climbed to the roof of the bridge, he found a spaghetti-like mess of wires—some of which had been cut—and antennae, but he did not find a transponder.

While he was there, O'Dea discovered a less ambiguous sign of deception: *Viarsa*'s call letters—CXYU, which were painted in large white letters against a black roof—had been covered with equipment. The letters would have made it easy to identify the ship: CX meant it was a Uruguayan vessel and YU was specific to the ship.

For the next couple of hours, the Australians searched the crew's cabins. Some of the rooms had six bunks, others had four; all of them were so small that they felt like cages. Their doors were only four feet high: to get inside a room, the men had to simultaneously step over a foot-high bulkhead and duck under a transom. There was so little space above the narrow bunks that Webb thought they looked like they belonged on a submarine. There was no natural light. Portholes had been shuttered to prevent them from being shattered by a wave.

Most of the crewmen were lying in their bunks. Without hooks to bait or fish to process, they did not have much to do. Some of them were weaving basketlike ornaments out of the branch lines. One was so large that it could have been used as a lampshade.

The overabundance of free time concerned Duffy. Coupled with anxiety, it could lead to confrontation or rebellion. Although he guessed that the crewmen thought of themselves as fishermen rather than criminals, their seamen's papers suggested that most of them had repeatedly worked on vessels that were believed to operate illegally. They may have rationalized their work with the belief that countries like Australia should not have the exclusive right to fish in places like Heard Island, but Duffy thought that on some level they must have been aware that they had crossed a line between right and wrong. And having done that, he worried about how far they would go.

Most of the crewmen did not object when they were asked to leave their cabins so the Australians could rummage through their drawers and under their mattresses. However, when Webb entered the cabin of a Spaniard he had nicknamed "rat tail man" because he wore his hair in a ponytail, he began screaming in Spanish. One of the shotgun-wielding South Africans, who was stationed in the hallway, responded immediately, stepping toward the fisherman and shouting, "You better pull your fucking head in or we're going to take it off."

The search turned up very little of value until O'Dea pulled several pieces of paper from the bottom of a clothes-filled drawer under one of the bunks. It appeared to be an employment contract, a single piece of letterhead that said "Viarsa Fishing Company" across the top. This was the first document to hint at the identity of the ship's owner. O'Dea took a spent roll of film from the same drawer. When the man who had signed the contract and owned the camera saw what O'Dea had taken, he became distraught, crying and shaking his head as he spoke rapidly in Spanish.

"He's very worried," another *Viarsa* crewman told Webb. "We were supposed to throw things away. You can't take that from him."

"We have to take it," O'Dea replied.

"The film is personal."

"We have to take it for now. We will give it back later."

For the most part, Webb was trying to play the good guy, hoping to befriend members of *Viarsa*'s crew who could speak a bit of English in the hope that someone might spill the beans and admit that the ship had been fishing during the days just before the start of the chase. The collection of circumstantial evidence would be helpful, but he needed something closer to direct proof—or personal testimony—to take the uncertainty out of the legal proceedings. But most of the crew seemed reluctant to be seen chatting with him. The lone exception was Marius Vacareanu, the one Romanian member of the crew. Close to six feet tall and muscular, Vacareanu was quick to smile, and he seemed to enjoy the opportunity to practice his English by talking to Webb.

"What kind of money do you make?" Webb asked during one conversation.

"Eight hundred dollars is deposited in my bank account every month—for me that's very good money."

Hoping that the owner had stopped paying the crew, thereby increasing the odds that someone would turn against him, Webb asked, "Are you still getting paid?"

"I don't know. When I spoke to my wife two weeks ago, she said that I was paid for the last month, but no one knows if we're getting paid now."

A day later, Webb decided to ask the big question: "What was going on when the ship was intercepted?"

"I don't know—I was asleep."

This was basically the same story the observer had told, causing Webb to conclude that everyone was given specific instructions and that Vacareanu would stick to the script.

A few minutes before sunrise on Monday, September 1, Duffy spotted Gouth Island, the first land he had seen since leaving Fremantle five weeks earlier. The ships would reach Cape Town in four days, and the proximity to South Africa appeared to make Cabrera nervous. "I want some answers and I want my passport back," he said to Webb shortly after they passed the island. "We have to know what you are going to do."

"We need to hold onto your passport, but I can try to answer your questions."

"Are we going to Cape Town?" Cabrera asked.

"You will not be going into Cape Town. You will be refueled off the coast."

The plan was that *Viarsa* would approach Cape Town but stay at least twenty-five miles offshore so as to ensure that the ship did not become entangled in any legal actions there. Webb did not explain the reasons for this to Cabrera, but the Australians had two specific fears: first, that *Viarsa*'s owners could ask a South African court to prevent Australia from taking the ship to Fremantle; and second, since South African officials believed *Viarsa* was one of the ships that had stolen its toothfish population, they might seize the vessel and initiate their own legal proceedings.

Cabrera then asked, "Will we be disembarked and flown to Australia?"

"No, you are not going by plane. You are going onboard *Viarsa*."

Webb expected Cabrera to be annoyed by the prospect of spending another three or four weeks at sea, but the captain did not react to this at all. Perhaps another long voyage did not seem any worse than the other possibilities. In fact, now that he had asked some of his questions, Cabrera became much more relaxed and the conversation turned personal. Cabrera told Webb that he lived with his second wife and their eleven-year-old son.

Encouraged by the rapport, Webb decided he would also ask a question: "One thing we need to know—who is the owner of the vessel?"

"The company's name is Navalmar."

CHAPTER 21

Early Thursday morning, Commander Paul Bartlett of the Royal Australian Navy climbed into a small launch that would take him to *Viarsa*. Tall and broad shouldered, the forty-five-year-old was an imposing figure. He was also a popular officer who was able to maintain an easy rapport with junior sailors without diminishing his authority. Duffy and Bartlett already knew each other: Bartlett, who was born in Britain, was the weapons officer on a British destroyer a dozen years earlier when Duffy served on the ship as part of a military exchange program. Bartlett subsequently immigrated to Australia and transferred from the Royal Navy to the Royal Australian Navy.

On August 16, he was asked to lead a twenty-seven-man contingent that would bring *Viarsa* back to Fremantle. It was the kind of role that appealed to him: he liked unique assignments and the challenge of quickly turning a group of men who had never worked together into a team. A few days before he met Duffy aboard *Viarsa*, Bartlett and his crew, most of them men in their twenties, boarded *SAS Drakensburg*, a South African naval vessel, and set out to intercept *Southern Supporter* and *Viarsa*.

Seeing Duffy, Bartlett laughed and jokingly asked, "What the hell are you doing out here?"

"Good day, Paul," Duffy replied. "Glad you could make it."

Bartlett was, at least initially, agreeably surprised by *Viarsa*'s condition. Like most naval officers, he had the impression that commercial fishing vessels, particularly those registered in developing countries, were poorly maintained and only marginally seaworthy. The lack of rust on *Viarsa* and the way the equipment appeared to be carefully secured took him by surprise.

"They obviously take some pride in their ship," he said to Duffy.

"They do—let me show you around," Duffy said, motioning Bartlett and Steve Young, a lieutenant commander who was serving as Bartlett's deputy, to the bridge, where they met Captain Cabrera.

"Commander Bartlett will be taking over from me today," Duffy told Cabrera. "He is in charge of the Royal Australian Navy contingent that will escort *Viarsa* back to Australia. Do you understand?"

Smiling broadly, Cabrera said, "Yes, yes—I do."

Bartlett also met Antonio Perez, who, as usual, was aloof and unwilling to look directly at the Australian officer. A few minutes later, after Bartlett and Duffy left the bridge, Bartlett said, "Perez seems devious."

Nodding, Duffy said: "I've never trusted him. The rest of the crew pretty much stays to themselves, and they have been basically compliant. I'm pretty sure they won't try anything. It's harder to say with Perez."

Duffy then led Bartlett to the factory, where his positive impression of the ship suddenly evaporated. The South Africans' attempts to soak up the water with flattened cardboard boxes had produced soggy piles of pulp. Bartlett was appalled by the mess as well as the stink of fish and the steel tank that was lined with cardboard and used as a bed.

"That thing looks like a stainless steel coffin," he declared. "We're not going to sleep here."

"I know," Duffy replied. "It wouldn't be great for a three-week passage. We were only here for a week."

"I wouldn't use it for a day!" Bartlett thundered. "What about commandeering some of the crew quarters?"

"Good luck. They have forty-one people onboard and forty-one bunks. I didn't want to make their lives any more difficult than I had to. It's up to you, but I think you'll find it difficult to find another secure place without upsetting them."

Later, after Bartlett walked down the narrow corridor that led through the crew quarters and peered into the crowded rooms, he reluctantly agreed with Duffy's assessment. By then, the web of lines that had been constructed over *Viarsa*'s deck had been removed and a helicopter had landed, carrying the rest of Bartlett's team and an array of weapons, along with sleeping bags, crates of bottled water, and enough combat rations to sustain Bartlett and his twenty-seven men for five weeks. The rations, more than anything else, made it clear that this would not be anything like a pleasure cruise. Called "rat packs," their contents looked nothing like the "chicken curry" and "sausages and spaghetti" that their labels promised.

Just before noon, Duffy, O'Dea, and Webb thanked the South African fishing officers and security guards who then boarded the helicopter that took them to the *Drakensburg* for the trip back to Cape Town. Shortly after that, Duffy and the Australian fisheries officers returned to *Southern Supporter*. Once they were gone, Bartlett gathered his men on *Viarsa*'s deck near the bow. "For the time being, we'll all stay onboard," he told them, "but at some point we'll split up into watches and give everyone a chance to have a break on *Southern Supporter*, which will accompany us back to Cape Town and then to Fremantle. While we're here, our accommodation will be in the front of the ship in the factory area and the conveyer belt compartment. We aren't going to use their galley—we'll live off our rat packs. And we're not going to use their showers or heads, but we are going to shave every day and maintain a military bearing."

Young, who would be responsible for navigating, spoke next. "It's going to take somewhere between eighteen to twenty-five days to get from Cape Town to Fremantle—three weeks is the best guess." Unlike modern naval vessels, which cruise at close to twenty knots, making currents and wind virtually irrelevant, *Viarsa* and *Southern Supporter* were so slow that Young planned to head south to follow the Great Circle Route, which takes advantage of the eastbound currents that once pushed Dutch clipper ships from Africa to Indonesia. "We'll drop pretty far south," Young said. "That will give us an extra knot, which will get us home a day earlier."

Early the next day, Friday, September 5, almost a full month after the chase began, the *Drakensburg* entered Cape Town's majestic harbor. It was a perfect morning: the city's skyline was a golden silhouette against Table Mountain, and the only cloud anywhere in the sky was sliding slowly across the flat top of the mountain until it spilled off the side to become a virtual waterfall.

"Spectacular!" Duffy said. "What a great way to return to the world."

Officials from South Africa and Australia—as well as journalists and diplomats from Britain, Spain, and Germany—were waiting on the dock to greet the ship. Ian Wilcock, Australia's high commissioner to South Africa, called the operation "wholehearted, imaginative, courageous, and highly effective" during a congratulatory press conference. "We want illegal fishing vessels, those that would plunder our oceans, those that would defy Australian, South African, and international law, to understand that we're coming after you. You can run, but you can't hide—even among the icebergs."

A few minutes later, an Australian diplomat, Tim Huggins, pulled Duffy aside. He began by offering his own congratulations, but his manner seemed restrained, giving Duffy the impression that some kind of bad news would follow. It did. Huggins said that Eduardo Schultz might be allowed to return to Uruguay with all of his records.

Duffy was so stunned, he did not have an immediate response. He felt like he had been punched in the stomach. "He's the crux of the case," he declared. "How could we even *consider* letting him go?"

"I know—I know," Huggins said. "I completely understand your frustration."

"If we can get him back to Australia without giving the Uruguayan government a chance to contaminate him, there's a chance he'll cooperate."

"Listen," Huggins said. "I don't have the whole story yet. The ministers for Justice and Fisheries agree with you, but the decision is going to be made by the Foreign Minister."

"I can see where this is going to end up."

Enraged, Duffy called Keith Johnson. "We can't let this happen," Duffy said. "Everything we've worked for would be compromised."

"I totally agree, but it's out of our hands," said Johnson, who added that the issue had become part of a larger negotiation involving, among other things, an upcoming round of international trade talks. "There's all sorts of negotiating going on—and things seem to be moving against us."

Paul Bartlett was equally frustrated. *Viarsa* had already been loaded with provisions: twenty-five thousand gallons of fuel, twenty kilograms of engine grease, along with pasta, soap, toothpaste, meats and pota-toes, and fruit and vegetables (*Viarsa*'s chef also requested forty liters of wine, half white and half red, claiming it would be used for cooking, but Duffy struck it from the list). But the ships could not set out until gov-ernment officials made up their minds about Schultz. Since it had to stay at least twenty-five miles off the coast, where the water was too deep to drop anchor, *Viarsa* was cruising back and forth along the coast, thereby damaging the impression of decisiveness Bartlett had hoped to project to *Viarsa*'s crew.

It was Friday, so Bartlett assumed, correctly as it turned out, that a decision would not be forthcoming until after the weekend. Before they finally left for Fremantle on Tuesday, September 9, the observer was taken by a small boat to Cape Town. The diplomats had agreed that he would be allowed to go to Uruguay but would go to Fremantle at a later date to respond to questions.

Bartlett divided his crew into three teams. At any given time, one would be on duty, one would be off duty but on call, and the third would be resting aboard *Southern Supporter*. The commander thought a general uprising by *Viarsa*'s crew was unlikely, but it was impossible to forget the unfavorable ratio of his crew to the fishing vessel's or to rule out smaller-scale confrontations. And while his men had guns, *Viarsa*'s had knives. Scores had been collected and secured in the factory, but many others were still scattered throughout the ship. For times when they were off duty but aboard *Viarsa*, most of the men decided that the conveyer belt provided the best place to sleep, although some preferred the steel coffin and a hammock that had been strung in the factory.

Bartlett spent much of his own time walking around the ship looking for signs of trouble—arguments, expressions of animosity, hushed voices. He also received intelligence from two Spanish-speakers who were part of his team. He asked one of them, Frank Alacantara, a thirty-five-year-old air force sergeant whose family lived in Madrid until he was six, to roam around the ship and become a part of as many conversations as he could. Alacantara, who had been trained as a nurse, was well suited for the job, and the fishermen immediately understood that he was different from the others, in part because of the green and brown Air Force overalls he wore. "They're happy with our presence," Alacantara told Young a couple of days after they departed Cape Town. "They feel the captain put them at great risk when they went into the ice, and they were angry that they didn't have a chance to say anything." Bartlett had asked the second Spanish-speaker to keep his proficiency a secret so he could listen surreptitiously, particularly to any phone calls placed by Cabrera and Perez.

One of Bartlett's concerns was over-familiarity between the two crews. "We have to maintain some distance," he told his men. "These people have nothing to do. They're going to talk to you and try to teach you Spanish, and that's okay, but we have to keep a clear delineation. The more interactions we have, the more difficult it becomes to keep our authority in place. And if we have an incident, they're going to be confused about why someone who had been friendly is pulling a gun on them. So avoid personal conversations. If someone asks you about your family or where you come from, change the topic to professional issues. If you're in the engine room, talk about the engines."

But knowing precisely where to draw the line was difficult. For example, a few days after the ships left Cape Town, Carlos, the chef, told Steve Young that he needed to have access to a locked closet in order to get two bottles of brandy.

"I need it for cooking," the chef explained.

"Cooking what?"

"Roast beef."

Young was astounded by the volume of brandy the chef intended to use as well as the idea that *Viarsa*'s crew might enjoy such lavish cuisine while his men made do with almost inedible combat rations.

"That's a lot of brandy for roast beef!" Young said.

"It's also for a cake—I put brandy in the cake."

A decision was required. Young could not say yes to everything, and the use of brandy seemed like a perfectly reasonable place to put his foot down. On the other hand, given the so-far friction-free voyage, it also seemed like too trivial a thing over which to risk a confrontation, and it presented an opportunity to earn some additional goodwill. "Okay," Young said to Alacantara, who was translating. "If he gives his personal assurance that it's only for cooking—that no one will drink any of it—he can have it." Later that morning, Alacantara told Young that the chef was indeed flambéing the beef. Not long after that, the chef delivered several pieces of cake to the bridge. Young thought it was delicious, the best food he had had in many days, the brandy very much in evidence.

Inevitably, in spite of Bartlett's warnings, the interaction between the crews expanded. The progression came in small steps, and many of them related to food. Following the brandy cake, the chef started delivering fresh-baked bread to the bridge. The Australians had already stopped brewing their own coffee; *Viarsa*'s brew, which included powdered milk, was vastly superior.

The only member of *Viarsa*'s crew who was unfriendly was Perez, who often appeared angry, particularly when someone opened the door of the bridge to battle the constant haze of cigarette smoke. There were also times when Perez made what Bartlett judged to be curt comments to the captain, giving Bartlett the sense that Cabrera deferred to Perez and that there was some underlying tension between the two, perhaps because Cabrera was more compliant than Perez thought he should be. The only times that Perez's demeanor changed was on a couple of occasions when he spoke to the Australians about soccer, conversations he conducted in broken English.

On October 2, Young told Cabrera that they would reach Fremantle the next day. "When we get there," Young added, "I would like you to berth the ship. I'll stand beside you and tell you where I want you to go, but I'd like you to be at the helm." Young had decided that he did not want to do it himself because of the complexity involved in maneuvering *Viarsa* at slow speeds. The only way to manage it was to take the engine out of gear, and Young did not want to risk a mishap when he knew his wife—and several senior government ministers—would be watching from the dock. Young had also arranged for Alacantara to learn the Spanish words for several nautical terms—ahead, astern, stop, port, starboard—and asked him to station himself near the helm during the docking. "I want to make sure they don't try to play their last card by running it into the pier or doing something silly," Young explained.

In fact, the docking occurred without incident. Afterward, Young and Cabrera shook hands and smiled as they said good-bye. "Thank you for a safe passage," Young said. Feeling sorry for him, he found himself adding, "And good luck."

When *Viarsa*'s crew was taken to the Australian Fisheries Management Authority's office in Fremantle a few days later to be interviewed, Cabrera gave his name and said: "I am fifty-eight years old. I am a citizen of

Uruguay. And I am not going to answer any of your questions." When the other crewmen were questioned, they all said essentially the same thing.

Eduardo Schultz was not much more helpful a couple of weeks later when he arrived at O'Dea's office, accompanied by Uruguay's consul general, Anna Maria Estevez, and a lawyer who worked for DINARA. The lawyer said Schultz would answer questions through a translator but could not be sworn in and that the interview could not be recorded. Without a sworn statement, O'Dea knew that nothing Schultz said during the interview could be used as evidence, but he did not have a choice: there was no way to compel him to provide sworn testimony.

"Can you tell us," O'Dea asked, "how you came up with *Viarsa*'s positions, the ones that were sent to Montevideo?"

"I just reported what the master of the ship told me to report."

"Is that the usual practice on Uruguayan ships?"

"No, it's the only time it ever happened."

This was something, O'Dea thought: confirmation from a Uruguayan official that Cabrera had disregarded the rules. But it did not provide direct evidence of illegal fishing.

"Didn't you think you should call Captain Flangini and tell him what was going on?"

Schultz shrugged his shoulders.

"According to the position reports you sent," O'Dea continued, "your ship was in the Atlantic Ocean. You must have known that wasn't true!"

This statement clearly angered Schultz, who began speaking heatedly in Spanish. When he stopped, the translator said, "He says that he's not here to be accused of anything because he did not do anything wrong."

"But you sent your position reports to DINARA from the bridge," said O'Dea. "You must have seen the actual positions from the GPS units there."

At that point, the consul general, who spoke English fluently, interjected, "This is not an interrogation. He's given his reasons. You should not be accusing him of any wrongdoing."

Looking directly at Schultz, O'Dea said, "You're just wasting our time."

"You're suggesting I'm a liar!"

Although it seemed obvious to O'Dea that Schultz was going to stick to the same story he had told on the ship, O'Dea decided to try one more question: "Okay, what we're really interested in comes down to one thing—what was going on in the days just before we found you?"

"I cannot tell you that. I was sick."

Making no effort to mask his anger, O'Dea declared, "You promised to help us! I have a very hard time believing that you were so ill that you never left your cabin or had any idea what was going on before we found you."

Without looking at O'Dea, Schultz replied, "I was asleep when you came up to us. I had not left my cabin more than once or twice in the previous four days."

"But you would have known whether the ship was steaming or fishing, wouldn't you?"

"He's already answered your question," the lawyer said. "I'm sorry—that's the way it is."

Shaking his head, O'Dea said, "Then there's really not much point in talking any further, is there?"

Webb, who also attended the meeting, was furious. Until then, he still thought there was some chance that Schultz would come through. After the Uruguayans left, he said: "It never should have happened this way. He should have come directly back to Australia, we should have been able to interrogate him—and we should have charged him with aiding and abetting a crime." One day later, Schultz returned to the office to deliver a three-page statement in which he repeated his claim that he did not know whether *Viarsa* was fishing when it was in the Australian Fishing Zone.

"Will you come back to testify at the trial?" O'Dea asked.

"No, no, no. I have to go and make a living. I can't come back here."

The Uruguayan government was not much more helpful than its observer. Captain Flangini publicly questioned Australia's right to claim the exclusive right to fish within two hundred miles of Heard Island. The Minister for Agriculture, Livestock, and Fisheries, Martin Aguirrezabala, admitted that *Viarsa*'s crew was guilty of "several irregularities," including the manipulation of the navigational positions it reported, but he insisted that "it is not acceptable" to call the vessel a "pirate" because the Uruguayan investigation did not find any evidence of that. Following a parliamentary investigation, DINARA "deflagged" five toothfish vessels, suspended permits for three others, and tightened some of its fisheries regulations. But Uruguayan officials also acknowledged that their actions would not stop the same vessels from continuing to hunt for toothfish because they could easily be registered somewhere else.

"When these companies don't get what they want in one country," said Pedro Mo Amaro, the Uruguayan ambassador to Australia, "they just go to another country. They change the name of their company and change the name of their vessels, but in the end, nothing really changes."

CHAPTER 22

Perth, Australia

Leaning forward in his seat with his mouth agape, Ricardo Cabrera was obviously puzzled. Eleven months after arriving in Australia, he was sitting in "the dock" of a crowded fifth-floor courtroom in downtown Perth. Every seat was taken, and there were so many people standing in the aisles and the area near the entrance that it was difficult for the lawyers to reach their places near the front. The assemblage included journalists, government officials from Spain and Australia, as well as a number of Perth residents who had read about the chase and wanted to get a glimpse of the toothfish pirates. One of the spectators, a woman who had managed to get a seat near the back of the room, appeared to be as confused as Cabrera. She was trying to decide whether the captain looked more like her grandfather, whom she adored, or the environmental bandit she had read about in the papers. As she studied his face and noticed the deep wrinkles, the deep-set eyes, and the thickness of his wavy gray hair, all she could be sure of was that he had had an interesting, probably mysterious life.

Cabrera was straining to hear every word, and his gaze was shifting between the judge and his lawyer, who were both wearing the elaborate robes and horsehair wigs that are still required in Australian courts. When it was his turn to enter a plea, Cabrera rose from his chair, shook his head vigorously, and declared, "Not culpable."

Antonio Perez, who was sitting next to the captain, looked pale and drawn. He had lost weight. He did not like the food in Australia, at least what was served at the Flying Angels Club, the seamen's boardinghouse in Fremantle where he and the other defendants had been living while they waited for the trial to begin. As always, he was difficult to read. Sometimes he appeared to be angry. At other times his head was cocked backward and his lips were pursed into something closer to a smirk, one of the looks that had annoyed Duffy and O'Dea aboard *Viarsa*. In fact, Perez's shifting expressions reflected his thinking quite accurately. He had originally assumed the trial would be a sham—rigged, or, as he put it, "prepared." But after spending time with his lawyer, Phillip Laskaris, a feisty defense attorney who defended his clients with the same single-minded doggedness that made Perez such a productive fisherman, he began to think that he just might have a chance. When he was asked for his plea, he stood and looked directly at the judge before offering his own, "Not culpable."

A lot was at stake, including Australia's credibility in the fight against large-scale illegal fishing. The government had spent several million dollars on the chase and bringing *Viarsa* back to Australia, and a quick look around the courtroom made it clear that the costs continued to mount. The prosecutor, Hilton Dembo, who was sitting on the left end of the long bar table near the front of the courtroom, had spent months preparing for the trial and arranging to get more than twenty witnesses to Perth. Mike O'Dea, Mike Flanagan, and Scott Webb sat just behind Dembo and next to more than twenty binders' worth of materials that they had assembled. Steve Duffy was also sitting in the courtroom. He had recently left the Customs Service and moved to the United Arab Emirates, where the government had hired him to help build its coast guard; but he had flown back, at government expense, for the trial. Australian taxpayers had also made subsistence payments to Cabrera and Perez along with two other defendants: Francisco Fernandez Oliveira and Jose Gonzalez Perez, *Viarsa*'s two other officers.

The fifth defendant, Roberto Enrique Reyes Guerrero, was the only one who was allowed to leave Australia and return for the start of the trial. Although he was just an ordinary seaman on *Viarsa,* he was charged because he was aboard the *South Tomi* when it was arrested for illegally taking toothfish from Australian waters several years earlier.

The trial itself would add to the tab, at a rate of about $30,000 a day. The courtroom was staffed by two interpreters, three guards, a clerk, an usher, a sheriff, and of course a judge—a senior magistrate named Paul Healy. Unseen were three typists who were creating an almost instantaneous transcript of the proceedings, as well as another staffer whose job it was to ensure that the microphones functioned properly.

The defendants had requested a jury trial, so eighteen jurors—twelve regular jurors and six alternates—were sitting on the left side of the courtroom, facing the defendants. Judge Healy believed it would be an unusually long trial—he had scheduled it for four weeks but knew it could take more time than that—which was why he swore in so many alternates. All but three of the jurors were women, and the men were young. Having decided that middle-aged men would be instinctively inclined to convict foreigners accused of stealing Australian resources, the defense attorneys rejected almost all of the prospective male jurors.

Before the prosecutor could even begin presenting his case, the attorneys representing the fishermen launched a multipronged legal blitz aimed at excluding major portions of the evidence that the prosecutor hoped to introduce. They started by suggesting that *Southern Supporter*'s hot pursuit had been broken. Citing entries in Stephen Duffy's log that described how the ship did not follow *Viarsa* into the ice on August 18, Laskaris asserted that the pursuit was illegal.

"*Southern Supporter* either terminated or interrupted the hot pursuit at that point," Laskaris claimed. "They called off the chase!"

"I don't think so," Duffy whispered from his seat near the back of the courtroom.

The judge also disagreed, saying, "It doesn't sound like terminating the pursuit to me."

Laskaris went on to argue that Australia did not have the right to claim ownership of the fish surrounding Heard Island because the island is "an external territory" thousands of miles from the Australian mainland that "cannot support human habitation or economic life." He even claimed that it was not clear that the defendants were aboard *Viarsa* when it was within the Australian Fishing Zone.

Obviously baffled by the last point, the judge asked, "What were they doing, swimming?"

"No, they weren't swimming."

"Well, where were they, then?"

"They were on a boat."

"There's some *other* boat that suddenly mysteriously appeared?"

The judge was obviously exasperated. He knew that *Southern Supporter* had detected other boats in the area hours before the chase began, but Laskaris's contention that the defendants could have been anywhere else but onboard *Viarsa* seemed ridiculous. Healy pointed out that Cabrera had admitted in his radio conversations with O'Dea that he and *Viarsa* were in the Australian zone at the start of the chase. After noting that

Cabrera and the rest of the crew were on the ship when it was boarded, the judge asked: "Can't it be inferred that if the vessel was in the Australian Fishing Zone, those people on the vessel were also in the Australian Fishing Zone?"

"No."

"Why?"

"The prosecution has to *prove* against each," Laskaris said. "The admission by the master is not evidence against any of them, which means that that admission can't be used as one link in the circumstantial fact chain."

Although his unwillingness to concede even the obvious seemed unnecessarily tedious, under the rules of evidence he had a point. Australia's legal system gives a great many rights to defendants, and Laskaris, who had previous experience representing fishermen but spent most of his time defending people accused of complex white-collar crimes, was committed to using each and every one of them in full. At the very least, his claims demonstrated the zealousness with which he would defend his clients. Judge Healy ultimately rejected all of Laskaris's arguments, but the defense did not come away empty-handed. By seizing the initiative, Laskaris seemed to have taken control of the proceedings.

He made so many objections that Duffy, the first witness, gave just four minutes of testimony during the first week of the trial. Shortly after Duffy returned to the stand on Monday of the second week, he and the jury were again asked to leave the courtroom because of another objection. Duffy had begun describing how lines had been strung over *Viarsa* on August 25. Just as he was about to say *Viarsa*'s crew strung the lines in order to prevent a helicopter from landing, Curt Hofmann, one of the two other defense attorneys, objected, asserting it would be "prejudicial" to present such an "interpretation" because "there are many other possible scenarios." This time the judge ruled in favor of the defense, which Duffy considered outrageous. He was not going to offer an *interpretation*. There could be no other reason for the lines. But although the judge said Duffy could describe the lines and say the ship did not appear to need them for any structural reason, he was prohibited from suggesting that they had been erected to thwart a helicopter.

The defense attorneys scored more points when they cross-examined Duffy. "You didn't see anyone engaging in fishing, did you?" Laskaris asked.

"No," Duffy acknowledged.

"You didn't see anyone on *Viarsa* set a line?"

"No."

"Retrieve a line?"

"No."

"Nobody else on *Southern Supporter* saw such a thing take place?"

"To my knowledge, that is correct."

"You did not find any high-frequency fishing beacons in the water, did you?"

"No, we didn't stop."

Attempting to use Duffy's naval experience to help the defendants, Laskaris then suggested that only *Viarsa*'s captain could be held responsible for *Viarsa*'s wrongdoing, if there was any, because the others were just following orders. "You know that the first rule of the sea," Laskaris added, "be it if you're on a military vessel or whether you're on a merchant vessel, is this: the master is the master?"

"Yes."

"The master on a vessel has incredible power over its crew and its passengers?"

"Correct."

"If you were the master of the *Viarsa* and you decided not to stop, having been chased by a vessel like *Southern Supporter*, you would expect every member of your crew to do exactly what you told them to do?"

"That's a fair expectation," Duffy said.

"And if they didn't, what's that called?"

"Mutiny."

"It doesn't matter what the Australian government thinks," Laskaris continued. "For the purposes of the members of the crew of the *Viarsa,* what the master tells them to do, they have to do, don't they?"

"Yes."

Laskaris then went on to suggest that Cabrera, too, had had no choice but to accede to an authority greater than that of the Australian patrol boat. "Let's put you in this scenario," the lawyer said: "You are the master of an Australian fishing vessel and you have been sailing around the continent of South America, and for one reason or another you come across a Uruguayan patrol vessel. You get an instruction, as the master of that Australian fishing vessel, from someone in Canberra telling you that you are required to return to the port of Fremantle. If you're an Australian flagged vessel, you would follow that instruction, wouldn't you?"

"Yes, I would."

"If you were being told to stop by the Uruguayan vessel, you wouldn't, would you?"

"Most probably not."

Mark Trowell, the third defense attorney, chipped away at the prosecution's case from another angle, challenging Duffy on the role that the South

Africans played during the boarding. Trowell, one of the top criminal law-yers in Western Australia, has represented many high-profile clients, including Robert Hughes, the well-known art critic and author, when he was charged with dangerous driving. Quick-witted and relentless, Trowell fired off a barrage of rapid-fire questions at Duffy, claiming at one point that the South Africans were "mercenaries."

"I don't believe the definition of mercenary fits," Duffy said.

"You just don't like the term, but you know it's accurate, don't you?"

"No."

Trowell kept pushing. "The South Africans seized the vessel, didn't they?"

"No."

"Who was first up the ladder?"

"A South African."

"Who was second up the ladder?"

"A South African."

"Once they had seized and secured the vessel, then Mr. O'Dea came on board?"

"No, that's not true."

"No?"

"No."

Duffy never lost his composure, but he was convinced that his testi-mony was a disaster. "I feel shattered," he said over dinner a few hours after he was grilled by Trowell. "I think I sounded like a goose." It hap-pened to be Duffy's forty-fourth birthday, but he was so frustrated that it was difficult to celebrate. It seemed to him that the defense had hijacked the trial and that the facts had become less important than legal gamesmanship. "It's just not right," he declared. "The accused get so many rights that I'm beginning to question the Australian legal system."

The pace and character of the trial did not change when Mike O'Dea took the hot seat one day later. Jury trials rarely move quickly, and in this one, the official day usually began at 10:00 a.m. and ended at 4:00 p.m. With breaks for lunch and coffee, there was rarely more than four hours of testimony in a day. The need to translate everything into Spanish for the defendants was an additional burden. Witnesses had to speak slowly for the interpreters, who sometimes requested breaks beyond the regularly scheduled ones.

And then there were the objections. Tuesday, October 26, O'Dea's fifth day of testimony, provides an example of how bad it could get: the proceedings did not begin until 10:23 a.m. because two of the jurors were late. Twelve minutes after O'Dea began answering questions, the jurors were asked to leave the room after Laskaris raised a technical objection. They returned at 10:42, but four minutes after that, just as O'Dea started to recount how he found the diary that appeared to belong to Jose Gonzalez Perez, Laskaris raised another objection. As they filed out of the courtroom and into the small, soundproof room where they had already spent much of the trial, the jurors were obviously bemused by the lack of progress. Several of them were chuckling.

The diary was an important—possibly crucial—piece of evidence: its author appeared to have written that *Viarsa* had been fishing during the hours just before the start of the chase. "It is a vital piece of evidence for the prosecution because it helps shore up their otherwise weak circumstantial case," Laskaris told the judge. "There are, however, significant problems with that piece of evidence." First, he noted that the supposed author had never been questioned about the diary and had never admitted it was his. Second, the person who said the diary was found in a bunk that belonged to Jose Perez was the Uruguayan observer, a person who would not be in court to testify. "Real caution needs to be taken in the admission of this document," Laskaris asserted. "It seems to me they are trying to get it in through the back door." The legal debate over the diary's admissibility continued through the afternoon, so the jury heard just sixteen minutes of testimony during the entire day. On the following morning, Wednesday, the judge ruled against Laskaris. "What use the jury is to make of the diary will depend upon what evidence comes out in relation to it," Healy said, "but the diary is clearly admissible."

When the jurors returned later that morning, Trowell began his cross-examination of O'Dea by asking about the conversation he had with Cabrera about fishing buoys on the morning the chase began.

"How many buoys did you think were in the water?" Trowell asked.

"I didn't know."

"Why did you use the term 'buoys' when you spoke to Cabrera over the radio?"

"I don't know."

"It could have been one buoy, couldn't it?"

"Yes."

"Could it have been on board *Viarsa*?"

"Well, I guess that's possible, yeah."

Shortly after that answer, the judge broke for lunch. Over sandwiches at a nearby restaurant, Laskaris admitted that the judge's ruling about the diary was a significant blow. Deciding how to respond to that was not the only challenge facing the lawyers. Curt Hofmann said he was trying to decide whether he should ask O'Dea if he felt pressured to ensure a conviction because of the millions of dollars the government spent on the chase. "The problem," Hofmann said, "is that if I tell the jurors how much the government spent, that in itself might make them feel more compelled to find our guys guilty." The lawyers also acknowledged that their work was complicated because the interests of the defendants and the owner of the vessel, who was paying the legal bills, were not the same. For example, while Laskaris's effort to pin the blame on Cabrera by suggesting that the others had no choice but to follow the captain's orders might help some of the defendants, it did not serve the interests of the owner, who wanted to reclaim the boat and the money Australia obtained from selling its cargo. For him, nothing short of a complete vindication was good enough.

"We need to get them all off," Laskaris said. "If just one of them is guilty, the owner loses the ship."

After lunch, Trowell returned to the topic of the beacons, asking O'Dea, "There had been two other vessels in the area—that's true, isn't it?"

"Yes."

"You can't exclude the possibility that if there was a fishing beacon in the water, it may well have belonged not to *Viarsa* but to the other two vessels?"

"I can't, no."

Trowell then moved to discredit the idea that *Viarsa*'s crew had attempted to conceal the vessel's identity by painting over its name and that they had repainted the letters while at sea. "Are you assuming," he asked, "that there were crew members on the side and the back of the vessel painting numbers and letters on it during the night? It would have been a bit difficult, wouldn't it?"

"It wouldn't be the ideal time to do it, I suppose, at night."

"Would you paint your house at night, without lights?"

"No."

"I'm told by the master of the *Viarsa*," Trowell continued, "that they had placed grease, that's engine grease, over the markings. That's why they were blacked out. They did so to protect it in the conditions and the weather they were encountering, and all they did is simply hose it off. Are you able to say that couldn't have happened?"

"Well, I've never heard of that being done."

"Well, have you heard of people painting the names and the markings on a vessel at night with no lights?"

"No, I haven't seen that done."

"You prefer to believe they painted these things on at night?"

"Yes."

"Right, okay. These Spaniards have amazing talents . . . ."

Trowell then turned to a subject he had been gearing up for since the start of the trial—Eduardo Morello Schultz. The fact that the government observer would not appear in court provided an irresistible set of opportunities. Trowell initially planned to suggest that Schultz was actually in charge of the vessel and that the rest of the crew had no choice but to follow his instructions. Given that the observer worked for the

Uruguayan government, it seemed like a plausible scenario, and one that would be difficult for the prosecutor to debunk. But exploring the observer's role would not be without danger: Although he told O'Dea that he did not know whether the ship was fishing when it was in the Australian Fishing Zone—an obviously valuable bit of information for the defense—Schultz also said things that could be damaging to the case. For example, he told O'Dea that Cabrera had deliberately provided him with false positions and forced him to report those positions to Uruguayan officials.

The strategy Trowell devised provides a perfect example of the benefits that go to those who can afford first-rate legal talent: he intended to get O'Dea to tell the jury about the favorable elements of the statement Schultz provided when he visited Fremantle, but prevent O'Dea and the prosecutor from introducing any of the unfavorable ones. The key was to get O'Dea to testify about the statement but to avoid giving the prosecutor a chance to introduce it into evidence. Trowell had to walk a narrow line; he could let O'Dea read Schultz's statement for the purpose of refreshing his memory, but he could not cross-examine him too closely about the document or let him read it aloud, which would give the prosecutor the right to introduce it into evidence.

As an opening gambit Trowell asked, "Schultz told you that he had witnessed no fishing whatsoever between August 3 and 8, didn't he?"

"He said he was sick."

"He said he did not see any fishing or hear any fishing activity on the boat from August 3 to 8, 2003. That's what he said, isn't it?"

O'Dea felt trapped. He could see how Schultz's role and statement would be used to the defense's advantage, and there was nothing he could do to stop it. He hesitated before he responded to the question, glancing around the room as if searching for a better answer. In the end, he looked down at the floor and muttered, "That's what he said, yes."

When the defense attorneys went to lunch that day, all three said they believed the tide of the trial had changed. *Given what the observer—a government official—had said, how could the jurors convict?* Each of the lawyers put the chance of securing not-guilty verdicts for all of the defendants at better than fifty–fifty. They did not, however, claim most of the credit. As much as anything, they believed Dembo was losing the case because of inadequate preparation, miscalculations, and outright mistakes. For example, he described Schultz as a truthful person and someone he wished would be available to testify. Having done that, it would be difficult for the prosecutor to later discredit statements attributed to the observer. The prosecutor's questioning had also seemed unfocused. He forced Duffy and O'Dea to provide exhaustive and overlapping accounts of seemingly unimportant aspects of the chase, but he did little to develop themes or highlight crucial facts. He frequently seemed to be on the defensive, spending more time responding to the defense attorneys' assertions than making his own.

"Prosecutors sometimes unravel," Hofmann said, and the lawyers intended to do everything they could to exacerbate the process. Trowell was the ringleader. As a senior barrister who had been designated a Queen's Counsel, he often sought to present himself as a learned intellectual in the courtroom, but as he walked back to the courthouse after lunch, he sounded more like a schoolyard bully. Rubbing his hands together with devilish glee, he asked, "What should we do to Dembo this afternoon?"

The theatrics began as soon as the jurors entered the courtroom and Trowell began joking with the defendants in a voice loud enough for everyone to hear. "Are you enjoying yourselves? Are you ready for the next chapter of the fictional account of what happened?" As the defendants laughed, Trowell stepped back and whispered, "Prosecutors hate that." In addition to putting a bit more pressure on the other side, he said the wisecracking humanized the defendants.

The effort to rattle Dembo went into overdrive later that afternoon. In the presence of the jury and judge, the defense attorneys criticized the manner in which he asked questions and accused him of presenting misleading evidence and even of boring the jury. Some of this is standard operating procedure, but Trowell and Laskaris took it to another level, threatening at one point to tell a legal organization that the prosecutor had behaved unprofessionally. About an hour after the lunch break, Laskaris was presented with a perfect opportunity to bait the prosecutor when Dembo asked O'Dea some innocuous questions about the crew that was aboard *John Ross*. When the fisheries officer said he did not know their nationality, Dembo, who was born in South Africa, asked, "Did they sound like me or did they sound like . . ."

"Did they sound like Zimbabweans?" Laskaris asked. "Is that what my friend is asking?"

"I'm not a Zimbabwean."

"Or Rhodesian?"

"I'm not a Zimbabwean or Rhodesian! You sit down and don't make racist comments."

Since it was not at all clear why Dembo, who is white, considered Laskaris's comments to be racist, Laskaris stood up and said, "I object to that."

"Sit down," Dembo shouted.

Trowell and Laskaris were not about to let it go. During the next break, as they stood in the corridor just outside the courtroom, they made a point of loudly talking about the fact that Dembo's legal career had begun in South Africa during apartheid. "Now that things have changed, everyone claims they were a freedom fighter," Trowell said as he glanced toward Dembo, who was well within earshot. The prosecutor just scowled and strode away.

O'Dea did not complete his testimony until Tuesday, November 2, exactly one month after the trial began. It was also the day the trial was originally supposed to end, but the jury had heard from just three witnesses. The defendants did not know what to think. "Some days are better than other days," Antonio Perez said a few hours after O'Dea completed his testimony. "It changes day by day."

Wednesday was one of the good days for the defendants. Phillip Shelverton, an Australian fisheries officer, had come to court to explain how the fishing buoys taken from *Viarsa* were handled after they left the ship, but Trowell knew Shelverton accompanied Eduardo Schultz from Cape Town to Montevideo after he left *Viarsa* and that Shelverton was present when the observer was interviewed by Uruguayan officials at DINARA's headquarters. When Trowell first asked about the meeting, Shelverton said it was conducted in Spanish. "I'm not too sure exactly what questions were asked and what answers were given," he claimed. However, after further questioning, Shelverton acknowledged that a female interpreter was sitting at his side throughout the interview.

"Do you recall her telling you that Schultz had said that he wasn't aware of any fishing gear being lifted during the period when *Viarsa* was in the Australian Fishing Zone?" Trowell asked.

"I do recall her telling me that," Shelverton said.

"Do you also recall her telling you that Schultz had said that if it had happened, he would have seen it?"

"Yes, I do recall that."

This was a real victory for the defense. The jury was told that the observer, whose sole purpose was to monitor *Viarsa*'s fishing operations, said it had not fished in the Australian Fishing Zone. In fact, this version of his story was different from what he told O'Dea aboard *Viarsa* and in Fremantle: the observer had told the Australians that he was so sick that he did not know whether *Viarsa* had taken fish from within the Australian Fishing Zone. When he was questioned by officials in Montevideo, he said he would have known if there had been any fishing, regardless of his health. Perhaps even more important, Shelverton, an Australian official and one of O'Dea's colleagues, had been exposed as being willing to mislead the court about an important meeting, presumably because it was damaging to the government's case.

The defense called just one witness—Ricardo Cabrera. The lawyers had decided that he would testify in English. Given his imperfect understanding of the language, there was a risk that he might answer questions without fully understanding them, but they thought it was more important for the captain to appear empathetic to the jurors. Using their language was crucial. Jurors tend to acquit defendants with appealing personalities, and Trowell hoped they would see in Cabrera a colorful old salt—a rogue, perhaps, but a likeable one.

"I have been sailing thirty-seven years," Cabrera told the court, explaining that he graduated from a nautical college in Montevideo in 1965 and had been working as a merchant mariner ever since. He said the voyage that landed him in this courtroom began on June 30 when *Viarsa* set out from Mauritius for "North East Bank," which he said was a toothfish fishery located in international waters to the north of the Australian Fishing Zone. After almost a full month of fishing there, he said he planned to go to "Williams Bank," another high seas toothfish fishery. However, because of forecasted bad weather, he said he altered his destination to "Elan Bank," an area to the south of the Australian Fishing Zone. "When I took the decision to go to Elan Bank instead of Williams Bank, I took the decision to cross directly through" the Australian Fishing Zone, Cabrera said.

"Are you able to tell the jury," Trowell asked, "how long it took for you to sail from the entry point into the Australian Fishing Zone to the point you reached south-southwest of Heard Island?"

"About twenty-five hours."

"Arriving at what time?"

"Arriving at five o'clock in the morning."

"That's on the morning of the seventh?"

"Yes."

"Did you have any mechanical problems?"

"Yes—we need to stop," the captain said, "because we've got a problem in the seawater pump due to high temperatures of the main engine. We stop about fifty minutes."

Dembo had previously sought to use *Viarsa*'s engine room log to suggest it could not have entered the Australian Zone at the time Cabrera claimed it had—4:00 a.m. on August 6—and reached the point where the captain said it had stopped for repairs early the next morning. The RPMs recorded for that period were too low to propel the ship fast enough to reach the position Cabrera claimed it did, Dembo posited. But Cabrera told Trowell that the ship was easily capable of traveling what he calculated to be 239 miles during the twenty-five-hour period, even if the engine had operated at less than top speed, because the strong winds and waves coming from the north sped the ship's passage.

"Before you were sighted by *Southern Supporter*," Trowell asked, "had you been fishing in the Australian Fishing Zone?"

"No, no. Never."

"Did you have any beacons in the water?"

"No, no, no beacons in the water. Never. I didn't fish and didn't drop any beacon. Nothing. Was only crossing."

Cabrera went on to say that all of *Viarsa*'s fishing beacons were aboard the ship. He said the two beacons that Webb and Duffy believed were missing from the racks—numbers thirteen and fifteen—were broken and were replaced with two other beacons, which carried numbers that were out of sequence from the other beacons. The two broken ones, he said, "were in the forward locker and that's why I substituted them—or I made them substituted by numbers sixteen and seventeen."

Cabrera responded to some of the questions with impatience, sometimes mangling the syntax, but he also managed to maintain what Trowell thought would come across as a European kind of gentility. He readily admitted that he had done everything he could to evade *Southern Supporter*. He said his actions had had nothing to do with whether he broke the law. Regardless of whether he had been fishing, he said he believed the Australians would "seize the catch, seize the vessel, and my career will be finished, like now." Besides, he said the Uruguayan government ordered him not to stop. He said Schultz had told him to keep going shortly after he saw *Southern Supporter* and that Captain Flangini personally called the ship and ordered the vessel to return to Uruguay. This order, he continued, was later confirmed by the two facsimiles that were sent to the ship, one from the Uruguayan Navy and the other from DINARA. "I had no option," Cabrera said. "I had to keep sailing to a Uruguayan port."

When it was time for Dembo to cross-examine the witness, he did what he could to challenge the captain's account and also to assert that Antonio Perez was the man in charge. But Cabrera never wavered: he maintained that he was the fishing master as well as the captain even though he had worked on fishing vessels for only three years and, unlike Perez, he never earned a fishing master qualification. He said Uruguay automatically allowed captains to also act as fishing masters, so there was no need for any special qualification. The prosecutor's evidence about Perez's role was far from conclusive, and since Dembo had not done much to explain how the hierarchies on fishing vessels are different from the more familiar command structures on other kinds of ships, it seemed unlikely that the jury would accept Dembo's contention that Cabrera shared a cabin with several other men while the much younger Perez stayed in the ship's best accommodation. Indeed, as Dembo hammered away at the issue, what seemed more likely was that the prosecutor was creating a hurdle for himself that he would not be able to clear.

"What I'm putting to you again," Dembo said at one point, "is that cabin which contained some clothing and the wallet and some personal information and cards was actually the cabin of Mr. Perez."

"No, no."

"And that Mr. Perez was in fact the fishing master?"

"No, no—I disagree with that. Sorry Mr. Dembo, but the cabin, the best cabin on the vessel, was the cabin at the side of the chartroom—and this cabin was my cabin during the whole trip."

Cabrera was equally steadfast in maintaining that the ship's identifying marks were covered with engine grease and that this was done to protect the paint. "It is normal where we go fishing, when we go to the south of the Indian Ocean, because of the weather that ends up damaging the paint," he said. He did not explain why elements powerful enough to remove paint from a ship would not also wash away a layer of grease.

Cabrera admitted to a single untruth. He said the ropes strung over *Viarsa*'s deck—the ones he told O'Dea were required to secure the mast—were, just as Duffy had wanted to say, intended to thwart a helicopter boarding. Although the admission might have endangered Cabrera's credibility, Laskaris had a ready defense, pointing out that O'Dea, too, had lied: he told Cabrera that he found fishing gear in the water, when he had not, and also that there were no other fishing vessels in the area even though *Southern Supporter* had detected two others. "Mr. O'Dea lied to Captain Cabrera consistently and systematically," Laskaris told the jury, suggesting to the jury that Cabrera was no more guilty in that respect than the government's own representatives.

When Dembo made his final address to the jury, he focused on Jose Gonzalez Perez's diary. The entries for August 4 through 6 had been crossed out and overwritten, but the prosecutor read what he said were the original words for August 6: "We started again with fishing activities, preparing the gear. We finished the day with good weather, nothing to report, and a good catch."

In their final addresses, the defense attorneys stressed that the prosecution failed to present a single piece of direct evidence and asserted that all of the circumstantial evidence, with the possible exception of the diary, was weak and equivocal. Hofmann said Duffy and O'Dea could not have known how long *Viarsa* had been near Heard Island before the chase because they could have easily confused it with one of the other ships that was also in the area. "If there are other contacts, are you satisfied beyond reasonable doubt that they were in fact the *Viarsa*?" Hofmann asked. "The fact of the matter is we don't have a clear understanding as to what boat was the *Viarsa*" until it appeared on *Southern Supporter*'s radar screen on the morning of August 6. "Prior to that, it's anybody's guess."

When Laskaris addressed the jurors, he reminded them that Stephen Duffy himself said he would have fled from *Southern Supporter* if he had been in Cabrera's shoes: "Duffy said, uncontrovertibly, that if he was the master of a fishing vessel in the same position as the *Viarsa*, he would not stop if he was being chased. If he was being chased by a Uruguayan patrol vessel, he would not stop. That's a very important piece of evidence." As for the seemingly incriminating diary, Laskaris acknowledged that it appeared to belong to Jose Perez and seemed to say that *Viarsa* fished in the Australian Fishing Zone, but he said the interpreters who translated the diary might have made a mistake. He also pointed out that Eduardo Schultz, who had kept the official records, said there had been no fishing.

The jury commenced its deliberations on Monday, November 29, almost eight weeks after the start of the trial. The defense attorneys were hoping for a short deliberation, which, they felt sure, would mean not-guilty verdicts. Their biggest worry was the diary. In most criminal trials, the final reckoning comes down to just one or two pieces of evidence, and as the day wore on, the lawyers feared it would be the diary in this case. "It's the Trojan horse," Laskaris said late Monday night.

On Tuesday morning, it became apparent that the jury was in trouble. In a note to the judge, the forewoman said, "One jury member has made it absolutely clear that she will not change her position. She refuses to engage in discussions and has isolated herself from the group. Without her participation, there seems little hope for anyone wishing to take an alternate position. And all discussions going on without her seem pointless." Asking the jurors to return to the courtroom, the judge told them they had "a duty to listen carefully and objectively to the views of every one of your fellow jurors."

Wednesday began with a glimmer of hope. The forewoman requested that several sections of the transcript be read, most of them focused on the prosecution's claim that *Viarsa* had been virtually stationary near Heard Island for ten and a half hours before the start of the chase. "We are querying that ten-and-a-half-hour period," the forewoman said in a note. The defense attorneys were encouraged: the jury appeared to be concentrating on Hofmann's point that there was not enough evidence to conclude that *Viarsa* was in the area during that entire period. It was a crucial issue. If the jury concluded that the ship remained in that area for ten and a half hours, they would have to reject Cabrera's assertion that *Viarsa* could not have done any fishing because it had entered the Australian Fishing Zone just twenty-five hours earlier.

The jury continued its deliberations all day on Wednesday, and on Thursday, after the judge received another discouraging note, he invited its members back into the courtroom and asked, "Have you, the jury, been able to reach verdicts on which you all agree on *any* of the charges?"

"For one," the forewoman said.

"All right," the judge said. "What we should do is take that verdict if you all agreed."

As the judge said this, two female jurors, one in the front row and one in the back, began shaking their heads. At that point, the forewoman began to sob. "There was . . ." she started to say.

"I don't want you to discuss it now," the judge said. "If you have agreed on any charge—all agreed on any charge in relation to any of the accused—I can take that verdict. But you all have to be agreed."

"No, no," the forewoman said.

"You're not agreed in relation to any of the accused on any of the charges?"

Now the forewoman shook her head.

"That's the position. Right. Any further time isn't going to help you reach a decision on any of them?"

"No."

With that, Judge Healy declared a mistrial. The nine-week trial that had cost taxpayers about $2 million had ended without a verdict, but his tone was calm and measured. "I will discharge the jury because these things do happen," he said. "It is important you don't feel that you've let anyone down."

The defense lawyers cast the result in a high-minded light. "Here were a bunch of foreigners who were caught in Australian waters, and the jury could not agree," Trowell said. He had no doubt that the defendants were guilty. "Of course they were fishing in Australian waters," he said a few weeks after the trial. "They didn't tell me that—but give me a break!" But in Trowell's way of thinking, the lack of a guilty verdict was actually a tribute to the Australian legal system. "Foreign nationals who thought they were going to be put up against the wall got justice. We didn't shoot them just because they were on the property."

But for government officials in Australia and elsewhere, the mistrial was an embarrassment and a terrible setback in the war against illegal fishing: authorities would inevitably become more reluctant to pursue suspected pirates unless they somehow managed to obtain actual evidence. The already high hurdles had just become even higher. The outcome was particularly wrenching for Mike O'Dea, who had been in court every day for nine weeks. Throughout the trial, he had a deep sense of foreboding. He did not think the trial would be lost, but he had a gnawing sense that there would not be a unanimous decision. As he thought about the consequences, particularly the need to prepare for another trial, which he was sure the government would demand, he felt numb. After he left the courtroom, he went home, drank several bottles of beer, and went to bed.

The defendants did not feel like they had won anything. The judge said that all of them except for Roberto Guerrero would be required to stay in Australia until the commencement of another trial. This was particularly painful because the defense attorneys were sure that the jury, with the exception of the one or two holdouts, had been on their side. "I know in my bones that we were very close to acquittal," Hofmann said. During the last days and hours of the trial, he and the other lawyers noticed that most of the jurors regularly looked directly at the defendants. Jurors who are about to convict people of crimes rarely do that; they do everything they can to avoid eye contact. About an hour after the end of the trial, Hofmann's belief turned to near certainty. He was walking away from the courthouse when he happened to run into the forewoman and another juror who were both waiting for a bus. Jurors in Australia are forbidden from talking about their deliberations, even after the end of a trial, but the forewoman, with tears in her eyes, approached Hofmann. Before he could do anything to stop her, she said, "I'm so sorry. I'm so, so sorry."

For Antonio Vidal, *Viarsa*'s owner, it was a mixed result. Although there would be more legal bills to pay, he was, in a fundamental sense, the only winner: Australia had done everything it could to prove that his ship had fished illegally—and it had failed. A couple of hours after Healy declared a mistrial, Laskaris had his first conversation with a man whom he believed to be Vidal. "The boss wants to talk to you," Perez said as he handed the receiver of a public phone in the lobby of the Flying Angels Club to his lawyer. The man at the other end of the line, who spoke in near-perfect English but did not introduce himself by name, was obviously familiar with the intricacies of the trial. He told Laskaris that he was worried about Perez's spirits. More than that, though, he wanted to make it clear that he wanted to continue the legal fight.

"We need to go on with it," the man said. "The money is not an issue."

CHAPTER 23

Perth

Waiting for the retrial, which would not begin until September 2005, was an agony for Antonio Perez. During the final days of the first trial, he had come around to thinking that he probably would be declared innocent—and even a guilty verdict would have been better than a mistrial. If he had been convicted, he would have been ordered to pay a substantial fine, up to $400,000, but he was sure it would have been paid by Vidal. Now he was stuck in Australia for another year.

It seemed grossly unfair: an offense for which the maximum penalty was supposed to be a fine would end up separating him from his family and making it impossible to work for at least two years. His daughters, who were about to enter their last year of high school, and his wife visited twice between the trials, but Perez was still desperate to get home. As the months passed, he told friends he was thinking about getting it over with by pleading guilty. Or stowing away on one of the outbound cargo ships he watched from the Flying Angels Club, the boardinghouse where he continued to stay. Or asking Vidal to send a boat to somewhere off the coast where he could sneak aboard.

Perez wanted to get back to the business of catching toothfish. He said that nothing he heard during the trial had persuaded him that the fish needed to be protected, and he dismissed the idea that continued massive catches would endanger the species. His reasoning, however, was far from reassuring. "There are men fish and women fish, and we usually catch the men fish," he said at the Flying Angels Club one night. "And when we do catch women fish, we don't use their eggs—they go back in the water." Both assertions are absurd. There is no way Perez could avoid catching male and female toothfish in basically equal numbers, and any eggs that are flushed from the factory along with the rest of the fish guts would be immature and unfertilized. In another impossible-to-accept assertion, Perez said it really does not matter if the toothfish population were to go the way of cod's because there will be another species to take its place.

Perez went on to say that he has already identified one possible successor—the Antarctic toothfish—such a close relation to the Patagonian version that it is difficult to distinguish their fleshes.

Back in January 2002, Perez took *Arvisa*, one of Vidal's vessels, to search for Antarctic toothfish in Prydz Bay, an often-frozen body of water just off the coast of Antarctica. It was an exploratory expedition during which *Arvisa* and *Dorita*, another one of Vidal's ships, came within sixty miles of Antarctica and caught a very substantial number of Antarctic toothfish. But while Perez had discovered a promising new source of fish, the vessels ran into problems when they were spotted by an Australian research ship. Vidal had made a mistake. Like *Viarsa, Arvisa* and *Dorita* were registered in Uruguay, and they were fishing in an area that falls within the jurisdiction of the Convention on the Conservation of Antarctic Marine Living Resources. Vessels registered in CCAMLR member nations—Uruguay is one of them—are required to have permits to fish there, but neither of Vidal's boats had one.

Therefore, while the Australians did not board the vessels, they did their best to track down the fish that had been caught. They eventually learned that some of *Arvisa*'s catch had been unloaded in Mozambique, where a Uruguayan government official had flown and signed a document that "certified" that the fish had been taken from a high seas location that was outside of CCAMLR's jurisdiction. Certain that the certification was fraudulent, Australian fisheries officers then alerted their counterparts around the world. And on May 30, 2002, when a container carrying thirty-three tons of *Arvisa*'s catch arrived in Boston, it was seized by U.S. Customs agents.

The U.S. government portrayed the seizure as a major step in stemming the inflow of illegal toothfish.[1] The seizure was clearly noteworthy in one respect: the United States had effectively accused officials from another government of lying. But the fact that the seizure required something so unusual only underscored the difficulties involved in defeating the smugglers.

In the aftermath, Lawrence Lasarow, the California-based seafood merchant who had bought the fish, was forced to forfeit half of the $320,218 that the government realized when it sold the shipment—but he said he did not know the fish had been caught illegally and was not charged with a crime. Nor was Vidal or Antonio Perez or Ricardo Cabrera, who was *Dorita*'s captain for the expedition, or anyone else who was onboard either of the fishing vessels. And while some of the fish had been confiscated, most of it was landed in Kenya, transshipped to Singapore and Hong Kong, and sold in China and Japan.

In fact, *Arvisa*'s history as a toothfish vessel goes a long way to illustrate

---

[1] *Highlighting the similarities between Antarctic and Patagonian toothfish, a press release issued by the government inaccurately said the seized fish was the Patagonian variety.*

the difficulties of stopping the pirates. Once called *Merced*, it was the vessel that launched Vidal in the toothfish business. In 1999, when it was known as the *Camouco*, it was arrested by French authorities for illegally taking toothfish from near Kerguelen Island, the fishery directly north of Heard Island and the one where Vidal had once worked legally in partnership with a French company. But although the officers who were onboard the boat were found guilty and fined, the vessel, which had been flagged to Panama, was returned to Vidal. It was then renamed *Arvisa*—like *Viarsa*, an anagram of Vidal Amadores SA—and registered in Uruguay. After it was spotted by the Australians in Prydz Bay, it was given yet another name, *Eternal,* and registered in the Netherlands Antilles.

On July 3, 2002, it was once again arrested for poaching toothfish from French waters. Antonio Perez, who was the fishing master during that voyage, his sixth aboard *Arvisa*, was assessed a $100,000 fine. This time the vessel was confiscated, but there was nothing to prevent Perez from continuing to work on other toothfish vessels.

During the time he was in Australia, Perez had formulated a specific plan for what he would do after he was released: he would take one of Vidal's boats back to Prydz Bay or somewhere else close to Antarctica. Thanks to his exploratory voyage, he believed there were enough Antarctic toothfish to keep him occupied for the rest of his career. He knew its habitats were covered or blocked by ice for much of the year and that the fishing season would be short. But thanks to the soaring price of toothfish—by then it regularly sold for more than $20 a pound at retail fish markets in the United States—Perez thought he could spend less time at sea and still make almost as much money as he had before.

From a different perspective, it is difficult to escape the conclusion that in going to this extreme—what is literally the end of the earth—Perez and his industry are approaching the ultimate end of the road. Indeed, if Antarctic toothfish turn out to be something less than an adequate substitute for their Patagonian cousin, either because of the inaccessibility of their habitats or the size of their population, it may be that the industry is even closer to the terminus, and that Patagonian toothfish will turn out to have been the world's last unexploited big fish. That is a possibility Perez is unwilling to acknowledge. Or perhaps he is so focused on capturing fish before someone else does that he is incapable of thinking in those terms.

By the time the second trial began, Australia had committed $66.8 million to enhance its fisheries enforcement efforts near Heard Island, which meant that Heard Island patrols would be more frequent and that they would carry armed boarding parties. But Perez said that would have no impact on his plans because he had come up with a risk-free way to catch Antarctic toothfish in CCAMLR-regulated waters. His strategy was based on the fact that the organization's regulations are essentially voluntary: they apply only to vessels that are flagged to countries that choose to be CCAMLR members.

"It will not be difficult for me," Perez explained. "We will just get a flag from a country that isn't a member—Panama or Colombia—and we will have no problems."

CHAPTER 24

"**B**e careful about jumping to conclusions," Mark Trowell told the jury shortly after the start of the second trial. "We do it every day, don't we? We get half the story and we jump to a conclusion. Well, we can't do that in a criminal trial. It's too dangerous and there is too much at stake."

The jury he was speaking to was quite different from the one that had been deadlocked a year earlier. While the defense had sought to have a predominantly female jury in the first trial, the new one was mostly male. Several of its members described themselves as students, but it seemed unlikely that any of them were currently enrolled because they would not be able to attend classes during the eight weeks or so the trial was expected to take. The defense attorneys, having concluded that the juror or jurors who opposed not-guilty verdicts in the first trial were women, hoped the young men were not fully in sync with school or work or perhaps society itself, and that they were therefore not instinctively inclined to fall into line with what they heard from law enforcement officers.

"You might be sympathetic to Australian fisheries officers for the job that they do on our behalf," Trowell told them, "but fisheries officers are not always right."

As in the first trial, the most important questions focused on what had been going on during the hours just before the start of the chase. When Stephen Duffy took the stand, Trowell forced him to admit that the "exercise book," a log maintained by the military men who operated the radar detection equipment, said nothing about radar emissions being received during the evening of August 6, the night before the chase began. The first entry in the log appeared to be at 6:57 a.m. on the morning of August 7. Duffy acknowledged that to be the case but said that was only because large sections of the log had been censored for reasons of national security.

"There is nothing about the fifth or sixth of August in the book?" Trowell asked.

"No, there isn't."

"So your document, an exercise book compiled by various persons on board *Southern Supporter*, makes no mention whatsoever of what happened before 6:57 a.m. on August 7, 2003?"

"That's right."

"So the jury has to rely on your say-so and the say-so of others?"

"Yes."

Trowell believed the log contained position reports that had come from American military satellites and that it had been censored to prevent the lawyers from asking questions in open court about U.S. intelligence capabilities. Whenever the questioning threatened to veer in that direction, an Australian government attorney who was sitting behind the prosecutor— Trowell repeatedly called him a "spook"—stood up to object. While Trowell regarded this as unfair to the defendants, he also recognized that it created an opportunity. "I know exactly what I'm going to tell the jury in my closing statement," he said over a cup of coffee a few hours after he questioned

Duffy about the log. "I'll tell them that the government won't let them see the only real evidence because the government doesn't trust the jurors."

When Phillip Laskaris, the other defense attorney, questioned Duffy, he zeroed in on the fishing beacons that supposedly had been detected shortly after the start of the chase. He pointed out that Mike O'Dea had been untruthful when he told Ricardo Cabrera that "we can confirm" there was fishing gear in the water and that there were no other fishing vessels nearby given that no one on *Southern Supporter* actually saw any beacons and that two other fishing vessels were believed to be in the area. From Duffy's perspective, it seemed outrageous that the tables were being turned to make it seem as if he and Mike O'Dea were the ones who were in the wrong. Duffy was doing everything he could to maintain the unflappable calm of a military man, but his patience was wearing thin.

"I was not in charge of Mr. O'Dea," he told Laskaris.

But the lawyer kept pressing: "You were the group commander. You were in charge?"

"I suppose if we were all perfect we wouldn't be here, Mr. Laskaris, would we?"

Duffy regretted those words even as he said them. While they would not damage the prosecution, he felt as if he had let down his guard and fallen into a trap by making an inappropriate show of his personal feelings. He was still feeling that way after he completed his testimony later that day and a few hours after that when he sat down to dinner. "I was close to losing it," he said as he sipped a glass of red wine. "We knew *exactly* where *Viarsa* was the night before we actually saw them—we had a position for them every hour." The more he thought about it, the angrier he became. Once again, it seemed as if the truth of what had happened was being overwhelmed by legal maneuvers.

And as good and bad turned into a muddle of confusion, it also seemed to Duffy that everyone had lost sight of the bigger issue—namely the unintended chain of consequences that occurred because people in the Northern Hemisphere had fallen in love with a creature that comes from faraway places where pirate fishermen are happy to go, even if it means they will destroy some of the world's last unexploited fisheries. No longer concerned about suppressing his feelings, Duffy lashed out against the lawyers, particularly Laskaris. "I don't know how he can live with himself," Duffy said toward the end of the evening. Noting that the attorney had married a few months earlier, he said, "He has a wife and kids now. Does he just not care about the environment and sustainability?" As if to demonstrate that he had not lost any of his own bearings, Duffy then declared: "It's very simple: poaching is a crime. If you steal fish from a private pond, it's a crime. If you steal them from Australia, it's a crime against that nation. And these guys are crooks!"

While he had the sense that his side of the story was not getting an adequate hearing, Duffy still believed the fishermen would be convicted. He would have felt even better if he had known about something that had happened in the United States one day earlier: a federal grand jury in Miami had indicted Manuel Antonio Vidal Pego, *Viarsa*'s owner, on charges of importing and attempting to sell "illegally possessed toothfish," false labeling, and obstructing justice. Although it was not at all clear whether Spain would extradite him, Vidal now had a new set of very personal issues to worry about: if he ended up in a Miami courtroom, he could face a maximum penalty of twenty years in jail for obstructing justice and up to five years for each of the other charges.

Mike O'Dea testified after Duffy. The sheer length of the legal process had taken a toll on the fisheries officer, and he was already worrying about the possibility that this trial might go the wrong way. "It would have been one thing if they got off shortly after the chase, but this has become a big part of my life," he said outside the courtroom. "And it's taken away some of my enthusiasm for the work." Like Duffy, he was particularly annoyed by the need to defend his own behavior. "The lawyers can pick apart everything we said and did, but the defendants can just sit there without doing anything to explain what *they* did. It's totally ridiculous that it's so difficult to get a conviction, particularly when you know so many other pirates are still out there."

The prosecutor for the second trial, Geoffrey Scholz, was a dour man who seemed incapable of small talk or even a smile, but he presented the government's case far more persuasively than Hilton Dembo had a year before. However, when Ricardo Cabrera, the only defendant to testify, gave his account of *Viarsa*'s actions, the prosecutor was unable to establish that any significant aspect of what the captain said was untrue.

Scholz understood that the end of the story was very much dependent on what had happened at the beginning, in particular the question of exactly where *Viarsa* had been during the hours just before the start of the chase. "Mr. Cabrera says his vessel was only ever in that area near Heard Island for fifty minutes," Scholz said during his final address to the jury. "Mr. Cabrera's evidence is completely divergent in that respect from Duffy's. They both can't be right, obviously." Scholz said the choice of who was telling the truth was also obvious. Citing Duffy's long experience as a naval officer, he declared: "The evidence discloses beyond a reasonable doubt that the vessel was in the zone on the sixth and seventh. Sure, it wasn't seen with a longline in the water, but all of the evidence points to the inevitable conclusion that it was engaged in fishing activity—and we ask that you return a verdict of guilty against each of the accused."

Mark Trowell, of course, asked the jurors to reach the opposite conclusion. And just as he had promised, he suggested that the government had withheld crucial evidence from the jurors. "You are asked to take a lot on trust," he told them. "There was a lot of information that had been, to use Duffy's words, censored on the basis of national security. The prosecution, representing the Australian government, really says to you something like this: 'We trust you to administer justice, but we don't trust you with any detailed information about how we caught them.' It's a slightly arrogant position, isn't it? It's really 'We entrust you to fulfill one of the most critical obligations of any citizen—that is, to determine the guilt and innocence of other people—but we won't trust you with some of the evidence that you need to reach that position.' It really is a bit of 'Don't worry about the facts—just accept what we say.'"

On Wednesday, November 2, 2005, eight weeks after the start of the trial, the judge, Valerie French, a veteran magistrate who had assiduously sought to prevent Laskaris and Trowell from taking control of the trial with their endless objections, summed up the evidence and instructed the jurors on how they should reach a verdict. "If you have a reasonable doubt that the prosecution has not proved the guilt of any of the accused persons before you, then the only thing you can do is to find that person not guilty. I can't tell you what a reasonable doubt is in this case—or in any case—because that's always for your assessment. However, I can tell you that the standard of beyond a reasonable doubt is the highest standard in our justice system."

The jurors, who would be sequestered in a hotel until they reached a conclusion, then left the courtroom. They deliberated for the rest of Wednesday and for eleven hours—from 9:00 a.m. until 8 p.m.—on Thursday without once asking the judge for any additional information or guidance. Late Friday morning, it became obvious that the jury was not making much progress when the foreman sent the judge a note: "Please may we have some guidance as we cannot reach a unanimous verdict." Returning to the courtroom, the judge encouraged them to keep trying, but she received another discouraging note that afternoon. After asking the jurors to return to the courtroom just before 3:00 p.m., she asked the foreman, "I take it that means you have been unable to reach a unanimous verdict in relation to any of the charges?"

"Yes."

"This is obviously a very significant matter," she said in exhorting them to keep at it. "I appreciate the stress, but I am going to have to ask you to continue with your deliberations."

Two hours later, Judge French asked the lawyers to come back to the courtroom and told them it was probably time to give up. "Unless I get some indication that progress has been made, I propose to discharge them." But then the foreman entered the room and reported that the deliberations had "progressed considerably" and that the jurors wanted to continue with their deliberations.

As Trowell and Laskaris walked to Trowell's nearby office, where they were joined by Laskaris's wife, Antonia, they were convinced that they would lose. Given that it was Friday afternoon and the jurors would probably be eager to avoid spending the weekend sequestered, he feared the increased pressure would push the jurors toward guilty verdicts. The lawyers talked about the briefs they would have to prepare before their clients were sentenced and attempted to find other things to talk about until a court officer called at 7:30 p.m. "They've reached a unanimous verdict," she said.

On the way back to the courthouse, Trowell told Antonia, "If they make eye contact with us or the accused, we'll be acquitted. If they don't, we're in trouble."

When the jurors filed into the courtroom a few minutes later, they did not look directly at either the lawyers or the defendants, but they seemed lighthearted—at one point the foreman appeared to be smiling—and Laskaris was sure that was a good sign. Once the jurors had found their places, the foreman was the focus of everyone's attention because he would announce the verdicts, starting with the charges against Cabrera.

The court clerk asked the questions. "Members of the jury, are you agreed on your verdict?"

"We are," the foreman replied.

"How say you: is the accused Ricardo Mario Ribot Cabrera on Count 1—intentionally using a foreign boat for commercial fishing in the Australian Fishing Zone—guilty or not guilty?"

Seemingly enjoying the attention, the foreman, one of the young men who had said he was a student, hesitated before he spoke. Then, while the rest of the jury remained standing, he delivered the news everyone had been waiting for: "Not Guilty." Cabrera fell back against his chair, took a deep breath, and smiled broadly. A few seconds later, as the enormity of the decision sunk in, he started slicing both of his hands through the air in short hatchetlike motions and chanting, in English, a single word, quietly but forcefully: "Yes. Yes. Yes."

During the next couple of minutes, the rest of the verdicts were announced, and all of them were the same: each of the defendants was pronounced not guilty on every one of the charges. Jose Gonzalez Perez, the man with the seemingly incriminating diary, and Francisco Fernandez Oliveira, one of *Viarsa*'s other officers, began to cry. By the time the judge said, "I direct that verdicts of acquittal be recorded in relation to each of the accused and they are free to go," both men were weeping uncontrollably.

Antonio Perez was fully in control of his emotions. A hint of happiness—as always, it looked more like a smirk—briefly crossed his face, but he otherwise expressed nothing even as he embraced the other fishermen and the lawyers. What he really wanted to do was to share the good news with two people in Spain. Once the jury was ushered away, Perez stepped into the partially lit corridor outside the courtroom and used a cell phone to call the first of them: his wife. He then phoned the second, Vidal, who did not answer the call but returned it seconds later. When Perez got on an elevator with the other former defendants and their lawyers a few minutes later, he said, "The boss is very happy."

It had been raining for much of the day, but when the fishermen and their lawyers left the courthouse, it was a cool but pleasant spring evening. Walking a half block, they entered the bar at the King's Hotel, where Laskaris ordered champagne. Perez was buoyant and eager to talk about his plans. "Tonight we drink!" he said. "And tomorrow Ricardo and I go fishing . . . in the Swan River," the meandering waterway that runs from Perth to Fremantle. After that, he said he was looking forward to returning to Riviera and spending a couple of months with his family. "I will relax a little, but after Christmas, I go fishing—for toothfish, of course!"

ACKNOWLEDGMENTS

I could not have written this book without the most exhaustive kind of cooperation of its main characters. Steve Duffy and Mike O'Dea answered every imaginable question during my trips to Australia and in innumerable phone calls and e-mails. I am also grateful to them and to Scott Webb for the rich collection of photographs and video they shot throughout the pursuit.

The Australian officers will no doubt be surprised to learn that Antonio Perez and Ricardo Cabrera also took time to answer my questions and that Perez was particularly forthcoming. I am still not entirely sure why they were willing to talk to me at a time when they were being prosecuted as criminals, but I suspect their motivation was fundamentally no different from Steve's and Mike's or, for that matter, my own when I set out to write this book: they understood that this is, quite simply, a remarkable story and one that involves all of the most important issues that face one of mankind's oldest industries.

Beyond helping me to reconstruct one of the longest pursuits in maritime history—it may well be the longest—the main participants in this drama made every effort to recall their words and feelings. Words that are surrounded by quotation marks were either recorded or remembered by at least one person. Unspoken thoughts, some of which are rendered in italics, were recalled by the person to whom they are attributed.

Several other people also played a crucial role in the creation of

Hooked, starting with Patrick Gallagher, the managing director of Allen and Unwin, my Australian publisher and the person who first recognized the potential for a book. Kathy Robbins, my agent, provided me with her usual wise counsel and introduced me to Rodale, which is publishing *Hooked* in the United States and Canada. At Rodale I am particularly grateful to Pete Fornatale, my editor; Zach Schisgal, the executive editor; and Liz Perl, the publisher.

Harry van Dyke gave the book a name and read several versions of the manuscript, making valuable suggestions throughout. Adam Glick recommended several major editorial improvements that were crucial to the final product, and I am enormously grateful for his enthusiasm throughout the project. Kathy Chetkovich and Marcus Brauchli, gifted editors both, suggested a great many important midcourse corrections.

Martin Exel and David Carter, who run a legitimate toothfish catching operation, gave me a thoroughgoing education in the ways of big-time commercial fishing. Linda Greenlaw, the author of *The Hungry Ocean,* vetted my description of longline fishing. I also benefited from Mark Kurlansky's wonderful book *Cod: A Biography of the Fish that Changed the World* and John Butcher's incredibly well researched book *The Closing of the Frontier: A History of the Marine Fisheries of Southeast Asia.* Scott Corrigan, a talented criminal defense lawyer, helped me to describe several legal matters accurately. Stuart Karle and Linda Steinman provided me with another kind of legal guidance, which is also very much appreciated.

Finally, I am grateful to Paul Steiger and the *Wall Street Journal* for granting me the leave of absence that enabled me to write this book and for providing me with a professional home now that it is done.

G. Bruce Knecht

New York City

BRAZIL

Rio de Janeiro

CHILE

ÚRUGUAY

Valparaíso
Santiago
ARGENTINA

Montevideo
Buenos Aires

St. Helena (UK)

ATLANTIC

OCEAN

Walvis Bay

NA

Tristan da Cunha (UK)

Cape To
Cape of Good

Gough Island (UK)

08/28/2003

08/26

08/24

08/22

08

Falkland Islands (UK)

S. Georgia Island (UK)

Bouvet Island (Nor)

Punta Arenas

S. Sandwich Islands (UK)

Cape Horn

S. Orkney Islands (UK)

S O U T H E R

Weddell Sea

A N T A